LUTHERAN QUARTERLY BOOKS

Editor

Paul Rorem, Princeton Theological Seminary

Associate Editors

Timothy J. Wengert, The Lutheran Theological Seminary at Philadelphia
and Steven Paulson, Luther Seminary, St. Paul

Lutheran Quarterly Books will advance the same aims as *Lutheran Quarterly* itself, aims repeated by Theodore G. Tappert when he was editor fifty years ago and renewed by Oliver K. Olson when he revived the publication in 1987. The original four aims continue to grace the front matter and to guide the contents of every issue, and can now also indicate the goals of *Lutheran Quarterly Books:* "to provide a forum (1) for the discussion of Christian faith and life on the basis of the Lutheran confession; (2) for the application of the principles of the Lutheran church to the changing problems of religion and society; (3) for the fostering of world Lutheranism; and (4) for the promotion of understanding between Lutherans and other Christians."

For further information, see www.lutheranquarterly.com.

The symbol and motto of *Lutheran Quarterly,* VDMA for *Verbum Domini Manet in Aeternum* (1 Peter 1:25), was adopted as a motto by Luther's sovereign, Frederick the Wise, and his successors. The original "Protestant" princes walking out of the imperial Diet of Speyer 1529, unruly peasants following Thomas Muentzer, and from 1531 to 1547 the coins, medals, flags, and guns of the Smalcaldic League all bore the most famous Reformation slogan, the first Evangelical confession: the Word of the Lord remains forever.

TITLES

Living by Faith: Justification and Sanctification by Oswald Bayer (2003).

Harvesting Martin Luther's Reflections on Theology, Ethics, and the Church, essays from *Lutheran Quarterly* edited by Timothy J. Wengert, with foreword by David C. Steinmetz (2004).

A More Radical Gospel: Essays on Eschatology, Authority, Atonement, and Ecumenism by Gerhard O. Forde, edited by Mark Mattes and Steven Paulson (2004).

The Role of Justification in Contemporary Theology by Mark C. Mattes (2004)

THE ROLE OF JUSTIFICATION
IN CONTEMPORARY THEOLOGY

Mark C. Mattes

WILLIAM B. EERDMANS PUBLISHING COMPANY
GRAND RAPIDS, MICHIGAN / CAMBRIDGE, U.K.

Wm. B. Eerdmans Publishing Co.
255 Jefferson Ave. S.E., Grand Rapids, Michigan 49503 /
P.O. Box 163, Cambridge CB3 9PU U.K.

Printed in the United States of America

09 08 07 06 05 04   7 6 5 4 3 2 1

ISBN 0-8028-2856-6

www.eerdmans.com

Contents

Contents

Foreword

During the last decade or so, there has been much ado about justification within some churches, and among them. Was this "much ado about nothing" — that is, about merely some ideas of certain theologians? So it seems, in parishes and even among some other theologians. It may be well known that Martin Luther once wrote, "Nothing in this article can be conceded or given up, even if heaven and earth or whatever is transitory passed away. . . . On this article stands all that we teach and practice" (Smalkald Articles 2.1.5). Yet, such a conviction is often considered merely a concern of the sixteenth century; we in our time have enough trouble of our own, it is argued. And, as a matter of fact, we do. No wonder that many theologians, clergy, and church members seem prone to let the sixteenth-century antagonists bury their own problems so that we can concentrate on today's problems. After all, the world has totally changed since then, and so have our problems, our questions, and the answers that we seek and need. So the debates and quarrels about problems of yesterday appear to be out of date.

I would agree with this modern view if justification were but an article, simply one point of doctrine. There are many articles, after all, as we see in the creeds, in dogmatics, and in theology in general. It sounds wrong if one of them is elevated to be *the* article. Each such scholarly promotion is open to contradiction and will indeed be contradicted, scholarly disputation being what it is. Unless the faith itself reveals an article to be fundamental and therefore *the* major article, any doctrinal declaration of an article's priority is merely a declaration — that is, mere words. But the reverse is also true: to demote what is essential to the faith is equally wrong.

So, the question here is whether or not the faith itself is at stake with the article of justification. If it is, this article is obviously much more than one article among others. In this case, the "article," as it were, stands for the creed. But who dares to define it? What, after all, *is* our creed? Now, things get personal. The question is just as deep and serious as the question "Do you love me?" To that question, an evasive answer becomes a clear answer — in the negative! Yet a clear answer in the affirmative carries with it real consequences as to attitudes, goals, schedules, and other decisions. Otherwise, a "yes" is but a lie. The loved one who hears a "yes" rightly expects those other consequences to follow. For in the case of love, it is about my very self; I cannot hold part of it back.

At this point, faith and love are equal: I myself am at stake. Otherwise, faith would be only a worldview, and you can get them a dime a dozen, be it "Christian," "modern," "postmodern," or whatever. No one need take a worldview that seriously, and no one will. For it does not impose any real obligation, either on myself or on anybody else. Faith, however, is not one worldview or another but a personal commitment and obligation, like love. Therefore it is crucial that the question be answered clearly. So, what is our creed? What is my creed? And if it is one of the formulae we recite in the worship service, what does it imply, entail, or require? For if it is really our creed, we ought to be clear about what it implies.

Here is the very place to focus on justification, not as *an* article or a sort of clue that unlocks any secrets of faith, but rather as a short summary of the faith itself: *God saves us lost humans, and does it only from mere love. This becomes real in the life, teaching, passion, death, and resurrection of Jesus Christ. Thus, his name holds and incorporates God's will and deed.* God's will, word, and work, as revealed and accomplished in Jesus Christ, is the content of the "article" of justification. Why so, and why call it an "article"? Because, on the one hand, around God's will, word, and work there are many things to learn, to see, to consider, to do or to turn from — as with love. On the other hand, since all these other items have to be dealt with, we must be clear that they are not the basis or center of the faith but the implications of the basic and central "article," namely justification itself.

Consequently, the "article" of justification is both quite simple and at the same time highly complicated. It is as simple as Christ saying, "Stay close to me, I am your rock and castle. Your ransom I myself will be; for you I strive and wrestle; for I am yours, and you are mine" (*Lutheran Book of Worship,* #299, 7). And it is more complicated than a learned dogmatics of several volumes, for it holds the fathomless abyss of God's will, word, and work. Thus, throughout history justification has been considered both a short summary of the Christian faith and a sophisticated article inviting deep and broad research. This research has challenged dogmatic theology, especially since the meaning of the summary has to be worked out ever more precisely. Through the centuries, scholarly research has provided a flood of insight into aspects of what "justification" means or implies. Yet, amid all this scholarship, perhaps the major matter is disappearing, as can happen in other fields.

At the famous London Ciba Symposium of Nobel prize winners half a century ago, Albert von Szent-Györgyi reported that the further his Massachusetts team progressed in their research on muscles, the less they knew about the muscle itself; they were even in danger, he said, of "losing" it. Perhaps something similar has happened with the article of justification in Protestant theology. We know an endless number of theological, historical, sociological, philosophical, and miscellaneous other details, and many of them are weighty and important. Yet at the same time, there is very little knowledge of the "article" itself. Specifically, we have forgotten that this "article" is not an "article" at all like the others but rather is the very kernel of theology.

So the task now is to bring together both sides — that is, to know the "article" of justification itself, but also with regard to the results of vast theological research. Since this is far from being the normal or natural way to proceed, I am all the more appreciative of the opportunity to write this foreword for an author who shares in this task. Indeed, Mark C. Mattes always keeps clearly in mind the "article" of justification, and does so taking careful account of recent learned literature. Along the way he makes it clear that this "article" has its pivotal role not because Luther put it at the center of faith and theology. The opposite is the case: as the quotation above shows, Luther held it to be the basis of all his teaching and preaching because it sums up God's whole action upon humankind. Therefore, Luther never presented it as a clear formula. In the Smalkald Articles he seems only to compile quotations from the Bible in order to express the "article" of justification, thus showing that it is by no means a formula but the sum of Scripture itself.

Mattes follows Luther in avoiding any definition of *the* "article" as such. Although chapter by chapter he summarizes his results with regard to justification, he keeps it in flux, as it were. By the structure of his summaries, he conveys that the matter is alive and cannot be locked in the cage of any formula or theory. Indeed, what happens is the reverse of a theologian domesticating a doctrine: "If the cross alone is our theology, then the theologian too comes to an end" (p. 170). Mattes knows that to give this "article" a special formula or wording would mean to encircle God. As a matter of fact, this has happened often enough in church history and theology. Many theologians seem to be "in the know" regarding God's will and possibilities and aims and intentions. But, Mattes says, "justification is corrosive to system-building" (p. 177). It is not by chance that he uses Luther's remarks on God's hiddenness with his warning against any attempt to penetrate it, remarks that have been so often critiqued or rejected in disgust. Old Adam (as well as Old Eve) cannot help trying to peek into God's plans — as if this were possible. There is a direct line from the medieval "decency" that obliged God to do or to reject something to the modern measuring of God by *our* conception of Christianity. The allure of this line is that it helps us construct the "overarching theories" (p. 178) that make theology attractive to the academy.

Here it becomes obvious why the "article" of justification is neither a formula nor a theological conception, as Mattes outlines quite clearly. It is no more a formula or a conception than is faith itself. Faith means a personal commitment, a reality, or even *the* reality of my life. Accordingly, the "article" of justification cannot be examined or handled as if it were a thing or a wording or something similar. *It describes and clarifies the reality of our lives as Christians.* It is therefore impossible to deal with it properly from any point of view "beyond" our own condition. There is no effective "beyond," any more than there is a place to stand "beyond" our solar system.

Here is the hidden snag in the systems that Mattes analyzes: they all argue from a point "beyond," be this a principle or a theory or a hermeneutic clue or whatever. In such systems there is no adequate consciousness of God's hiddenness, which, to put it sharply, crosses out all our supposed knowledge about God and his secret plans. Mattes also shows clearly that from this follows the neglect of the difference between law and gospel. To be sure, this is not a new clue for correct proclamation. As such it would itself attempt a position "beyond." The difference between law and gospel is something we become aware of passively, in that God is acting upon us. Then we start recognizing his will and the holiness of his will and become conscious of God's commands and our constant trespass. Thus we find ourselves within a horizon not made by human beings but given to us by God, a horizon surrounding us that gives us no chance to escape from being judged as disobedient and therefore lost. This is the situation in which any speaking of God's law becomes serious and significant. Here is precisely where we experience the wonder that God himself opens up this suffocating situation and leads us into a new sphere, as it were, where we can breathe freely and are freed from the oppression of not only a human law but even God's own law. In other words, we are bestowed with the gospel. It seems obvious; it may even be described. But every description can only be the outlining of what is happening to us. There is — to repeat it — no theoretical "beyond."

Mattes has a keen eye on the law/gospel difference. The way he deals with contemporary theological conceptions reveals that any neglect of this difference (or any position "beyond") turns the gospel into law, even if the law seems denied and mere gospel proclaimed instead. I find it not only intriguing but also rather fascinating to discover how clearly Mattes demonstrates all these interconnections and does so almost incidentally, by simply following his plan to ask about the "article" of justification in general and in the systems of these several scholars in particular. All in all, what makes this book so worth reading is not least the riches of insight and precise observations that are spread along the way. Or, to put it as an oxymoron, Mattes is too good a systematic theologian to follow the temptation of systematizing the "article" of justification; "the quest for a system hinders truth," he says (p. 181). Not in spite of this caveat but precisely because of it he is able to outline clearly the inner logic of justification.

I need not further anticipate what the reader will encounter in detail. Yet it may be useful to give a foretaste of some particular features. The table of contents regarding Jüngel, Pannenberg, Moltmann, Jenson, and Bayer shows a remarkable inner consistency: a map of God enclosing creation; a map of creation enclosing God; the "third use" of the law as founded in the Holy Trinity; the Holy Trinity unfolding in the church; and language as the medium that encloses and conveys all of this. That Mattes' preference is for the language conception is not surprising; nevertheless, that he does not simply copy this conception but rather develops it in his own manner is equally without surprise.

Another major point is Mattes' purpose to treat justification "also for discerning how theology should be done" (p. 8), which proves his awareness of its specific character. This is indeed worth mentioning, since it — notoriously — does not go without saying in the theological literature. Mattes bluntly states, "Justification is primarily a story about God and his claim on the world" (pp. 13-14). This reminds me of a young colleague working on justification to whom, therefore, I had given Gerhard Forde's book *On Being a Theologian of the Cross*. He handed it back to me with the remark that it was quite nice, but he was doing scholarly work. In the statement by Mattes just quoted, he probably would have analyzed the word "story" or "claim" — indicating a level of positivism where the heart of justification lies beyond the horizon. In a certain way, another statement by Mattes also applies: "How 'catholic' is the Roman Catholic Church? Is it not, in its own way, quite sectarian, quite *Roman?*" (p. 79). There is no arguing with sectarians. One should also bear in mind this observation by Mattes: "The best answer to bad politics is good theology" (p. 109).

I have succumbed to the temptation of divulging the contents of this weighty book instead of merely pointing to it. I am happy to be able to do both, for Mattes here helps us all assess justification, as I would put it, as a dimension of perceiving, thinking, arguing, and thus, last but not least, of *doing* theology — *good* theology.

Munkbrarup near Flensburg, Germany   KLAUS SCHWARZWÄLLER
27 June 2004

Acknowledgments

Some describe writing as a lonely task, but this author disagrees. Instead, as I have sought critique of my own work as well as critical engagement with others' work, I have discovered myself to be upheld by a community of churchly scholars that has sustained me and has pushed me to greater honesty, growth, and self-awareness. I'm profoundly grateful to the specific fellowship of scholars that has helped me in various ways with this project.

While this book is solely the responsibility of one person, the efforts of many have helped in its genesis. I am indebted to the following for their individual and team efforts. Chiefly to be recognized is Paul Rorem (Princeton Seminary), who in late August 2001 first helped me germinate the book's theme, has assisted with numerous editorial suggestions, and has stayed with the project to its completion. Gratitude must be offered to Steven Paulson (Luther Seminary), a theological friend for two decades, who thoroughly edited several chapters. Special recognition must also be given to Vitor Westhelle (Lutheran School of Theology at Chicago), who at the last stage of writing generously provided a thorough and critical reading of the text that allowed me to strengthen both its content and its style. My work is honored and graced by a thoughtful foreword from Dr. Klaus Schwarzwäller, former Professor of Systematic Theology at the University of Göttingen.

Additionally, the following scholars read chapters and offered insightful and critical comments: Matthew Becker (Concordia University–Portland), Kathryn Pohlmann Duffy (Grand View College), Ken Sundet Jones (Grand View College), and Dennis Bielfeldt (South Dakota State

University). Their attention to this project clarified the argument as it developed. In addition to the evaluations of these scholars, I wish to acknowledge the repeated copy-editing of Pastor Ronald R. Darge, mentor and friend.

Pam Rees and the library staff of Grand View College have been very helpful in providing materials through interlibrary loan. I'm especially indebted to the kindness of Louise Hay, Coordinator of Instructional Applications, for her generous technological support. Amy Marga and Andrew L. Wilson are to be thanked for indexing this volume.

An earlier draft of this volume was first presented, in a different format, as lectures in a course at Concordia Seminary Graduate School, St. Louis, Missouri, in July 2002. For the hospitality and sponsorship of Charles Arand, as well as the critical engagement of the participants in that seminar, I express my appreciation. Chapters were read to the Cedar River Theological Education Forum in Cedar Rapids, Iowa, in May 2004. I am grateful for the sponsorship of Pastor Randy Kasch. In its current format this book was presented as the focus of the Summer Theological Conference at Mt. Carmel Ministries in Alexandria, Minnesota, in June 2004. For the sponsorship of Pastor Johan and Sonja Hinderlie I am very grateful.

Also, the work here has benefited from engagement with colleagues in several other forums. In particular, cohorts in both the first Lutheran Academy of Scholars in Higher Education and the Rhodes Consultation on the Future of Church-Related Higher Education repeatedly stimulated my theological reflection and self-critique. An ecumenical awareness within these groups helped me to reflect on the significance of the doctrine of justification through non-Lutheran eyes. Also, a *Satis Est* Grant from the Fellowship of Confessional Lutherans helped to provide valuable time for the completion of this book.

I wish to recognize President Kent Henning, Provost Ronald Taylor, and the Board of Trustees of Grand View College for granting me a sabbatical during the spring semester of 2002, which permitted the writing of the first draft of this work.

Most importantly of all, I am indebted to my wife, Carol, for her love and support throughout the entire project.

My intent is to do theology *pro ecclesia* — for the church — in honor and respect of its heritage, with the ultimate goal that this project will contribute to the gospel's being proclaimed more clearly, faithfully, and passionately, and with integrity for the church's mission in the world today.

Abbreviations

AGL	Oswald Bayer. *Aus Glauben leben: Über Rechtfertigung und Heiligung.* 2d ed. Stuttgart: Calwer, 1990.
AK	Oswald Bayer. *Autorität und Kritik: Zu Hermeneutik und Wissenschaftstheorie.* Tübingen: Mohr (Paul Siebeck), 1991.
BC	*The Book of Concord.* Edited by Robert Kolb and Timothy J. Wengert. Minneapolis: Fortress, 2000.
BSELK	*Die Bekenntnisschriften der evangelisch-lutherischen Kirche.* Göttingen: Vandenhoeck & Ruprecht, 1976.
GMW	Eberhard Jüngel. *God as the Mystery of the World: On the Foundation of the Theology of the Crucified One in the Dispute between Theism and Atheism.* Translated by Darrell Guder. Grand Rapids: Eerdmans, 1983.
Jenson, ST 1	Robert Jenson. *Systematic Theology,* vol. 1: *The Triune God.* New York: Oxford University Press, 1997.
Jenson, ST 2	Robert Jenson. *Systematic Theology,* vol. 2: *The Works of God.* New York: Oxford University Press, 1999.
Jüngel, Justification	Eberhard Jüngel. *Justification: The Heart of the Christian Faith.* Translated by Jeffrey Cayzer. Edinburgh: T&T Clark, 2001.
LBF	Oswald Bayer. *Living by Faith: Justification and Sanctification.* Translated by Geoffrey Bromiley. Grand Rapids: Eerdmans, 2003.
LBW	*The Lutheran Book of Worship.* Minneapolis: Augsburg, 1978.
LW	*Luther's Works* (American edition). 55 vols. Philadelphia: Fortress and St. Louis: Concordia, 1955-1986.

LWRNK   Oswald Bayer. *Leibliches Wort: Reformation und Neuzeit im Konflikt.* Tübingen: Mohr (Paul Siebeck), 1992.

Pannenberg, ST 1   Wolfhart Pannenberg. *Systematic Theology.* Vol. 1. Translated by Geoffrey Bromiley. Grand Rapids: Eerdmans, 1991.

Pannenberg, ST 2   Wolfhart Pannenberg. *Systematic Theology.* Vol. 2. Translated by Geoffrey Bromiley. Grand Rapids: Eerdmans, 1994.

Pannenberg, ST 3   Wolfhart Pannenberg. *Systematic Theology.* Vol. 3. Translated by Geoffrey Bromiley. Grand Rapids: Eerdmans, 1998.

SA   Oswald Bayer. *Schöpfung als Anrede: Zu einer Hermeneutik der Schöpfung.* 2d ed. Tübingen: Mohr (Paul Siebeck), 1990.

TE I   Eberhard Jüngel. *Theological Essays I.* Translated by John B. Webster. Edinburgh: T&T Clark, 1989.

TE II   Eberhard Jüngel. *Theological Essays II.* Translated by John B. Webster. Edinburgh: T&T Clark, 1995.

TH   Jürgen Moltmann. *Theology of Hope.* Translated by James Leitch. New York: Harper & Row, 1967.

Theologie   Oswald Bayer. *Theologie.* Gütersloh: Gütersloher Verlaghaus, 1994.

WA   *Luthers Werke: Kritische Gesamtausgabe (Schriften).* 65 vols. Weimar: H. Böhlau, 1883-1993.

INTRODUCTION

Chapter One

The Question of the Doctrine of Justification's Role in Theology

It is said that the problem with the doctrine of justification by grace alone through faith alone is not that it has been tried and found wanting, but that it has not been tried. Of course, this supposition is not entirely true. If the doctrine of justification had not been tried, at least by some preachers through the course of history, there would be no church. After all, the church is a creature of the gospel *(creatura evangelii)*, and even the gates of hell will not prevail against it (Matt. 16:18), despite what we sometimes think. The word does not return empty (Isa. 55:11). However, the word is effective often in the face of and in opposition to our theology and cultural presuppositions. The fact that we do not receive the full impact of the doctrine of justification in the church's mission is due to our failure to use it thoroughly and consistently. At its core, the doctrine threatens all self-defense before God. If the doctrine is to be permitted to have its effect, then it must be freed from our theological and ecclesiastical defenses. The doctrine needs to be used in both theological construction and pastoral discernment. One purpose of this volume is to bring both theology and proclamation, as public endeavors, into greater alignment.[1] Theology needs to take leave of the quest for system and affirm its role as the art of discerning how to deliver the promise.[2]

---

1. As will be specified, this work builds on that found in Gerhard O. Forde, *Theology Is for Proclamation* (Minneapolis: Fortress, 1990).

2. Of "promise," Oswald Bayer notes that it "is the center of Luther's theology. When he says that God promises, he does not refer to something in the future that we may antici-pate. The promise is not only an announcement that will only be fulfilled in the future. It is a

We can see the misalignment between theology and proclamation in the supposition that the doctrine of justification is to be limited to first-order discourse — the attempt to discern the proper distinction between law and gospel, command and promise, in preaching — and thus is to have no bearing upon the attempt to establish an overall systematic theology.[3] We can likewise see this misalignment in the view that the doctrine of justification is to be seen as the foundation for systematics[4] but not its "hub" by which all aspects of doctrine and life are configured. In contrast to four of the theologians examined in this study, we must contend that the doctrine of justification is not to be limited to first-order discourse, nor is it to be a foundation for theology in contrast to a hub, but rather that it bears upon second-order discourse and affects all aspects of doctrine and life. The doctrine of justification itself sets appropriate boundaries in the quest for coherent, consistent, and comprehensive theological, metaphysical, and ethical systems, insofar as reflection can establish them in light of the law-gospel distinction.

These quests should be limited by the proper distinction between law and gospel;[5] this distinction cannot be subsumed under or margin-

---

valid and powerful promise and pledge that takes immediate and present effect. A good comparison is the text of English banknotes: 'I promise to pay the bearer on demand the sum of X amount of pounds. London, for the governor and company of the Bank of England, Chief Cashier.' With this understanding of the term 'promise' Luther was moving along the lines of medieval German legal thinking that used the word *promissio* to describe the way a ruler bound and committed himself at his enthronement. This was how God also committed himself in the *promissio* pronounced in his name. He was bound by it and will stick to it and keep it. Faith lays hold of God by accepting and counting on the given promise, and therefore it lays hold of the 'faithfulness of God, of his truth, his Word, and his righteousness.'" See LBF 51-52.

3. For instance, compare Niels Henrik Gregersen, "Ten Theses on the Future of Lutheran Theology: Charisms, Contexts, and Challenges," *dialog* 41 (2002): 268. Gregersen writes, "The distinction between law and gospel is necessary in order to safeguard the unconditional character of the gospel itself. However, Luther's dialectic of law and gospel should not be elevated into a theological principle that structures the interpretation of Christian faith from beginning to end. The law-gospel distinction belongs to a first-order theology of divine-human speech acts, not to the second-order reflection of the God-world relation in general."

4. This is done by many essayists in *The Promise of Lutheran Ethics*, ed. Karen L. Bloomquist and John R. Stumme (Minneapolis: Fortress, 1993).

5. Even to this day, *The Proper Distinction between Law and Gospel* (St. Louis: Concordia, n.d.) by C. F. W. Walther, recognized by Werner Elert (*Law and Gospel*, trans. Ed-

alized by a comprehensive theological, metaphysical, or ethical unity. This side of the *eschaton*, faith cannot and should not be transcended by understanding, by sight (2 Cor. 5:7). Sight entails a transparency that would be able to defend or explain human suffering, guilt, and finitude from God's point of view. This is simply not humanly possible. Because this is so, all people live from some form of faith, either in God or in an idol. The problem with idolatry, however, is that it is dissatisfied with such faith. It attempts to transcend faith as a means to escape our fundamental insecurity, which is a result of our finitude. But there is no escape. The only answer to our death is the new life awakened by God's promise. If it is true that all must live from some kind of faith, then this question arises: In what or in whom will we place our confidence? An idol promises a false security since it offers an attempt to transcend the fundamental uncertainty about our place in the cosmos with which we must always contend but which genuine faith can accept. Faith in God's promise allows us to entrust our lives to the care of God as faithful to this promise, even in opposition to God's own accusation against sin, or the terror that can arise from the experience of God's hiddenness.

All systematic theological frameworks are subordinate to the doctrine of justification, the "doctrine by which the church stands or falls" (*articulus stantis et cadentis ecclesiae* [Valentin Löscher [1673-1749],[6] or the "center and boundary"[7] of theological discourse. The doctrine of justification is the *basis* for theology, since it directs theology's task as giving Jesus Christ as *sacramentum* to those oppressed by the law, living under divine wrath, or being made uncertain by the hidden God *(deus absconditus)*. It is the *boundary* of theology in that it sets limits to all attempts to subordinate this activity to any other comprehensive task. As Luther expressed it in the *Smalcald Articles*, "Nothing in this article can be

---

ward H. Schroeder [Philadelphia: Fortress, 1967], p. 2) as one of the few nineteenth-century theologians to have discerned the proper distinction between law and gospel, remains a helpful study. One of the most important aspects of Walther's thinking — taken directly from Luther — is that the proper distinction between law and gospel is an *art* which engages and embraces all of industry. See *The Proper Distinction between Law and Gospel*, p. 46.

6. See Gerhard Sauter, "God Creating Faith: The Doctrine of Justification from the Reformation to the Present," *Lutheran Quarterly* 11 (1997): 44.

7. Ernst Wolf, "Die rechtfertigungslehre als Mitte und Grenze reformatorischer Theologie," in *Peregrinatio*, vol. 2, *Studien zur reformatorischen Theologie, zum Kirchenrecht und zur Sozialethik* (Munich: Kaiser, 1965), pp. 11-21.

conceded or given up, even if heaven and earth or whatever is transitory passed away."[8] Further, Luther states, "This doctrine, I say, they [our opponents] will not tolerate under any circumstances. We are able to forgo it just as little; for if this doctrine vanishes, the church vanishes. Then no error can any longer be resisted."[9] Neither theoretical nor practical reason can give us the assurance that God is for us. The quest for a comprehensive system of all knowledge, the unity of truth, insofar as it seeks to transform faith into sight, ironically hinders truth, which must be satisfied with the conviction of Johann Georg Hamann (1730-1788) that "our knowledge is fragmentary."[10] It is not that the criteria of four of the theologians examined in this study are "alien" to theology's agenda, as a Barthian "revelatory positivism" might have it, but that these criteria are always tantamount — in one way or another — to law, or even to the mask of the hidden God.

In other words, if we relate the doctrine of justification consistently to the quest for system in theology, then it applies not only to first-order discourse, as most Protestant theologians would affirm, but also to second-order discourse as well. Particularly in light of the current attempt to situate theology as an "integrating" discipline in the curriculum of the university,[11] this supposition entails that we must forgo situating theology within an encyclopedic scope for truth, whether it be metaphysically, morally, or existentially grounded, overviews which by their very nature revert to theological claims. Even those scholars who deny an ultimate spiritual

---

8. BC 301:5 (BSELK 415:20-416:2).

9. "Warning to His Dear German People," in LW 47:54 (WA 30/3:319-20).

10. Hamann, Letter to Herder (May 8, 1785), in *J. G. Hamann, 1730-1788: A Study in Christian Existence* (New York: Harper & Brothers, 1960), p. 245.

11. One can hardly ignore John Leith's point: "Theology written in German universities and in the tradition that began with Schleiermacher fascinates many American theologians today. This theology has many striking qualities: generally a wide philosophical background, an intellectual cleverness, and not infrequently a pedantic quality. Yet those who are fascinated with this theology have not, to my knowledge, taken seriously the ineffectiveness of this theology in Germany itself and in Europe. Why has this theology so little effect on the vitality of a declining church in Europe and so little impact on social and political life? Every seminary professor needs a reality check: What do the students who have taken seriously the professor's courses accomplish when they go out as pastors? Is the theology of the university preachable so that it can sustain congregations over a period of time?" See *Crisis in the Church: The Plight of Theological Education* (Louisville: Westminster/John Knox Press, 1997), p. 38.

reality appeal to some alternative ultimate, such as chance, nothingness, matter, or the self in order to explain the cosmos. From the perspective of the doctrine of justification, we can say that at its most fundamental level, truth is not finally the coherence of all propositions in an overarching metaphysical or ethical system, nor the correspondence of all statements to reality as such, as perceived for our time. While such comprehensive approaches to reality are not to be dismissed and do in fact have meaning within an attempt to narrate our understandings of the world (we are born metaphysicians),[12] we must affirm that, more than anything else, truth is fundamentally agreement with God's judgment with respect to humans, given in the promise that God is well-pleased *only* with sinners for Jesus' sake. In such a "solemn exchange,"[13] we give God his due by giving God glory.

It is this theocentricism[14] which is challenged in today's church. True: the Sabbath is made for the human and not the human for the Sabbath (Mark 2:27). Jesus' critique of pharisaical self-righteousness reveals God's desire to save. It does not, however, serve to justify the supposition that the truth of faith is to be found in its relevance. Quite the contrary. The above dominical saying must be remembered in light of this other: one does not live by bread alone, but by every word that proceeds from the mouth of God (Matthew 4:4). The Sabbath and its word are God's generosity, God's service to us. To acknowledge this service as God's gift, and to give him glory for it, is to render God his due, and thereby receive liberation from the tyranny that we could serve as our own gods for ourselves. More than anything else, this word of promise — "I am the Lord your God" (Exodus 20:2) — is delivered with the stipulation that is bound to ignite conflict: "you shall have no other gods before me." All purported gods must be tested and challenged in light of this command, if we are to hear and receive God, who wants to be gracious. Humans exist for God's good pleasure, not vice versa. In this truth, humans can find liberation from their self-imposed tutelage arising from the belief that their freedom could be secured in exercising their self-expression. The need to actualize this

---

12. "Moreover he has put a sense of past and future into their minds, yet they cannot find out what God has done from the beginning to the end" (Ecclesiastes 3:11).

13. See Eberhard Jüngel, *The Freedom of a Christian: Luther's Significance for Contemporary Theology*, trans. Roy A. Harrisville (Minneapolis: Augsburg, 1988), pp. 62-65.

14. Phillip Watson, *Let God Be God! An Interpretation of the Theology of Martin Luther* (Philadelphia: Muhlenberg, 1948), pp. 34-38, 59-64.

potential becomes a compulsion to authenticate and establish the self. In such self-expression, we become like Atlas, bearing the whole world on our shoulders, and in that way are doomed to be free (Jean Paul Sartre [1905-1980]).[15]

The purpose of this study, then, is to encourage and promote the doctrine of justification so that it will be used in the church — not only with respect to preaching, pastoral conversation, and administration of absolution and the sacraments, but also for discerning how theology should be done. While the doctrine of justification might have implications for all creation, and thus be far more than the "article by which *the church* stands or falls," it applies at least to the church. If we fail to get the doctrine of justification right with respect to theology, then we fail not only the doctrine itself and theology, but also the church.

The Purpose of This Study

The theme examined in this study is the extent to which five contemporary leading Protestant theologians — Eberhard Jüngel, Wolfhart Pannenberg, Jürgen Moltmann, Robert Jenson, and Oswald Bayer — integrate justification by faith alone as a standard for systematics. These thinkers are pivotal for current theology; their works are paradigmatic, offering trajectories of thinking which apply to other theologians. Similarly, criticisms of these prominent authors also apply to others. This study finds the first four thinkers wanting with respect to justification *sola fide,* since each subordinates justification to the quest for a comprehensive system in different ways. The intellectual strategies employed to articulate a system take precedence over justification as a test of genuine theology. These systems seek either to accommodate to some aspect of modernity, perceived as having the greatest apologetic potential for theology, or, in contrast, to affirm a catholic identity as a hopeful alternative to modernity, perceived as wholly bankrupt. When presenting these theologians, we will not primarily examine the development of their theologies but instead bring to the fore those features in their thinking that bear on the doctrine of justification.

This study aims to show that, overall, with respect to justification, extraneous and even false assumptions are employed by the first four

---

15. Oswald Bayer, "Zukunft und Schöpfung," in SA 147.

thinkers. These assumptions situate the doctrine so as to give it a secondary status in theology. Its secondary status is that the doctrine serves as a foundation but not as a hub for all other doctrines. Systematics can then be developed on the basis of other goals and agendas than those set by the doctrine of justification itself. At best, law and gospel apply to individuals' consciences but not to the overall goal of systematics, which should be developed within a matrix of theory, ethics, an existential experience, or various combinations thereof. Thereby, systematics becomes dislodged from proclamation, and vice versa. However, these quests for theory, ethics, or a meta-experience are themselves subject to the doctrine's critique, and thus are in no position to situate the doctrine. The typology offered here is not meant to be exhaustive but illustrative of pitfalls one encounters when one seeks to render faith as sight.

The critique of the first four theologians benefits from an analysis of the fifth theologian presented: Oswald Bayer. Bayer's theology provides helpful tools by which to assess the quest for system in the other theologians. The concepts employed from Bayer used to critique the other theologians include the following: (1) rejecting the tendency of modern theology to situate the gospel within overarching frameworks of psychology, metaphysics, and ethics, (2) unmasking the Hegelian "natural theology of the cross" as structuring these other theologies, (3) rejecting reason as a "monarch" to which theology must systematically conform, and (4) specifying the gospel linguistically as a promise. It is, however, appropriate to include Bayer in the overall outline, since his work, as a theology indebted to the linguistics of the speech act, also undergoes an internal critique with respect to its consistency and fidelity. Bayer's work is especially to be contrasted with Jenson's. Although both seek a robust theology that does not accommodate to modern foundationalism, the gospel for Bayer maintains its integrity with respect to the church; it is not conflated with the church, something Jenson tends to do.

The discerning reader will also see the author's dependence not only on Bayer's theology but also on Gerhard O. Forde's theology.[16] The themes of Forde claimed in this analysis include the following: (1) that theology is for proclamation, not speculation or social reconstruction; (2) that the gospel creates the new being in opposition to human effort *coram deo;*

16. For an overview of Forde's theology, see Mark C. Mattes, "Gerhard Forde on Reenvisioning Theology in Light of the Gospel," *Lutheran Quarterly* 13 (1999): 373-93.

(3) that law, when used for salvation, is always deadly for the old being, but finds its appropriate place in creation through the agency of the gospel; and (4) that through the gospel we can be restored to creation as God intends it. In concert together, Bayer and Forde permit Luther's voice to be heard today. They help us understand that when humans acknowledge God's divinity in faith, then concomitantly they are free to accept their creatureliness. They can live free of the pretension that they can provide their own meaning for themselves. They are free to live "outside of themselves," so that they can listen to and receive from God and others, and serve others and the earth free from any quest for gain or merit.

A consistent approach to distinguishing law and gospel will resist a strategy of accommodation as the means for theology to secure a place in the wider academy. Rather, distinguishing (not separating) law and gospel mediates other disciplines by analyzing how law is operative in them. Here, we do not appeal to faith fideistically as faith in faith itself, but instead to faith in the God who is ever speaking to us, not only directly and clearly in Scripture but indirectly and sometimes obscurely in all creation (Psalm 19), in every experience and encounter with both humans and the non-human creation. Ultimately, discerning how to speak the gospel can help us acknowledge providential grace in creation, and not only the accusing law. This study affirms that justification, properly understood, is not solely a discrete theological *locus*, or theology's starting point, but rather the evaluator of all theology — including the standard of reason operative in theology. It is not one topic, or even foundation, but rather the basis by which to evaluate all. When the doctrine of justification is honored as a principle of pastoral discernment, then it no longer appears as a late medieval concept needing translation in order to address modern "meaninglessness," the supposition which crippled the Helsinki convention of the Lutheran World Federation (1963). Rather, the doctrine of justification serves as a *discrimen*[17] by which to discern law and gospel, insofar as God interprets our lives in both Scripture and nature.

David Kelsey's definition of the concept of *discrimen* in contrast to *norm* and *criterion* can be useful in our attempt to understand Luther's

---

17. See Oswald Bayer, "Gesetzt und Evangelium bei Luther," in LWRNK 38. The reference in Luther is WA TR 5, Nr. 5518: "do ich das discrimen fande . . . , da Riss ich her durch." As such, it is comparable to Luther's claim that the proper distinction between law and gospel is an art.

view of justification.[18] A norm is absolute, excluding other theological norms. A criterion is not absolute but is derived from norms. A *discrimen* is a configuration of criteria that are organically related to one another as reciprocal co-efficients. For example, for Roman Catholics, the church is a part of the *discrimen*, while for Protestants, it is the context of the *discrimen*. The criteria organically related to one another in justification include law and gospel, death and resurrection, God's hiddenness and revelation, God's wrath and grace, and the distinction between *coram deo* and *coram mundo*. Hence, as a *discrimen*, the doctrine of justification is the critical point that shapes other doctrines and church practices. Our teachings need to conform to it, as well as our pastoral practices. Is the prophetic word to be spoken so as to afflict the comfortable or comfort the afflicted? The doctrine of justification is bound fundamentally to pastoral practice. It calls for an imaginative act of assessing how to discern law from gospel in any given context. The argument of this study is that the quest for system is also subject to justification as *discrimen*. The distinction between law and gospel subverts system. Theology exists primarily for pastoral discernment.

If justification by faith alone is taken as this discernment, then we must dethrone reason as the "monarch"[19] that offers a grand unified theory of everything, subordinating the rest of reality under the modern paradigms of knowing, doing, and feeling, or perhaps instead the ancient paradigm of the true, beautiful, and good. We can affirm that reason is "something divine."[20] But reason offers its good only when it is limited to penultimate matters — particularly when it is subordinated to love as the quest to serve others. When it is inflated in the assumption that it can penetrate into ultimate matters, it violates its own boundaries, its own finitude, and manifests an *ambitio divinitatis*[21] inappropriate for it. Humans

18. See *The Uses of Scripture in Recent Theology* (Philadelphia: Fortress, 1975), pp. 160-69.

19. See Oswald Bayer, "The Being of Christ in Faith," *Lutheran Quarterly* 10 (1996): 146.

20. LW 34:137 (WA 39/1:175 [thesis 4]).

21. This concept is a central concern to this essay, and it behooves us to examine it in several passages in Luther. In his letter to George Spalatin (June 30, 1530), Luther writes, "Be strong in the Lord, and on my behalf continuously admonish Philip [Melanchthon] not to become like God [Genesis 3:5], but to fight that innate ambition to be like God, which was planted in us in paradise by the devil. This [ambition] doesn't do us any good. It drove

are bound to speculate about questions of origins and the future. When they attempt to situate God on the continuum arising from the process of this inquiry, their thinking becomes "justifying" thinking.

Undoubtedly, many ecumenists[22] seek greater institutional unity for the church in Western culture, in which religion is increasingly privatized. This affects the perception of how or whether the doctrine of justification *sola fide* should be central to the church's teaching. For these ecumenists, bondage to sin and consciences bound to law do not seem nearly as relevant as ecclesial solidarity or countercultural uniqueness in the face of Christianity's apparent marginalization due to secularism and nihilism. In contrast, this study affirms that a visibly unified Christendom is not nearly

---

Adam from paradise, and it alone also drives us away, and drives peace away from us. In summary: we are to be men and not God; it will not be otherwise, or eternal anxiety and affliction will be our reward" (LW 49:337 [WA B 5:415, 41-46]).

Also, in the *Disputation against Scholastic Theology* (1517), thesis 17 (LW 31:10 [WA 1:225]) Luther wrote, "Man is by nature unable to want God to be God. Indeed, he himself wants to be God, and does not want God to be God." Luther noted that we are humanized by God's judgment that evaluates us as sinners. Hence in his exposition of Psalm 5:3 (WA 5:128, 39–129, 4), Luther wrote, "Through the kingdom of his humanity, or (as the apostle says) through the kingdom of his flesh, occurring in faith, he conforms us to himself and crucifies us, by making out of unhappy and arrogant gods true men, i.e., miserable ones and sinners." For Luther (in the *Treatise on Good Works* [LW 44:32, WA 6:211]), one makes oneself into one's own idol if one looks to works and not faith alone *coram deo*. Hence, "Now it may well be that if these things are done with such faith that we believe that they please God, then they are praiseworthy, not because of their virtue, but because of that very faith by which all works are of equal value, as has been said. But if we have any doubt about it, or do not believe that God is gracious to us and pleased with us, or if we presume to please him first and foremost by good works, then it is all pure deception. To all appearance God is honored, but in reality the *self has been set up as an idol.*"

Further, in the *Lectures on Galatians,* 1535 (LW 26:257-58 [WA 40/1:404-5]), Luther wrote of those attempting to "keep the law" that "they not only do not keep it, but they also deny the first Commandment, the promises of God, and the blessing promised to Abraham. They deny faith and try to bless themselves by their own works, that is, to justify themselves, to set themselves free from sin and death, to overcome the devil, and to capture heaven by force — which is to deny God and *to set oneself up in place of God.* For all these are exclusively works of the Divine Majesty, not of any creature, whether angelic or human." For further references, see Eberhard Jüngel, *The Freedom of a Christian: Luther's Significance for Contemporary Theology,* pp. 24-25.

22. For the single best study on the doctrine of justification in ecumenical discussion, see Gottfried Martens, *Die Rechtfertigung des Sünders — Rettungshandeln Gottes oder historisches Interpretament?* (Göttingen: Vandenhoeck & Ruprecht, 1992).

as important as delivering God's gifts of forgiveness of sins, life, and salvation. The former quest, noble as it seems, is accountable to the latter.

Current spirituality, so steeped as it is in therapeutic modes of thinking, is apt to present, in the famous phrase of Reinhold Niebuhr (1892-1971), "a God without wrath bringing men without sin into a kingdom without judgment through the ministrations of Christ without a cross."[23] No wonder anxious consciences are not to be found! They are anesthetized with antidepressants, alcohol, entertainment, therapy, and in this case, religion itself, spirituality, as a narcotic. However, from the perspective of Reformation theology, the quarrel about the gospel's distinctiveness is less a dispute about how to secure anxious consciences and more a matter of how to honor God properly.[24] Can *more than* faith be offered by humans to give God the worship that is God's due? If the doctrine of justification is to be understood, it must be freed from the highly anthropocentric modes in which it has often been interpreted. It is, in contrast, a thoroughly theocentric doctrine, concerned not just (let alone solely) with the anxious conscience but also with how God is honored. God is not only humanity's solution but also humanity's problem. God is the threat that humanity is not and can never be self-sufficient. The human is not self-generative. All human creativity, as *poiesis, praxis,* and *theoria,* presupposes that life is given, in biblical perspective, as a gift. To honor the First Commandment — to fear, love, and trust in God above all things — can be done by faith alone. No effort or energy on our part can render God the honor that is his due. Only faith in the promise which introduces the commandments, "I am the Lord your God," frees us from the bondage of attempting to secure ourselves in the face of our fundamental insecurities and apparent meaninglessness. It allows our humanity to be free. Such freedom opens *poiesis, praxis,* and *theoria* as forms of service. Free from *ambitio divinitatis,* we are returned to creation.

Only such faith actually fulfills the law, since the law, after all, is a custodian leading us to Christ (Gal. 3:24). The issue with justification, then, is establishing truth: Do we want God to be God even in our theologizing? In this regard, we must keep in mind that all people are theologians in one way or another! Justification is primarily a story about God

---

23. *The Kingdom of God in America* (New York: Willet, Clark & Co., 1937), p. 193.

24. David Yeago, "The Catholic Luther," in *The Catholicity of the Reformation,* ed. Carl E. Braaten and Robert W. Jenson (Grand Rapids: Eerdmans, 1996), pp. 17-18.

and his claim on the world, not especially a story about one's inner turmoil, or social inequalities and their amelioration, or a purported metaphysical unity of reality. Righteousness is of two kinds.[25] *Coram deo*, it is God's loving, self-giving affirmation and claim which permits humans to live as creatures for this earth, entrusting life into God's care. Before God, we are completely passive. *Coram mundo*, it is the active service to the neighbor unleashed through us by God's generosity. With respect to creatures and the earth, we are ever active. When *ambitio divinitatis* comes to its end, when it suffers its death, through God's own agency upon it in re-creation through the word, the human is liberated to cooperate with God in his creativity and work.[26] Yet, such *cooperatio* must not ignore, beyond ethics, a fundamentally aesthetic reception of this world in all its manifold plurality, its sheer gifted beauty and lavish abundance, a treasure to be honored and savored. Counter to all heroism promoted in society, religion, and the academy, it is not the moral person but the sinner, not the wise man but the fool, who agrees with God and his decrees (1 Cor. 1:22-25).

Unlike metaphysics (the overarching structure of reality) or ethics (the overarching structure of moral order), theology is a universal discipline that discerns God's action as the source of both metaphysics' being and ethics' doing. Theology discerns how God confounds the self-secure, hardens the impenitent (such as Pharaoh), and consoles, by means of the promise, those who lament or accuse themselves. The promise must be "held up to God,"[27] even in the face of human attempts to establish metaphysics or ethics. In this regard, Oswald Bayer's contention that faith should not be transformed into "existentializing," "theorizing," or "ethicizing" about the divine is particularly insightful.[28] In such attempts, we will encounter God in hiddenness, just as Moses was offered only the *posteriora dei* (Exod. 33:17-23).[29] God's works appear in contradictions and oppositions. Faith alone is the appropriate response to revelation as pre-

---

25. For further discussion, see Robert Kolb, "Luther on the Two Kinds of Righteousness: Reflections on His Two-Dimensional Definition of Humanity at the Heart of His Theology," *Lutheran Quarterly* 13 (1999): 449-66, and Charles P. Arand, "Two Kinds of Righteousness as a Framework for Law and Gospel in the *Apology*," *Lutheran Quarterly* 15 (2001): 417-39.

26. Luther, *The Bondage of the Will*, LW 33:241-45 (WA 18:753-55).

27. Luther, "Large Catechism," in BC 443:21 and 444:28 (BSELK 667:21 and 669:28).

28. See Theologie, C, 4.

29. Compare LW 31:52 (WA 1:263, 1f.)

sented under the sign of the opposite *(sub contrario)*. Hence, justification is not to be seen as the foundation for the structure of one's theology. Rather, it is the *discrimen* by which all theological *loci* are to be evaluated.

Luther Our Contemporary

This brings us to the question, Can Luther really be our contemporary? Is it really appropriate to evaluate contemporary theologians in light of Luther? Must he not rather be updated?

Of course, Luther does not need to be "updated" if there is no difference between him and us with respect to the question of salvation, whatever his scientific or ethical liabilities or lapses. Indeed, our attempts to update Luther might simply be tantamount to neutralizing his power. We see our problem as finding alternative salvations that exercise our potentiality with respect to a perceived ultimate, because of a fundamental misgiving about faith. Admittedly, faith is necessary for salvation. But no one believes it is sufficient. We want more. Ultimately, we want an assurance derived from elsewhere than faith. However, if the gospel is to be taken seriously, we must affirm that faith is not only necessary but also sufficient for life. The gospel is enough. It does not need to be supplemented and perhaps even verified by our feelings, metaphysical schemes, or dreams for an ideal future state, or even a perfected church. Faith (trusting in God's promise) is enough. Although it hardly needs saying, Luther has no status as a prophet, as if his writings were to be thought of as a second revelation alongside Scripture (though he may well be that messenger of the "everlasting gospel" [Rev. 14:6] foretold in Scripture).[30] For all of that, justification *sola fide* is not a sectarian but a wholly catholic

---

30. Hence, of this passage R. C. H. Lenski wrote, "Sometimes it was thought that Luther was prefigured by the third angel. The other two were thought to be Wycliff and Huss. When commentators reject this interpretation, they do so without sufficient reason. The text for Reformation Day is well chosen, for the fathers of Reformation days selected it not because they identified the first angel *wholly* with Luther. The Reformer, too, preached only the old apostolic gospel. The angel with the eternal gospel is the messenger from heaven for the *whole* New Testament Era and thus most certainly includes a man like Luther who once more made the eternal gospel ring out in all its saving power and purity in the whole wide world despite all the devil's effort to hush his voice." See *The Interpretation of St. John's Revelation* (Minneapolis: Augsburg, 1963), p. 428.

doctrine.[31] As such, it too sets boundaries for catholicity, which as a tradition is itself constituted as an argument about the nature and criteria of catholicity itself.[32]

For Luther, justification can be seen as (1) wholly for the sake of Christ and his righteousness, (2) by virtue of the imputation of this righteousness through the forgiveness of sin for our benefit, (3) through the faith that receives this forgiveness, not as a new quality in us but as a laying hold of the gracious promise, (4) happening as an instantaneous act and not gradually, (5) offering a renewal of life based on this forgiveness, and (6) bound to the proper distinction between law, which brings an end to the old being, and the gospel, which creates the new.[33] Correlated with these affirmations is the discernment that as saving, God is a promising God — promising to be for us, to provide for us, to forgive sin. Insofar as this promise finds its good in its pastoral usage, in its appropriation, we must discern God as "preached," in which these goods are delivered, from God "not preached," and must therefore discern God as "revealed," even in the darkness of Jesus' death on the cross, from God as "hidden," masked in various forms in creation. For Luther, we deal with God in the faith that clings to the promise and not in the doubts that arise from encountering God as hidden, the God who "works life, death, and all in all."[34] This latter view of God, the *deus absconditus*, we daily encounter behind the terrifying and chaotic power of nature that can threaten to consume us, in theological abstractions of God's power, in his seemingly callous indifference to our plight, and in the threat of dealing with a deity who rejects as well as accepts us. God's acceptance is specific, physical, and concrete. It is mediated — administered and instituted — in a word that is a body, and a body that is linguistic,[35] as bread and wine, water, and the

---

31. Most recently, this has been acknowledged by Thomas C. Oden; see *The Justification Reader* (Grand Rapids: Eerdmans, 2002) for abundant quotes from the church fathers affirming justification *sola fide*.

32. Alasdair MacIntyre, *After Virtue*, 2d ed. (Notre Dame, Ind.: University of Notre Dame Press, 1983), p. 222: "A living tradition then is a historically extended, socially embodied argument, and an argument precisely in part about the goods which constitute that tradition."

33. There are many fine expositions of Luther on justification. For this list I am indebted to Uuras Saarnivaara, *Luther Discovers the Gospel* (St. Louis: Concordia, 1951), pp. 9-13.

34. Luther, *The Bondage of the Will*, trans. J. I. Packer and O. R. Johnston (Old Tappan, N.J.: Fleming H. Revell, 1957), p. 170 (WA 18:685).

35. Theologie, C, 1.1.2, p. 399.

voice of the preacher. For Luther, nature then needs not perfecting, as Aquinas (1224/6-1274) thought, but liberating from incurvation. Luther — *eleutheros* — the very name means "freedom."[36]

An Overview of This Study

This study examines five theologians, three seeking accommodation to modernity and two not. Other than Bayer, these thinkers can be seen as offering "natural theologies of the cross" when they are evaluated with respect to their ability to honor justification *sola fide* as a *discrimen*. In the first three thinkers, justification is seen as beneficial within the university, structured in Weberian[37] terms as having the goal of distinguishing facts from values. In the first three thinkers, theology's primary role is not to challenge but to accommodate to the assumptions of the university and wider culture. We begin, in Chapter Two, with Jüngel's theology of interpreting justification in light of the "word event," because Jüngel is the best current representative of the Neo-Orthodox thinking that prevailed in theological circles in the mid-twentieth century. This movement sought relevance for justification as an experience that unleashes human authenticity. In Chapter Three, we examine Pannenberg's reaction against Neo-Orthodoxy's privileging the "word" as a unique, positive revelation in opposition to the academy's supposition that truth is always a claim to universality, not specificity. In contrast to seeing truth as mediated in such particularity, Pannenberg positions justification within a general metaphysics. Not seeing justification through the lens of either a unique experience or a universal metaphysics, Moltmann, in Chapter Four, presents justification as an affirmation of the individual who is enfolded within the ethical quest for universal justice for victims and the earth. All three theologians work within a framework in which the theoretical and the practical, fact and feelings, nature and spirit, and explanation and understanding are opposed. In addition, when they challenge these oppositions, they

---

36. Bernd Moeller and Karl Stackmann, "Luder — Luther — Eleutherius: Erwägungen zu Luthers Namen," in *Nachrichten der Akamemie der Wissenschaften in Göttingen,* vol. 1, Philologisch-Historische Klasse (Göttingen: Vandenhoeck & Ruprecht, 1981), and Hans-Walter Krumwiede, *Glaubenszuversicht und Weltgestaltung bei Martin Luther: Mit einem Ausblick auf Dietrich Bonhoeffer* (Göttingen: Vandenhoeck & Ruprecht, 1983).

37. The perspective on Weber here is dependent upon MacIntyre, *After Virtue,* 2d ed.

do so only indirectly and *ad hoc,* not directly and systematically. Similar to Descartes (1596-1650), Kant (1724-1804), and Kierkegaard (1813-1855), each agrees that nature is a particular *locus* of experience subject to measurement, while the person as such is not.

These theologies can be typified in light of Schleiermacher's (1768-1834) fundamental categories of "knowing," "doing," and "feeling" as fields on which to develop theological categories.[38] In his quest to offer a comprehensive scope to Christian convictions, Jüngel, harkening back to Bultmann, and similar to Schleiermacher, associated theological truth with a meta-experience. More specifically, this feeling is termed an "experience with experience," mediated through the specific cross of Jesus Christ in which, similar to Hegelian metaphysics, infinite reality is made finite and finite reality is made infinite, a misunderstanding of the *finitum capax infiniti* doctrine. Here, justification serves not as a *discrimen* by which to deliver the promise, but as a basis in which the cross is the key that deciphers eternity, making it transparent, enfolding us within it.

Pannenberg, in contrast, appeals not to feeling, an existential meta-experience, but to knowing. He starts not with the specific cross of Jesus Christ but, indebted to Hegelian epistemology, with experience in general, arguing from it that God, as the most universal of categories, must be assumed if there is to be a reason for any intellectual comprehension whatsoever. However, the ultimate basis for this intelligence will be perceived only at the end of cosmic history; Jesus' resurrection is the guarantee that this potential completion in the divine life will be actualized. Here gospel and law will coincide in the future intelligibility that will be secured.

In contrast to the previous two thinkers, Moltmann grounds his theology not in feeling or knowing but in doing. Ultimate unity and coherence in the world should be based on establishing an ideal society that will fulfill all needs and expectations, particularly of those who are powerless. Faith currently gives individuals the courage to develop their potential and the motivation to establish a global community of equality.

In contrast to these strategies that *accommodate* the doctrine of justification to modern assumptions in one way or another, we will examine two thinkers who seek *non-accommodating* strategies. First, Robert Jenson

---

38. *The Christian Faith,* trans. and ed. H. R. Mackintosh and J. S. Stewart (Philadelphia: Fortress, 1976), §3, p. 5.

exposes the modern world as one that has "lost its story," that is fundamentally nihilistic, since it has rejected the medieval view of God as the final causality, the *summum bonum* of the world. Counter to the pervasive individualism fostered in the Weberian approach that separates facts and values, Jenson wants us to aspire toward an ideal community where reason is not instrumental (reducible to measurement) but participatory (as taught by Neoplatonism) in the Holy Trinity as humanity's highest good, restoring *the* story to the West. The scientific quest for explanation is mediated only through narration, relativizing "science," with its instrumental reason, to this comprehensive narrative, and providing "objectivity" to a catholic *ethos*. However, while formally Jenson works within a catholic narrative outside modern modes of thinking, he duplicates these modes of thinking in the content of his Hegelian-indebted approach to God, leaving his view markedly unstable.

Finally, Oswald Bayer offers us a systematics in which theology is subordinated to justification as its basis and boundary. In contrast to the other thinkers, and in loyalty to justification *sola fide*, Bayer acknowledges that our knowledge seeking an encyclopedic view will only and ever be quite fragmentary. In contrast to Jenson's catholicism as the comprehensive focus for the *telos* of experience, Bayer proposes that the church's role as the "true universal community of communication"[39] is open to God's address as both wrath and promise in creation and receives an identity shaped in word and sacrament. Bayer always points us toward creation-as-gift and refuses to construe the *telos* as self-potentiating. As responsible to justification *sola fide*, Bayer is skeptical of the theological methods based on the knowing, doing, or feeling outlined above. He notes that the quest for a pure spirituality, community, or knowledge apart from physicality, ambiguity, sensuality, and otherness is unrealistic. The gift-word of the gospel opens possibilities for mutual understanding, renewed communication, greater sense-awareness, and aesthetic appreciation. Here justification is not limited to primary discourse but is permitted to critique those overarching theoretical structures that aim to explain our experience. When reason recognizes its limitations, creation is opened experientially and socially as divine address, and the human is given permission to explore the full range of experience.

---

39. See *Autorität und Kritik: Zu Hermeneutik und Wissenschaftstheorie* (Tübingen: J. C. B. Mohr [Paul Siebeck], 1991), p. 7.

In summary, this study contends that the church must recover its confessional identity in the word of promise as the source of life. This is not for the purpose of reverting to an allegedly secure and insulated ideal past, but rather for delivering the word of salvation, a word that restores humans to creation by liberating them from incurvation. It is to acknowledge that Christ is unbound!

PART ONE

THE ROLE OF JUSTIFICATION IN THEOLOGICAL STRATEGIES OF ACCOMMODATION

Chapter Two

Eberhard Jüngel:
Justification in the Theology
of the Speech Event

Few contemporary Protestant theologians of international stature have sought to employ the doctrine of justification by grace alone through faith alone for their constructive work as rigorously as has the Tübingen systematician Eberhard Jüngel.[1] His work grows out of expertise developed in a number of theological fields.[2] His lifelong theological commit-

---

1. For collections of essays or books representative of Jüngel's systematic work, see *Unterwegs zur Sache* (Munich: Kaiser, 1972); GMW; *Entsprechungen: Gott, Wahrheit, Mensch* (Munich: Kaiser, 1980); *Wertlose Wahrheit: Zur Identität und Relevanz des christlichen Glaubens* (Munich: Kaiser, 1990); and Jüngel, Justification. For collections of Jüngel's essays in English, see TE I and TE II. For important interpretations of Jüngel's work, see John B. Webster, *Eberhard Jüngel: An Introduction to His Theology* (London: Cambridge, 1986), "Jesus' Speech, God's Word: An Introduction to Eberhard Jüngel," *The Christian Century*, December 6, 1995, pp. 1174-78, and "Who God Is, Who We Are: An Introduction to Eberhard Jüngel," *The Christian Century*, December 13, 1995, pp. 1217-20; Paul J. DeHart, *Beyond the Necessary God: Trinitarian Faith and Philosophy in the Thought of Eberhard Jüngel* (Atlanta: Scholars Press, 1999); Roland D. Zimany, *Vehicle for God: The Metaphorical Theology of Eberhard Jüngel* (Macon, Ga.: Mercer University Press, 1994); and *The Possibilities of Theology: Studies in the Theology of Eberhard Jüngel in His Sixtieth Year,* ed. John Webster (Edinburgh: T&T Clark, 1994).

2. For his work in ethics, see *Christ, Justice, and Peace: Toward a Theology of the State,* trans. D. Bruce Hamill and Alan J. Torrance (Edinburgh: T&T Clark, 1992) and *Mit Frieden Staat zu Machen: Politische Existenz nach Barmen V* (Munich: Kaiser, 1984). For his work in Christology, see *Paulus und Jesus: Eine Untersuchung zur Präzisierung der Frage nach dem Ursprung der Christologie,* 2d ed. (Tübingen: Mohr, 1964). For his research on Barth, see *God's Being Is in Becoming: The Trinitarian Being of God in the Theology of Karl Barth,* trans.

ment to this doctrine was quite evident in his initial response, a challenge, to the *Joint Declaration on the Doctrine of Justification*[3] made by the Roman Catholic Church and member churches of the Lutheran World Federation. Of greatest concern to Jüngel was his perception that the *Joint Declaration* failed to honor the doctrine of justification as *the* criterion that identifies Christian faith,[4] as well as the *simul iustus et peccator* doctrine, the view that the human *coram deo* is always fundamentally passive, and that through faith we live *extra nos* in Christ.[5]

Although he helped to initiate the draft of the first Position Statement of German Academics in response to the *Joint Declaration,* it is significant that Jüngel signed neither the first[6] nor the second[7] Position Statements. His final response to the *Joint Declaration* is that it allows Protestants and Catholics to move beyond traditional doctrinal condemnations[8] for further study, guided by the principle that it is not we who own the truth, but the truth that owns us.[9] His own recent book on justification,[10] written during the height of the conflict over the *Joint Declaration,* is far less a polemic against the *Joint Declaration* than a thorough

---

John Webster (Grand Rapids: Eerdmans, 2001) and *Karl Barth: A Theological Legacy,* trans. Garrett E. Paul (Philadelphia: Westminster, 1985). For his research on Bultmann, see *Glauben und Verstehen: Zum Theologiebegriff Rudolf Bultmanns* (Heidelberg: Carol Winter Universitätsverlag, 1985). For his Luther research, see *The Freedom of a Christian: Luther's Significance for Contemporary Theology,* trans. Roy A. Harrisville (Minneapolis: Augsburg, 1988).

3. *Joint Declaration on the Doctrine of Justification,* Lutheran World Federation and Roman Catholic Church (Grand Rapids: Eerdmans, 2000).

4. See Jüngel, "Um Gottes Willen — Klarheit!," *Zeitschrift für Theologie und Kirche* 94 (1997): 397-98.

5. Jüngel, "Amica Exegesis einer römischen Note," *Zeitschrift für Theologie und Kirche,* Beiheft 10 (1998): 260-63.

6. See "No Consensus on the 'Joint Declaration on the Doctrine of Justification': A Critical Evaluation by Professors of Protestant Theology," trans. Oliver K. Olson (from the *Frankfurter Allgemeine Zeitung* [January 29, 1998]), *Lutheran Quarterly* 12 (1998): 193-96.

7. "Position Statement of Theological Instructors in Higher Education to the Planned Signing of the Official Common Statement to the Doctrine of Justification," trans. Mark Menacher, http://wordalone.org.

8. The "condemnations" tend to be one-sided, though. See "An Opinion on the Condemnations of the Reformation Era, Part One: Justification," trans. Oliver K. Olson, *Lutheran Quarterly* 5 (1991): 8-13.

9. Jüngel, "Kardinale Probleme," *Stimmen der Zeit* 11 (1999): 734.

10. See Jüngel, Justification.

statement of his own understanding of justification as it has directed his thinking throughout his career, particularly as a critique of certain aspects of modernity.

While deeply indebted to Luther's theology, Jüngel has always distanced himself from what he would perceive to be a narrow, parochial Lutheran confessionalism (and this is, perhaps, a significant factor in his decision not to join the 251 German academics who signed the second Position Statement protesting the *Joint Declaration*). Jüngel's thinking interweaves his own initial work among the champions of the New Hermeneutic, Gerhard Ebeling[11] (1912-2001) and Ernst Fuchs[12] (1903-1983), with the theologies of Barth (1886-1968) and Bultmann (1884-1976) and the philosophies of Georg W. F. Hegel (1770-1831) and Martin Heidegger (1889-1976). His view of the doctrine of justification is forged in an intense engagement with these thinkers, although Barth has, for Jüngel, the strongest say by far in matters theological. While Luther's views are to be honored and upheld, they are best read through the lens of Barth's configuration of theology's proper agenda. Over the last three decades, Jüngel has been the closest and arguably the most authoritative voice for the Barthian "Word of God" theology, while Barth's overall influence has declined, at least in the academy.

Jüngel maintains that the doctrine of justification requires a responsible contemporary restatement precisely because it "is in every way the *articulus stantis et cadentis ecclesiae . . .* which can only be disavowed by a 'church' which does not wish to stand and which ignores its own foundation."[13] Given that the doctrine of justification has not been the central focus of contemporary systematic theologies that tend to emphasize issues of apologetics, why is it so central in Jüngel's thinking? Jüngel gives a clear

11. Ebeling's important works include the following, all published by Fortress: *Word and Faith* (1960), trans. James Leitch; *The Nature of Faith* (1961), trans. Ronald Smith; *Theology and Proclamation* (1966), trans. John Riches; *God and Word* (1966), trans. James Leitch; *The Problem of Historicity* (1967), trans. Grover Foley; *Luther: An Introduction to His Thought* (1970), trans. R. A. Wilson; and *Introduction to a Theological Theory of Language* (1971), trans. R. A. Wilson.

12. Fuchs' important works include the following: *Glaube und Erfahrung: Zum Christologischen Problem in Neuen Testament* (1965), *Marburger Hermeneutik* (1968), and *Hermeneutik* (1970), all published by Mohr (Paul Siebeck), and *Studies of the Historical Jesus*, trans. A. Scobie (London: SCM Press, 1969).

13. Jüngel, "The World as Possibility and Actuality: The Ontology of the Doctrine of Justification," in TE I:104.

answer. Protestantism has failed to mine this doctrine for its resources and energies, particularly with regard to ontology. The doctrine of justification by faith[14] is definitive of God's being[15] and humanity's being.[16] Jüngel appeals to aspects of the doctrine of justification which were not obvious to the Reformers but which are consistent with their intentions. He draws out the ontological implications ever implicit in the doctrine of justification in order to correct those intellectual traditions that misunderstand these ontologies and their proper relationships.[17] This chapter will analyze and critically assess Jüngel's view of justification, particularly as it has been defined from the experiential theology of the "word event" *(Sprachereignis, Wortgeschehen)* with respect to Luther's theology, and its importance for contemporary proclamation.

For Jüngel, God is properly a happening *(Ereignis)*, motivated by love for a creation threatened by the extinction of chaos. God is "Going-out-of-Himself into nothingness" *(a se in nihilum ek-sistere)*,[18] which nevertheless permits him to "correspond" to himself, and also allows humans

---

14. See his early essay "Die Freiheit der Theologie" in *Entsprechungen*, p. 28, where he says that justification is the center of all theology, defining God and humanity.

15. "Faith that justifies asserts, therefore, that God reveals who he really is in that he justifies men. And since the justification of the godless by God took place in the event of God's identification with the crucified man Jesus, theological thought must hear from this christological event what both God and man ought to mean." See GMW 231.

16. "Paul calls this event in which we are brought into correspondence with God through the being of Jesus Christ *justification*. Thus Luther (in *The Disputation Concerning Man*) correctly saw that justification is the real definition of human being. Justification by God can be regarded as definitive of human being, since it releases us from the clutches of human action, without denying that the concept of our being includes our actions. To put the matter in a different way: in the event of divine justification, human nature, threatened by itself, is affirmed by God against its constant perversion into abnormality. And so justification is an event of ontological relevance." See "Humanity in Correspondence to God," in TE I:133.

17. Hence in "Gottes umstrittene Gerechtigkeit," in *Unterwegs zur Sache*, p. 71, Jüngel says that the dispute about God's righteousness is always and necessarily a dispute about the right understanding of God and the right understanding of humanity. Early in his career he recognized that Bultmann really could not afford to ignore questions of ontology because if one wants to think about Christian existence, one must also concurrently think about the distinction between being and nonbeing, since justification entails God's creation of the new being from out of nothing. See Jüngel, "Nicht Nur Eine Geographische Bestimmung," *Evangelisches Kommentare* 2 (1968): 468.

18. GMW 223.

to "correspond" *(Entsprechen)* both to God and to themselves. God then is not properly being-itself, but its source. God affirms being by means of excluding and limiting threats to being: chaos, death, and nothingness. The doctrine of justification relates the divine and the human by properly ordering them such that the human is expanded through a relationship with God, who is a freely offered "plus"[19] to human experience. Thereby, Jüngel avoids the problems associated with ancient metaphysics, "Platonism," in which God is ordered to the world as its super-sensible double whose truth, beauty, and goodness are instantiated in the world but for whom the world offers no life-altering agency. He also avoids the problems associated with modern metaphysics, "Spinozism," in which God and the world are virtually identified, though distinguished in two modes as an active, mental, rational "naturing nature" and a passive, physical, though intelligible "natured nature."[20] In Jüngel's vision, God does not need the world (God is "not necessary but more than necessary" [*mehr als notwendig*]),[21] and, surprisingly, the world does not need God (an insight of secularism to be appropriated by Christianity). The advantage here for theology, he thinks, is that God can *freely* love the world, and the world can *freely* respond to God's love.

Luther's views of justification were forged in an entrenched polemic against medieval Roman Catholic theories of merit (the Indulgence Controversy) and Renaissance Humanism's affirmation of human power (the polemic against Erasmus [1466-1536] over "free will"). While clearly addressing the doctrine of justification to the former view, Jüngel also skillfully applies it to Erasmus's contemporary heir, modern secularism, with which he has a deeply ambiguous relationship. He applauds contemporary critiques of ancient metaphysics, while rejecting modernity's reduction of humans to their "works." Secularism as mediated through philosophical atheism can, ironically, offer important insights about the God who justifies. The ancient metaphysics of substance is unable to portray the drama

19. See "Das Sakrament — Was ist das? Versuch einer Antwort," in *Was ist ein Sakrament? Vorstösse zur Verständigung* (Freiburg: Herder, 1971), pp. 99-61.

20. "There is only one path open to faith, between 'Spinozism' and 'Platonism'; this path theology has to choose as its own path of thinking, though it may learn from Spinoza and Plato. For insofar as it reflects upon the Christian faith, theology has to conceive of God as the one who *came* to the world in Jesus Christ and as such does not cease to *come* to the world." See "Metaphorical Truth," in TE I:59.

21. See GMW, section 2.

of the biblical God's engagement in human history. Atheism has appropriately criticized the false theology grounded in the metaphysics of substance. A metaphysics of subjectivity which views the subject as a free self-defining agent — even a social ontology in which one's being is established via relationships — accords far better with the being of God as justifying the ungodly. God is knowable — indeed, even *thinkable*[22] — through faith, which is itself grounded in a meta-experience, an "experience with experience"[23] mediated through an encounter with "nothingness"[24] and for which the believer properly responds with gratitude and not anxiety. However, with regard to anthropology, Jüngel's insight, based on Reformation thinking, is that the modern world fails to distinguish one's "person" from one's "works."[25] Modernity consistently seeks to have humans ground themselves within themselves — in their ability to think, feel, or do — and thus reduces the dignity of the human to merit, the ability to contribute to modernity's own agenda. These agendas tend to be that of conquest or expansion. Modernity is unable to ground humanity in Another outside of humanity itself.

For Jüngel, we cannot turn our backs on the technologies that we have developed to harness nature. Nevertheless, the modern world can quickly dehumanize the very humanity it seeks to serve. The doctrine of

22. "Thought is never imitation. That kind of 'thinking after' which sees itself obligated to 'think after' God is always the thinker's own pursuing of his own way. For that reason, thought does not believe in that which is thought. It must as thought always begin itself and desires to see its own thoughts judged only by the authentic thoughts of others. To 'think after' means then not to believe in something which has been thought through by someone else. That which is 'thought after' never becomes something pre-thought for someone else, never becomes a thought. That which is 'thought after' becomes a *being*, which as such is something to be thought, that which most authentically is to be thought and remains that: the being of God. To the extent that this being of God is *coming* to itself on all its ways, the thought which 'thinks after' is a thought which is setting out on the way into the future, a thought which lays claim on the future in the act of thinking. To think means to set reason into movement, through a return to an origin not caused by reason, toward the future, so that reason departs from a movement of circling constantly around itself. Reason will be set into motion toward the future only when it is preceded by something which then should be 'thought after.'" See GMW 167.

23. GMW 32, 104, 168, 182, 279, and 377.

24. GMW 32.

25. See, especially, "On Becoming Truly Human: The Significance of the Reformation Distinction between Person and Works for the Self-Understanding of Modern Humanity," in TE II:216-40.

justification by faith acknowledges the fundamental passivity of the human *coram deo* and its worth, independent of merit, in the sight of God. It offers the possibility of a rehumanization of the human. Humans dehumanize themselves in the process of attempting to map[26] or wholly objectify both the physical and the social environments, and even themselves, thereby potentially extinguishing their own dignity. While the secular world as offering freedom of conscience and basic human rights needs to be affirmed,[27] its tendency to ground humanity in either human thinking or doing, particularly the agency of conquest and control, needs appropriate boundaries. Jüngel seemingly wants to accept modernity's configuration of faith as fundamentally private, while rejecting modernity's quest for control as what Luther would call *ambitio divinitatis*, asserting oneself as one's own deity, both legislator and judge. While clearly Jüngel offers great insights into the latter perspective, justification quickly becomes connected to a unique meta-experience or feeling, echoing Schleiermacher's "feeling of absolute dependence,"[28] and less connected to a linguistically mediated promise. Undoubtedly, with the concept of "experience with experience" Jüngel intends a meta-experience determined by the *extra nos* of the word. However, with this as a central focus for understanding the consequences of faith, he risks structuring theology

26. See George P. Schner, "Metaphors for Theology," in *Theology after Liberalism: A Reader,* ed. John Webster and George P. Schner (Oxford: Blackwell, 2000), pp. 11-12.

27. Jüngel's affirmation of aspects of secularism can be heard in this statement: "European Protestant Christianity also exists in a secular form. And the Protestant churches should rejoice at this their secular child, instead of lamenting it as a lost son or daughter. The church is not the parental home to which this secular child should be returned; the church is at its best if it fulfills its own task, as a pointer, for secular society too, towards the coming city of God, in which church and state will share a common future. The church should not therefore look with suspicion on the (correctly understood) worldliness of the world as a form of secularised Christianity. The Reformation with its doctrine of two realms itself laid the foundation for the existence of a world emancipated from the church and having its own justice and its own value. The Protestant Church should bless this its worldly child and wish it to become truly adult." See "The Gospel and the Protestant Churches of Europe: Christian Responsibility for Europe from a Protestant Perspective," *Religion, State and Society* 21 (1993): 142.

28. Schleiermacher, *The Christian Faith,* ed. H. R. Mackintosh and J. S. Stewart (Philadelphia: Fortress, 1976), §4, p. 12: "The common element in all howsoever diverse expressions of piety, by which these are conjointly distinguished from all other feelings, or, in other words, the self-identical essence of piety, is this: the consciousness of being absolutely dependent, or, which is the same thing, of being in relation with God."

within the horizon of experience. Thereby, his loyalty to Barth is potentially subverted by the very Schleiermacherian concerns that Barth opposed. It is here that Jüngel's attempt to bring together Bultmann's concern for experience with Barth's theology of the word is problematic. His view makes faith vulnerable to being grounded in an experience that constitutes language, instead of language constituting faith. Nevertheless, Jüngel is right to contend that our intellectual journeys to map both the world and the human experience need to recognize their boundaries, particularly in the face of the potential dehumanization of children, the vulnerable, the disabled, and the aged. Where and how such human intellectual and technological quests should or should not be limited is an important concern with respect to fidelity to the doctrine of justification.

In Jüngel's intellectualizing (the "thinkability" of God) and personalistic approach to faith (an "I-Thou" dialectic between God and the human), the gospel is presented as an "event of correspondence"[29] in which God, as defining himself as Trinity, corresponds to himself and allows humans to correspond both to God and to themselves, since in faith humans are healed from self-alienation. We passively correspond to God in faith and actively correspond to our humanity in love to the neighbor opened by faith. Jüngel clearly rejects modernity's tendency to look to ethics or politics as salvific.[30] Raised in the former East Germany, he is highly skeptical of the "promise" of politics to save! However, he has great faith in human reason's ability to "think" God, since he affirms that God allows himself to be thought in faith.

Theological Influences

For Jüngel, theologians have failed to apply the doctrine of justification appropriately to God. When it is seen as definitive of God's being, we have grounds for revising the traditional view of God as highest being, which, in his judgment, has so rightfully been rejected by modern atheism. This can even lead to a revision in our thinking about thinking itself and can open

---

29. GMW 286.

30. For a discussion of modernity's construal of politics as salvific, see Craig M. Gay, *The Way of the (Modern) World; or, Why It's Tempting to Live as if God Doesn't Exist* (Grand Rapids: Eerdmans, 1998), p. 31.

new horizons for theological anthropology, whose ontology has likewise been neglected by the doctrine of justification. Thus, Jüngel ontologizes justification and uses it as a way to codify God not as highest being but as the "union of life and death for the sake of life,"[31] a deity who is self-defining as "coming" to the world, transcending the opposition between presence and absence.[32] For him, the human as such is likewise a "mystery" who comes to self by means of God's grace, free of incurvation in the passivity of faith, but active in the love unleashed by faith. To understand how and why Jüngel comes to this viewpoint, it is imperative to understand the roles that Barth, Heidegger, Bultmann, and the advocates of the New Hermeneutic played in his thinking.

Jüngel has learned to think theologically on the basis of several factors. First, he accepts a Hegelian- and Heideggerian-influenced social ontology (in which being is "being-with," affirming the priority of the category of relation over that of substance). Second, he adopts a Heideggerian-influenced ontology that prioritizes the category of possibility over that of actuality (in contrast to Aristotle), since God creates new possibilities by raising the dead. Third, he sees "nothingness" as a threatening, non-neutral factor (in contrast to Heidegger), overcome in Jesus' resurrection, and out of which God creates the world and the new being. Fourth, he believes that subjectivity is unable to ground itself apart from its being upheld and preserved by God. Fifth, he claims that language mediates experience and truth (which is metaphorical, not discursive, and capable of pluriform meanings and referentialities),[33] even disclosing God's

31. "This discourse directs us toward the task of thinking of God himself as the union of death and life for the sake of life. Since the 'union of death and life for the sake of life' is a way of defining the essence of love, we shall have to think *God as love* together with the christologically understood humanity of God." See GMW 299.

32. GMW 300: "The God who comes only in the word finds his only correspondence in faith, because only faith lets God's being be a being that is coming, that is, lets God be present as the one who is absent." See also GMW 349-51 and 378-80.

33. Hence, Jüngel writes, "The alternative to the understanding of truth as correspondence between statement and state of affairs is to understand it much more primordially as that interruption of the ontological cohesion of the (created) world (the cohesion of its actuality), through which we attain to the position of being over against our world so that something like *adaequatio intellectus et rei* becomes possible. For this elementary interruption of the cohesion of our actuality ought to contain within itself an even more primordial correspondence and unconditional trustworthiness. Is invocation of God this kind of elemental interruption of our life and so of the world?" See "Invocation of God as the Ethical

own grace — God coming into experience via an "analogy of advent."[34] Sixth, he seeks to see faith as grounded outside itself in an encountering, external word (and not grounded in *praxis* or ethics), though this truth might be obscured by his concern to delineate a special meta-experience. Seventh, he believes that the human should be lord, not tyrant, over creation. Eighth, he affirms the Rahnerian[35] and Barthian[36] supposition that the immanent trinity (God as triune in himself) is the economic trinity (God as triune for human salvation) as its summarizing concept, and that the economic trinity is the immanent trinity as its historical embodiment (inferred from the crucified Jesus as the one with whom God "identified"). Finally, he sees the category of "correspondence" as serving as the overarching way of picturing the relationship of (a) the divine to the divine, (b) the divine to the human, and (c) the human to the human. In Jüngel's mind, these nine propositions are all legitimate inferences from the doctrine of justification as applied to both ontology and anthropology.

For Jüngel, the analogous relation that God establishes between himself and the world is that of a "still greater similarity in the midst of such great dissimilarity."[37] Jüngel is fond of repeating that the correspondence that exists between the justifying God and justified humanity acknowledges

---

Ground of Christian Action," in TE I:171. For Heidegger's views on truth, see his "Letter on Humanism," in *Pathmarks*, ed. William McNeill (Cambridge: Cambridge University Press, 1998), pp. 239-76.

34. Defined by Jüngel thus: "But when the analogy contains God as one of its members (x:a=b:c), then, on the basis of the relation of God (x) to the world (a), the world-relationship (b:c) which corresponds to that relation appears in a completely new light, in a light which *makes* this world-relationship *new*, an eschatological light. The world-relationship (b:c), which of itself can give no reference to God, now begins to speak for God: not as 'natural elements' *(natura)* which God has brought to their highest form and made perfect, but rather as a worldly obviousness speaking in the service of something even more obvious, and thus as a completely new case because of the new light which illuminates it. The God who comes to the world (x — a) makes use of the obvious in this world in such a way that he proves himself to be that which is even more obvious over against it. It is all too obvious that one will give everything for the value of the treasure buried in the field in order to have that greater value." See GMW 285.

35. See Rahner, *The Trinity,* trans. Joseph Donceel (New York: Herder & Herder, 1970), p. 15, and "Remarks on the Dogmatic Treatise *De Trinitate,*" in *Theological Investigations IV,* trans. Kevin Smith (Baltimore: Helicon, 1966), pp. 77-102.

36. See Alan Torrance, "The Trinity," in *The Cambridge Companion to Karl Barth* (Cambridge: Cambridge University Press, 2000), p. 82.

37. GMW 288.

the difference between them.[38] The difference, an "ontological divide"[39] to which Jüngel alludes, is at the heart of Barth's thinking, both early and late. For Barth, the accentuation of the ontological divide between the Creator and the creature is comparable at this point to a Lutheran understanding of law as accusing *(lex semper accusat)*, although this Lutheran doctrine was defined independently of ontological commitments. Of course, Barth — in direct contrast to Lutheran understandings of the distinction between law and gospel — would specify that the law is the "form"[40] of the gospel, affirming that God has only one word and not two. Nevertheless, Barth's claim here — and Jüngel's echoing of it — is a direct assault on human *ambitio divinitatis* as manifest in ethical, spiritual, and metaphysical endeavors.

The early Barth raised a prophetic voice against the idols of human potency demonically manifest in the trials of the First World War as a secularized Ritschlian faith, "culture Protestantism." He spoke against the Kantian and Ritschlian supposition that the kingdom of God is the *telos* of human moral aspiration and that practical reason can discern God's will by conforming itself to moral law by honoring others' autonomy as ends-in-themselves, resulting in a "kingdom of ends."[41] He challenged the Schleiermacherian supposition that "the constant potency" of Jesus' God-consciousness was a veritable existence of God in him[42] and that the church holds forth the image *(Bild)* of Jesus which enables one's own God-consciousness to connect spiritually with his.[43] He opposed the Hegelian

---

38. GMW 97, 157.

39. See George Hunsinger, *How to Read Karl Barth* (Oxford: Oxford University Press, 1991), pp. 71-72, 74-75, and 177-78.

40. See Barth, "Gospel and Law," in *Community, State, and Church* (Gloucester, Mass.: Peter Smith, 1968), pp. 71-100.

41. Hence, Kant notes, "Now a kingdom of ends would actually come into existence through maxims which the categorical imperative prescribes as a rule for all rational beings if these maxims were universally followed. Yet even if a rational being were himself to follow such a maxim strictly, he cannot count on everybody else being faithful to it on this ground, nor can he be confident that the kingdom of nature and its purposive order will work in harmony with him, as a fitting member, towards a kingdom of ends made possible by himself — or, in other words, that it will favour his expectation of happiness." See *Groundwork of the Metaphysic of Morals*, trans. H. J. Paton (New York: Harper, 1953), p. 106.

42. Schleiermacher, *The Christian Faith*, §94, p. 385.

43. Schleiermacher, *The Christian Faith*, §125, p. 578: "The Christian Church, animated by the Holy Spirit, is in its purity and integrity the perfect image of the Redeemer, and each regenerate individual is an indispensable constituent of this fellowship."

supposition that reason is a process of self-development in historical phases which culminates in Spirit coming to full awareness of itself in and through human consciousness and vice versa. The early Barth posited a deity with no native point of contact or continuum with the human. In this regard, he was indebted to Kierkegaard's "infinite qualitative distinction" between God and humanity.[44] From this view, he was able to expose modern European Protestantism as idolatrously justifying human aggression and violence — to which God renders the verdict of guilty, says "No!" The highest European intellectual traditions were complicit with this violence of world war. For the early Barth, the gospel proclaims a God who is utterly distant from humanity.[45] It is false for us to presume that God shares the same "one line" with ourselves,[46] and, as the later Barth concurs, human conceptions of God are simply "wrong."[47]

The later Barth appealed to a Christocentricism as the compass for all theology: God is self-disclosing in his election. The elect man is Jesus Christ, our substitute for sin, through whom the incarnate word has journeyed into the "far country"[48] of sin and death and has returned to reign in glory. Barth continued his rejection of "natural theology," ethics, and spirituality as offering access to God, but he now saw God as "self-revealing" in the life, death, and resurrection of Jesus Christ. God's being is "in act" as a triune self-unfolding: God is as God-for-us. In this regard, Jüngel thinks he can associate Luther's "theology of the cross" *(theologia crucis)* from the "Heidelberg Disputation" (1518) — God incarnate in the suffering and shame of Jesus' death — with Hegel's affirmation of the diremption of Spirit, "God's death" *("Gott Selbst ist tot")* in the man Jesus so that human community might be raised as Spirit. Jüngel builds on the Barthian supposition that God is self-electing in the humiliated Jesus Christ. This allows him to discern that the internal affairs of the triune life are compatible with Hegel's revamping of the old Lutheran principle that the finite bears the infinite *(finitum capax infiniti)*. Hegel's claim was that God's tasting death in Jesus' death on the cross permits the point of contact between the finite and the infinite such that we finite ones are capable

44. Barth, *The Epistle to the Romans,* 6th ed., trans. Edwyn Hoskins (London: Oxford University Press, 1968), p. 99.

45. Barth, *The Epistle to the Romans,* p. 28.

46. Barth, *The Epistle to the Romans,* p. 44.

47. Barth, *Church Dogmatics* III/1 (Edinburgh: T&T Clark, 1958), p. 358.

48. Barth, *Church Dogmatics* IV/1 (Edinburgh: T&T Clark, 1956), p. 157.

of understanding the infinite.[49] For Jüngel, the gospel is a "story to be told,"[50] but this is because God's life is precisely that story of diremption as well. This is rightly designated a "natural theology of the cross."[51]

Hegel, of course, misreads Luther's intentions. Thesis 20 of the *Heidelberg Disputation* — "He deserves to be called a theologian, however, who comprehends the visible and manifest things of God seen through suffering and the cross"[52] — is intended to be a statement of faith, not a clue by which to sleuth the divine. The point is that faith discerns God's sustenance and support of human life *sub contrario* even in the midst of trial and temptation. Luther certainly never intended that we might be able to *think into* God's life. For Luther, the paradox of God deep within the flesh can never be scripted as an analogy. The shamed and scorned victim is not an analogy of the divine love, because it is itself the gift of divine love. However, this is exactly what Jüngel, as faithful to Barth, makes of this paradox.

In this regard, it was the need of the younger Bultmannians, which included Jüngel's teachers, to draw out the character of the proclaimer, Jesus, on the basis of the proclamation. This stirred Jüngel to find commonality between Barth, who shunned human experience as a criterion for theology, and Bultmann, who affirmed it.[53] With Barth, theology begins and proceeds from the objectivity that it is God who rightly speaks of God, a word to which faith corresponds, while for Bultmann it is faith that corresponds to the word by means of a new existential self-understanding. Here the order of knowing is accountable to the order of being. This is Barthian "realism."[54] It is receptivity, not human construction, that defines epistemology. Since God alone can truthfully speak about God, then our thinking must follow after God's self-revelation, what Jüngel calls *Nachdenken,* and is held accountable to it. Jüngel's insight is that Barth has

---

49. See Mark Mattes, "Hegel's Lutheran Claim," *Lutheran Quarterly* 14 (2000): 249-79.

50. GMW, section 14.

51. Theologie, C, 6.2, p. 509.

52. LW 31:40 (WA 1:354).

53. See Bultmann, *Kerygma and Myth,* vol. 1 (London: SPCK Press, 1953), pp. 18, 24-25, 36. For Bultmann, we achieve our unique individuality by connecting unreservedly to the future.

54. See Ingolf U. Dalferth, "Karl Barth's Eschatological Realism," in *Karl Barth: Centenary Essays,* ed. S. W. Sykes (Cambridge: Cambridge University Press), pp. 14-45, and George Hunsinger, *How to Read Karl Barth,* pp. 43-49.

a theory of revelation that offered a hermeneutics concerned for human "authenticity" (although Barth did not discern this), while Bultmann has a hermeneutics that implicitly offered a theory of revelation (which would itself imply a trinitarian view of God similar to Barth's).[55] Once it is granted, as it was for the younger Bultmannians, that Jesus as the one proclaimed has a continuity with Jesus the proclaimer, then the Jesus whose ministry was "on the side of God" implies for Jüngel, as it would for Barth, that God was "on the side of Jesus."[56] Jesus is (self-) definitive of God. As mediated by the leaders of the New Hermeneutic, Fuchs and Ebeling, it is not just that Jesus rose into the kerygma, as Bultmann maintained, but that the kerygma has become a word *event* that gives rise to and nurtures the institution of the church. The Bultmannian quest for human authenticity can thus hardly ignore the role of faith as receptive, passive, and exocentric — a living outside oneself in the word — and thus is suspicious of human accounts of power, agency, and conquest.

For the later Barth, the question of how to acknowledge the distinctiveness between the divine and the human without robbing each of their proper agencies is pivotal. Jüngel does his theology within this horizon. How should the differences between the agencies of God and the human be construed such that neither robs the other of their appropriate power and freedom, but instead complement each other? The "logic of disjunction" in which divine and human agencies compete with and cancel each other out — as discerned by the classical atheists (Feuerbach, Marx, Freud) — is to be denied. With his overall relentless critique of both the ancient metaphysics of substance and the modern metaphysics of subjectivity, Jüngel has also utilized similar objections to metaphysics from Martin Heidegger's philosophy, such as (1) the understanding of being as "being-with,"[57] (2) the per-

55. "The foundation of this perspective is Jüngel's observation that Bultmann's hermeneutic is a theory of revelation and that Barth's theory of revelation is a hermeneutic. This means for Jüngel that Bultmann and Barth develop a *de facto* identical concept of the saving significance of the man Jesus — what Bultmann expresses as the paradoxical identity of 'historical' and 'eschatological' events is the same as what Barth describes as the sacramental character of the humanity of Jesus Christ: namely the objectively grounded revelation being chosen by God for himself — and in that way the being of God is speakable for the human." See Wilfried Härle and Eilert Herms, "Deutschsprachige Protestantische Dogmatik nach 1945," *Verkündigung und Forschung* 27 (1982): 22.

56. Jüngel, *Paulus und Jesus*, p. 283.

57. See Heidegger, *Being and Time*, trans. John Macquarrie and Edward Robinson (New York: Harper & Row, 1962), p. 28.

son as constituted by possibilities, not properties, (3) the priority of relation over substance, (4) the role of language as allowing being "to come," (5) the *physis* of language that subverts discursive correspondence between signifying word and signified thing,[58] and (6) the role of "nothingness" in the definition of human existence.

The overriding Barthian approach to a perspective on justification leads Jüngel to construe justification by faith in terms of an encounter with God in highly "personalistic" terms, an experience "with experience" or "eschatological spiritual presence," an "I-Thou" rapport between the divine and the human. He tends to be "existentializing" with respect to theological method, while "theorizing" (attempting to decipher the inner life of God) with respect to theological content.

It is appropriate to break here from our commentary to ask, How is the gospel to be delivered in all this? Is that not the purpose of theology?[59] How does the preacher "deliver the goods," the forgiveness of sins, life, and salvation, in word and sacrament, on the basis of Jüngel's thinking? Jüngel, we should affirm, is a noted preacher in Germany. Nevertheless, how does his existentializing and theorizing lend itself to proclamation? For Jüngel, God is not properly in the world with its buzzing, blooming diversity, but solely in a word that evokes a particular meta-experience. The world, for Jüngel, is not revelatory per se but is given over epistemologically to scientific dissection. Through science, it is demystified, decoded, and made ready for consumption, though this is exactly the kind of relation to the world from which he claims that the gospel can and should deliver us. However, his agreement with Bultmann that science "has no need of him [God], neither as a ground of its own legitimation nor as a reference to the ground of legitimation for that which science itself cannot legitimize,"[60] is telling. It indicates that Jüngel's relating of God to word is done in opposition to the world. The world can be measured; God and the self cannot. Jüngel's view here, like Bultmann's, is

---

58. See Gerald L. Bruns, *Heidegger's Estrangements: Language, Truth, and Poetry in the Later Writings* (New Haven: Yale University Press, 1989), p. 120. For a fuller statement of Jüngel's cautious and limited appropriation of Heidegger's thinking, see his article co-authored with Michael Trowitzsch, "Provozierendes Denken: Bemerküngen zur theologischen Anstössigkeit der Denkwege Martin Heideggers," *Neue Hefte für Philosophie* 23 (1984): 59-74.

59. See Gerhard Forde, *Theology Is for Proclamation* (Minneapolis: Fortress, 1990).

60. GMW 3.

configured by the perspective of Max Weber (1864-1920) on the "scientific" vocation of the university, which affirmed that "there are no mysterious incalculable forces that come into play, but rather . . . one can, in principle, *master all things* by calculation."[61] Outside of the one word of Jesus Christ, nature tells us nothing of God. This is Jüngel's "more natural theology."[62] Jüngel works within an Augustinian and Cartesian "I-Thou" personalism, not Luther's framework, where nature both "masks" God and sacramentally delivers grace. In opposition to Jüngel, we ought instead to agree with the Psalmist that "the heavens are telling the glory of God; and the firmament proclaims his handiwork. Day to day pours forth speech, and night to night declares knowledge" (Ps. 19:1-2). Rather than the "catholic" view, critiqued by Jüngel, that the world mimetically participates in divine truth, beauty, and goodness by means of an analogy of being *(analogia entis),* or his own view that the world is devoid of God unless God comes to it through an "analogy of advent" (with the exception of the human experience of love as analogous to divine love),[63] we should affirm, with Luther, that the universe, and all within it, serve as God's masks. Whatever we encounter in the world, even a "rustling leaf"[64] or a "grain of wheat,"[65] delivers either God's providential mercy or God's wrath. God's hiddenness in creation is a holy masquerade in which

---

61. See "Science as Vocation," in *Max Weber: Essays in Sociology,* trans. and ed. H. H. Geth and C. Wright Mills (New York: Oxford University Press, 1977), p. 149.

62. "It is in no way impossible, coming from the first thesis of Barmen, and without of course practicing any 'natural theology,' to acknowledge full well the truth of the problem of natural theology — although dealing with it in a manner quite different from the way in which natural theology itself would be able to deal with it. It is not at all impossible, coming from the one Word of God (to which alone the church has to listen, and which alone the church has to recognise as the source of its proclamation), to outline a *more natural theology* which knows Jesus Christ as the one who has reconciled both human beings and the world (2 Cor. 5:19). He is the one who, together with the prayers of Christians, also bears the groaning of the creation and who leads the children of God with the waiting creation to the redeeming *apokalypsis* (Rom. 8:9-23). It is a more natural theology therefore, which, along with the recognition of Jesus Christ as the savior of human beings, is learning to think anew the old notions of the salvation of phenomena *(sozein ta phainomena). Here* new ways open up: 'political theology' as well as ways which destine for each creature their own 'ecological theology'!" See *Christ, Justice, and Peace,* pp. 26-27.

63. See "Gelegentliche thesen zum Problem der natürlichen Theologie," in *Entsprechungen,* pp. 200-201.

64. See Luther, "Lectures on Genesis," in LW 1:170 (WA 42:127).

65. WA 31/1:443.

the mask comes off only in the promise "for you," mediated through earthly things as sacramental realities and bodily words.

The Ontology of the Justifying God

Jüngel has expended much energy on revising the doctrine of God in order to counter various charges of modern atheists and, in his mind, to be faithful to the doctrine of justification. His move has been to shift discussion about the doctrine of God away from a general metaphysics of substance that sees God as the world's highest being to a special metaphysics of subjectivity that sees God as the world's mystery. For Jüngel, God is a triune event of love, which relates to the world in terms of a "still greater similarity," the oneness of the Eternal Son of God in Jesus, "in the midst of such great dissimilarity"[66] of finitude and sin. As mentioned, the difference between God and the world is not between that of sensible and supersensible realms, as in Platonism. Nor is it a distinction within a spiritual monism in which God is the world's soul and the world is God's body, as in Spinozism. Unlike the latter position, God has agency with respect to the world not only as its creator and preserver *ex nihilo,* but also as the one who offers the world the possibility of new life. Jüngel construes God's agency such that any inherent conflict or power struggle between God and the world would misread it. If God's agency is sheer power that evokes a struggle for recognition, God would be seen as a minus, not a plus, to the world. But, since God is the one who offers new possibilities that the world is unable to provide for itself, such as life out of death, then God is not necessary but "more than necessary." Otherwise, the world can go about its business independently of God "as though God were not a given" *(etsi deus non daretur).*[67] For Jüngel, humanity genuinely corresponds to God not via mimetic participation in the theological virtues of faith, hope, and love that instantiate goodness as such, but by receiving life externally, allowing another, God, to be there for one, the gift of an alien righteousness *(iustitia aliena).* Human beings correspond *passively* to God as humans receive from God, living by faith in the alien righteousness of another, a "word event" that evokes new being within and in whose life humans participate

---

66. GMW 288, 294, 298.
67. GMW 18f., 58-60, 61f.

by faith. Humans correspond *actively* to God in works of love on behalf of the neighbor's well-being and love to God for his own sake.

Jüngel can affirm a "hidden work of God" *(opus dei absconditum),*[68] but not a "hidden God" *(deus absconditus).* Luther's supposition of a "hidden God" is far too closely tied to the notion of God as sheer power — *deus ipse* — who "works life, death, and all in all"[69] and whose power might very well seem to be opposed to his love, the "revelation of his glory under the antithesis of the cross."[70] For Jüngel, any view of God not defined completely by love — God self-defining as love — could border on the demonic and is to be rejected for faith. Such a "hidden God" threatens the kind of correspondence between God and the human in which divine and human agencies are not competitive but harmoniously synchronized.

From Luther's perspective, the question about whether we in our *Anfechtungen* wrestle with God, and do not solely experience God as gracious, is quite plausible. Believers and non-believers deal with this hidden God in their various life experiences, precisely in their attempts to master the world and their fate. It is the role of the gospel to turn us to the "preached God," who through Jesus Christ as *sacramentum* gives us assurance with regard to God's disposition toward us. The person of faith holds this "hidden God" accountable to the promise, even appealing to God against God! For Jüngel, in contrast, it is never against God that we wrestle, but against the forces of chaos that threaten to overwhelm the structures of order that sustain human well-being. If Jüngel agrees with Barth that God is the "One who loves in freedom,"[71] then there can be no "hidden God" because love as manifest in Jesus — the finite vehicle that allows the infinite to wholly *define* itself — offers a *transparency* between God and humanity. In Jesus Christ, we see into the very heart of God (a sight permitted by faith), since Jesus Christ is the definitive key to the divine's own self-definition for itself and for us. Divine mystery is not a result of our inability to perceive its depths but is due to the miracle of the narrative of God that is told. The logic of disjunction between human and divine power, maintained by many atheists, simply does not hold. God's agency offers new horizons and possibilities for an entrapped humanity. For Jüngel, as for Barth, God is the

---

68. GMW 131.

69. See Martin Luther, *The Bondage of the Will,* trans. J. I. Packer and O. R. Johnston (Old Tappan, N.J.: Fleming H. Revell, 1957), p. 170 (WA 18:685).

70. Jüngel, "The Revelation of the Hiddenness of God," in TE II:137.

71. Barth, *Church Dogmatics* II/1 (Edinburgh: T&T Clark, 1957), §28, p. 257.

"essence of the possible."[72] However, to say that God is self-defining and that our access to this definition is solely through the Incarnation is to say more of God than faith allows.

For Jüngel, it was not Descartes's attempt to think God per se that was misguided. Jüngel argues for God's thinkability in opposition to modern atheists. Descartes's error was that he interposed the "I think," the *cogito,* between God's essence, conceived in terms of the ancient metaphysics of substance as "that than which nothing greater can be conceived" and God's existence, a move at the origin and center of modern humanity's own self-invention.[73] Modernity would increasingly invest less in God as an explanation for the world and would center human worth, value, and dignity — even in the face of the emptiness and sterile cartography of cold matter and blind chance, the cosmos as "objectively" seen by science — within the human itself. Similarly, for Johann Fichte (1762-1814), to think something and to realize something is to render it under the conditions of space and time. In this view, cognitive judgments unite spatio-temporal intuitions with a category that has no essential relation to space and time. The mind produces schemata that adapt categories to spatio-temporal forms. "Thinking God" would always render God's being under such spatio-temporal forms and thus fall short of God's infinity. Hence, an infinite God cannot be thought![74] Likewise, Ludwig Feuerbach (1804-1872) understood God to be the essential limit of human thought. Thought magnifies but cannot transcend itself. God then is the essence of reason itself, and reason (not faith!) is the creator of divinity *(ratio creatrix divinitatis)!*[75] Finally, Friedrich Nietzsche (1844-1900) interprets God as the essence of the "bad infinity," one arbitrary thing following another indefinitely; yet, he asks, can we be expected to think higher and further than the creative will itself?[76]

All these atheistic responses, generated after Descartes, configure God's being in Platonic terms that accentuate God's unthinkability: God is beyond the limits of human thinking. However, this assumption fails to permit the divine to represent itself within finite experience. God is think-

---

72. See Barth, *Dogmatics in Outline,* trans. G. T. Thomson (New York: Harper & Row, 1959), 48.

73. GMW, section 9.

74. GMW, section 10.

75. GMW 146.

76. GMW, section 10.

able if he allows himself to be thought, if faith is able by means of thinking to follow the traces that he has left in the world, particularly that most important trace of all: the life, death, and resurrection of Jesus Christ. If we are to think God and thereby rethink thought itself, we must "de-Platonize"[77] our views of God. We must take leave of the metaphysics of substance and embrace a view of God as a subject[78] who divests himself of his own divine glory in order to embrace his sinful creatures. Acknowledging such *kenosis,* self-definition of oneself in the "otherness" of death, an embracing of death as a definitive moment of the divine life, "Hegelizes" Christianity. Theology as "schooled by Luther's Christology and Hegel's philosophy,"[79] at least with respect to the Incarnation, offers the thinkability of God. God is thinkable in the story of his own life, mediated in the life of Jesus Christ and his witness in the church.

If there is a "hidden God," a deity who says in all things, "am I not allowed to do what I choose with what belongs to me?" (Matt. 20:15), whose rationales are impenetrable, whose election seems unjust, one who appears to be no lover of life but its accuser and even destroyer, then this God would be everywhere in his creation other than in the promise! For Jüngel, such attributes of the "hidden God" do not belong to God whatsoever,[80] but to chaos, nothingness, and death. God *is* only as self-defined in the promise. He is a God about whom we can make inferences about the very electing will itself on the basis of the ministry of the elect one, Jesus Christ. Jüngel's view of God, akin to Hegel's and Barth's views, offers a God who is freely self-determining, subjecting himself to the powers of chaos, nothingness, and death for the sake of creatures lost to these powers.[81] Theology is a theorizing in which we are able to "reason into" God. The man Jesus, who labored in history, is the key that deciphers the historicity of

77. See Jüngel, *Death: The Riddle and the Mystery,* trans. Iain and Ute Nicol (Philadelphia: Westminster, 1974), p. 53.

78. GMW 158, 227.

79. GMW 373.

80. For Jüngel's overall understanding of the *deus absconditus,* see "The Revelation of the Hiddenness of God: A Contribution to the Protestant Understanding of the Hiddenness of Divine Action," in TE II:120-44.

81. Hence Jüngel writes, "God does not want to perfect himself without man. God's coming to himself must be understood as an act of freedom, in which God gives himself a future in such a way that he disposes over his future and thus over himself. That God does not desire to come to himself without man is to be understood in such a way that God has definitively decided about his future." See GMW 38.

God's deity. Election, covenant, and Christ all reveal God's very essence — a God who cannot but be true to himself. God is "coming" from himself to himself, but not apart from "coming" to us. Justification of the ungodly is God's covenant fidelity to his own creatures. God corresponds to himself in the imputative word of justification. He is never a God who stands against himself for the sake of the sinner.

From Hegel, then, Jüngel offers what was designated earlier as a "natural theology of the cross," the cross as God's "self-definition,"[82] in order to establish the point of contact whereby God as self-interpreting connects with our ability to interpret God by thinking faith. God's primal decision to be for creation and against nothingness and chaos,[83] his own decision in eternity to define nothingness as a part of his own life, limiting its threat to creation, accords with his goal to include his creation in his own eternal blessedness. Unlike the "hidden God," God is never an enemy before whom one must "hold the promise up."[84] Rather, he is the one who has domesticated chaos, nothingness, and death, the one whose will is unambiguous, permitting faith to be transfigured by sight.

Jüngel affirms that God "identified" with the dead Jesus by absorbing the death he suffered from us sinners, becoming our substitute,[85] in order to offer new life for life threatened by death. He does this not with the word "incarnation," developed from the perspective of the ancient metaphysics of substance, but from (1) Bultmannian existentialism's talk of a "paradoxical identity"[86] between myth and history, (2) Barth's analysis of

82. GMW 229.

83. GMW 159.

84. Luther, "Large Catechism," in BC 443:21 and 444:28 (BSELK 667:21 and 669:28).

85. "That Jesus suffers the death which the law foresees for the godless, because he identified with this godlessness as such, is the conflict of the law with the law which is decided in his own person. And that is what constitutes the God-forsakenness of the cross." See GMW 367. See also Jüngel, Justification, p. 166: "As the true atoning sacrifice, Jesus is our peace, because he restores to us that lost wholeness of being which is more than the sum of its parts and which thus deserves to be called *salvation*."

86. Bultmann wrote, "The paradox of the Christian faith is precisely this, that the eschatological process which sets an end to the world became an event in the history of the world and becomes an event in every true sermon, and in every Christian utterance, and the paradox of theology is precisely this, that it must speak of faith in objective terms, like any science, while fully realizing that its speaking becomes meaningful only if it goes beyond the 'objective' formulation." See *Myth and Christianity*, trans. H. Wolff (New York: Noonday Press, 1958), pp. 70-71. For Bultmann, the meaning of history, if it lies anywhere, lies always

the unfolding of the eternal divine election of Jesus Christ in time, and (3) German Idealism's claim that in the "System," being and thinking ultimately correspond, "the identity of identity and difference."[87] Within the divine life itself, Jüngel affirms that God "differentiates"[88] himself as this person of God, the eternal Son, who elects himself to be one with death, from the person who elects this other to be raised to life, the Father, and all this through the agency of the Spirit, who is the chain of love *(vinculum caritatis)* between the Father as the lover (in the Godhead and for the world) and the Son as the beloved, who reciprocates love back to the Father. Such trinitarian dynamics ultimately surpass a metaphysics of subjectivity as inadequate for the divine life and demand a social ontology, God perceived as an event of "mutual otherness." For Jüngel, we can read God's historicity from the script of history because God's being-in-self and being-for-us are one (in- and for-self). In other words, the divine ontology is one with the divine soteriology. Or, the one rational goal within the divine life is historically embodied in the man Jesus.

Despite the genuine attempt to respond to atheism, why should so much attention be paid to God's ontology? Should we not be skeptical of our ability to schematize the divine, not only because it transcends human imagination, but also because God is hidden outside Christ-as-promise? In this light, does not secularism's affirmation of a "naked public square" need demythologization? Do atheists not have, in fact, substitute deities and idols, usually tied in the modern world to our economy, the "god" of capitalism as "free enterprise" at work in the (providential) "hidden hand of the marketplace," while the god of communism is the collective will expressed as the liberation of the proletariat?[89] Like Barth, Jüngel is deeply

---

in the present. When the present is captured by an eschatological word in the Christian proclamation, then the meaning of history is realized. See *History and Eschatology: The Presence of Eternity* (New York: Harper, 1957), p. 153.

87. The early Hegel writes, "Philosophy must give the separation into subject and object its due. By making both separation and the identity, which is opposed to it, equally absolute, however, philosophy has only posited separation conditionally, in the same way that such an identity — conditioned as it is by the nullification of its opposite — is also only relative. Hence, the Absolute itself is the identity of identity and non-identity; being opposed and being one are both together in it." See *The Difference between Fichte's and Schelling's System of Philosophy*, trans. H. S. Harris and Walter Cerf (Albany: State University of New York Press, 1977), p. 156.

88. GMW 363.

89. See Robert H. Nelson, *Economics as Religion* (University Park, Pa.: Pennsylvania

concerned that the proper understanding of the relationship between God and humanity, in which each other's power is not expressed at the expense of the other, be defined. He is concerned that idolatry (human projections of power, *libido dominandi,* onto God) be prevented so that God is honored and not used. However, we need to ask, Is such a theory applicable or adequate when only faith will do? Is *defining* the proper relationship of the human to God nearly as important as *delivering the words* of law and promise that actually *establish the right relationship* of fear, love, and trust? The proper ordering between the divine and the human cannot adequately be established by theory, but only by preaching. Faith evoked by the proclaimed word permits human power to cooperate with God's creativity, spontaneously unleashing deeds of righteousness *coram deo.* The ontological attempt to map deity by following in the deity's footsteps and inferring thereby the landscape of the deity's interiority is a closeted attempt to walk by sight, and not faith. In the public forum Saint Paul knew that Jews (for us, popular religiosity?) sought miracles and Greeks (for us, the academy?) wisdom. In response, he offered Jesus Christ, a stumbling block to Jews and foolishness to Greeks (1 Cor. 1:22-25). Delivering the point of the First Commandment — God's rightful claim over his creation — actually brings an end to human idolatry and raises the new being.

In order to affirm a free relationship between God and humanity, Jüngel insists that we must support the secular supposition that God is "not necessary" for the human to be truly human. Yet, can the human really be human without God, as Jüngel wants us to believe? Is the only route to a free relation between God and humanity through affirming such secularization? Perhaps this secularization really is not the neutral turf that it pretends to be, such that religion must always be configured as a "private" matter. Secularization, rather, indisputably entails the affirmation of a theological claim. This claim is that the human can be human apart from God because, in fact, the human can serve as one's own god. Rather than a neutral turf that relegates religion to a private matter, secularism affirms deeply religious, though closeted, pagan views of the self. It offers a space for the Epicurean self,[90] who need not fear divine punishment, since there

---

State University Press, 2001), pp. 25, 110-12. See also Harvey Cox, "The Market as God," *Atlantic Monthly* 283 (1999): 18-23.

90. See Benjamin Wiker, *Moral Darwinism: How We Became Hedonists* (Downers Grove, Ill.: InterVarsity, 2002).

is no afterlife. Upon death one's atoms disperse, and this truth should pre-empt worry over future rewards or punishments in an imaginary afterlife. Or, it offers a space for the Gnostic sacred self,[91] which will eventually be unfettered from its loathsome earthly body and return to its divine heavenly source. Both fictive "selves" — trapped in incurvation — are at an advantage if the public square is divested of a highest good. The latter would entail their demise, expose them as not ultimate. Is not Jüngel on target when he affirms that the exocentricity that is evoked by faith unleashes a dynamic of love within human life and experience? If so, should we not assert that this other view of Jüngel's is to be preferred over that view which affirms a positive role for secularity? If secularism seeks a justification for humans in the public realm based on the merit of their works (a secular works-righteousness) as ultimate, it would seem to function as the cultural equivalent of the medieval quest for merit. Indeed, is not this the reason why Jüngel has so strongly tried to counter its self-deceptions, such as the attempt of the human to secure itself?

If it is appropriate to challenge Jüngel's accommodation to some aspects of secularism, then it is appropriate to question his configuration of the divine-human relation as an "I-Thou" personalism. If the public square is not really religiously neutral, then God is speaking to us not in the pure disembodied spirituality of the address that presents a "Thou," but in the impurity and always ambiguous mediation of many voices and bodies, ever leading one to rest one's confidence in the promise. Hence, given the ambiguity of the self-evaluation of our own hearts, resulting from the fact that we are *simul iustus et peccator,* as Jüngel affirms, how can we ever be sure of our own correspondence with the divine? "Correspondence" is too optimistic or intellectualizing a concept. It transforms faith into sight. The eschatological limit between the old and new being implies that an overarching mirroring of relationships of temporal behavior in an eternal reality falls short. Undoubtedly, we do cooperate with God. We have a synergy *coram mundo* in the charity unleashed by faith.[92] But given

91. See Harold Bloom, *The American Religion: The Emergence of the Post-Christian Nation* (New York: Touchstone, 1992), p. 49, and Philip J. Lee, *Against the Protestant Gnostics* (New York: Oxford University Press, 1987).

92. Remember Luther's response to Erasmus in *The Bondage of the Will:* "Before man is created and is a man, he neither does nor attempts to do anything toward becoming a creature, and after he is created he neither does nor attempts to do anything toward remaining a creature, but both of these things are done by the sole will of the omnipotent power

that, it is hard to see how Jüngel's view of correspondence to God accords with walking by faith.

The Ontology of Justified Humanity

For Jüngel, forensic and effective forms of justification are not to be separated.[93] However, Jüngel is apt to see their symbiosis by appealing to the existential aspects of forensic justification as a word *event*, happening within interiority. Luther's view of creation as mediating word and word as mediating creation is bypassed. Jüngel is fond of the Augustinian expression that God comes closer to me than I am able to come to myself *(deus interior intimo meo)*[94] in the word.[95] God's declaration that although we are guilty, we are forgiven for Jesus' sake, mortifies the "will to power," *libido dominandi*, of the self-securing self. This old self, who is able only to use *(uti)*, never enjoy *(frui)*, God or, for that matter, able only to use and not honor others, is replaced with a new identity grounded externally, outside itself, in Christ.

On the basis of the doctrine of justification, Jüngel challenges the theoretical and practical aspects of the modern view of agency and selfhood that sees the self autopoietically as a self-owner. This view ties human worth to merit within a system that seeks to conquer nature and control human social relations for the sake of a perceived human well-being. Modernity fails to leave room for faith and thereby inhibits the liberation from *libido dominandi* that the gospel effectuates. Insofar as society grounds itself on the basis of merit, it obtains a works-righteousness that fosters personal and social security, cohesion, expansion, and growth. In this regard, we can claim that it is not free but *bound* to seek such self-development. Ironically, we are bound, not free, because we are *driven* to

---

and goodness of God, who creates and preserves us without our help; but he does not work in us without us, because it is for this he has created and preserved us, that he might work in us and we might cooperate with him, whether outside his Kingdom through his general omnipotence, or inside his Kingdom by the special virtue of his Spirit." See LW 33:242-43 (WA 18:753-55).

93. Jüngel, Justification, p. 73.

94. GMW 296, 298, 341, 358.

95. And this is the only point of contact that he finds between his work and that of the new Finnish school of Tuomo Mannermaa; see Jüngel, Justification, p. 212.

establish ourselves on the basis of our own merit! Our quest for and defense of autonomy surprisingly results not in more but less freedom — indeed, bondage![96] We are imprisoned in our own self-securing quest for invulnerability in the face of disorder, chaos, and apparent meaninglessness. We are forced to look to our own inner resources to supply the strength and fortitude that would have been proffered by God. Secularity divests itself of God as the highest good for human life as the price to be paid for securing the self as its own legislator and judge. Yet, its choices are made on the basis of a compulsion to establish worth in the face of meaninglessness — and that by works-righteousness!

Jüngel exposes secularism as offering a messianic aura for self-grounding, both as attempting to map reality encyclopedically and as seeking to establish an ideal society through a specific social program. In response, Jüngel claims that we need to establish appropriate boundaries to such expansion.[97] Yet, these very attempts of the human to secure, even to save itself, in the face of such ambiguity indicates radical finitude and underlying need. The totally secured human would be a caricature.[98] To be truly human is to live by trust, allowing others to be for one,[99] allowing God to define one's self-definition.[100] Secularism fails to recognize this truth.

We must disagree with Jüngel about secularism. Secularism should be unmasked as itself a revamping and sanctioning of certain distorted Christian and non-Christian religious themes. Much of secularism is simply an attempt to legitimate a de-potentiating of the Lordly claim of the First Commandment. The privatization of faith perspectives is often a way to undermine their engagement with, even infringement upon, contemporary economic life. Debate between secularism and faith ought to be configured not as between "science" and "religion," but as between alternative faith perspectives with quite different deities.[101]

---

96. GMW 178.

97. Jüngel, *Death: The Riddle and the Mystery*, p. 133.

98. GMW 179.

99. GMW 180.

100. GMW 164.

101. That much of the contention between orthodox faith and modern secularism can be seen as an interreligious conflict is one of John Milbank's great insights in *Theology and Social Theory: Beyond Secular Reason* (Oxford: Blackwell, 1990). However, the same concept can also be gleaned from Ernest Becker, *The Denial of Death* (New York: Free Press, 1973), pp. 4-5, and Robert H. Nelson, *Economics as Religion*, pp. 110-12.

In Jüngel's view, faith is "allowing someone to be there for me," countering incurvation,[102] where that someone is the triune God. Such faith allows one to live exocentrically in God, to participate in the triune life, not by nature but by grace, and thus to live for the neighbor's well-being. Such faith spontaneously and naturally unleashes love, when anxiety from the threat of nothingness is properly given over to God, who, for Jüngel, has established nothingness within his own life. Such a view of faith parallels his view of language as address, advent, and interruption. It establishes an authentic human life when one is grounded not in oneself but in Another who freely shares Christ's righteousness with humanity. Such alien righteousness suggests several "correspondences": (1) the immanent trinity with the economic trinity and vice versa, (2) the triune God with humanity and humanity with the triune God in the ministry of Jesus Christ, (3) our humanity in Jesus by means of faith, allowing God in Jesus Christ as an event of love to be for one, and (4) earthly things with respect to the "analogy of advent," God utilizing earthly things to convey his own truth and presence in parables and stories.

Theology, for Jüngel, is not primarily construction, as it often is presented today, but *Nachdenken*, following after the triune God on the various paths that God has taken and takes. Its constructive work is wholly accountable to the divine journey as presented in the biblical narratives. Both the divine and the human are seen in terms of correspondence — not of mind to thing, but of words to realities which re-orient life and convey God's coming as transcending the opposition between presence and absence. The order of knowing then matches the order of being, being-as-arrival. The order of being is based upon concord, not a dissonance that recognizes the irreconcilable disharmony that faith never accords with sight this side of the eschaton. For Jüngel, the priority of the divine in relation to everything else is affirmed within his understanding of it as advent and interruption. Theological thinking is not primarily *poietic*. Using the technical language of phenomenology, the early Jüngel said that its "act-intentionality" is preceded by an "act-extensionality."[103] It offers images or reflections accountable to biblical narratives and metaphors. Truth happens in personal encounters that rearrange lives. The temporal order is interrupted by another, different horizon outside its scope that makes it analogous to the divine as

---

102. Jüngel, Justification, p. 114.
103. Jüngel, *Paulus und Jesus*, p. 5.

wholly gracious. Interruption is not dissonance but correspondence between eschatology and history. Here the Bultmannian paradox is flattened out. Historicity is characterized by a system of correspondences within the triune life. As an echo, history is capable of bearing historicity, and being is enfolded within this ontology as a concrete, living expression of it. While historicity does not need history (and vice versa, apparently), history gives concrete embodiment to historicity. Conversely, historicity makes history intelligible. Nevertheless, in Jüngel's thinking, the epistemological priority of the rational is to be preferred over the sensual — a Hegelian virus infecting his work.

In Jüngel, the Bultmannian paradox between history and eschatology is channeled into a Barthian analogy of faith, giving rise to the "analogy of advent." The Hegelian historicity of the divine unfolds itself so as to permit human agency via a fundamental passivity, mimicking its own self-giving life. The world as such is without analogy to God. Both a Thomistic analogy of being and Luther's view of the world as masking the divine are rejected. However, unlike Hegel, Jüngel affirms with Barth that God need not be embodied in the world: God's advent within the world is a "plus" to it. For Jüngel, as much as for Barth, God is the "One who loves in freedom." The divine rationality need not be embodied, but insofar as it is, its embodiment is rational.

Jüngel and Luther

Clearly Jüngel is indebted to Luther. With Luther, he takes justification by grace alone through faith alone to be the heart of theology. He skillfully appeals to Luther's thinking about the human attempt to establish itself meritoriously before what is ultimate in order to expose the modern "will to power" as both inherently self-justifying and violent. With Luther, he claims that we are fundamentally human in our passivity, our reception of God's gifts in both creation and renewal. With Luther, he believes that the old being cannot be reformed, but only annihilated. The word alone is the source by which the new being in Christ exists. With Luther, he believes that Christ is primarily sacrament *(sacramentum)*, and only secondarily example *(exemplum)*. With Luther (against Müntzer and the *Schwärmer*), he is skeptical of all human ethical attempts to create an earthly utopia to supplement faith. With Luther, he understands the inevitability of the will to bind itself to an idol in the face of its impotence. Nevertheless, his over-all theological orientation is committed to the mature Barth's project of rightly ordering human to divine agency.

In this light, several issues must be raised with regard to Jüngel's the-ology from the perspective of Luther. First, for Jüngel, God's being-for-self and being-for-us are identical. He seeks to honor God for God's own sake; yet, this presentation ties our understanding of God to what God has to of-fer for us — salvation. Are we dealing, finally, with a theocentric or an ego-centric approach to faith here?[104] Since the ontology of the divine is so closely associated with a relation to the human, can Jüngel deliver the theocentrism he apparently wants? For Jüngel, the human is God's "cove-nant partner."[105] Hence, partnership is a key metaphor for understanding God's justice.[106] If we, with Luther, are to fear, love, and trust in God above all things, must we not say that genuine filial fear of God is due to the fact that we as creatures are in no position to control God? Hence, we must not presume to be able to decipher God's deity. However, Jüngel pushes a kind of ontological and ethical parity between the divine and the human that is built into God's deity itself. Not only to know Christ is to know his bene-fits, but God *is* God's benefits. Here God's lordship is so defined through love that it is lost. Thereby, Luther's genuinely theocentric perspective is replaced with an egocentric one.

Second, in light of Luther, is there no *Anfechtung coram deo* for Jüngel? We are able to read into or decipher the inner life of the divine since, in Jesus' death, the finite serves as a vehicle for the infinite's self-definition. Indeed, this is the key that unlocks Christology and the doc-trine of election: God is choosing himself when choosing Jesus as the elect man. The doctrine of election is thus only and always gospel — never threat! What then becomes of actual human experiences of wrestling with God — as on Mount Moriah, when with Abraham we are asked to offer Isaac (Gen. 22), or at the Jabbok, when with Jacob we contest with God

---

104. See Phillip Watson, *Let God Be God! An Interpretation of the Theology of Martin Luther* (Philadelphia: Muhlenberg, 1948), pp. 34-38, 42, 59-62.

105. GMW 38.

106. Jüngel, Justification, p. 76: "God is *just* because he practices *grace*. Grace and jus-tice are for God not so separate that grace should be enacted before right. Rather, God ac-complishes his justice in the very fact of practicing grace. As a gracious God, who also re-mains *a faithful covenant partner* to ungodly human beings, God *acts in keeping with himself,* is faithful to himself, is *just* in himself and behaves rightly toward the ones he has created."

(Gen. 32)? What becomes of our certitude about God's character on the basis of our theory when life's experiences seem to contradict God's own commitment to us? Must we not, instead of reasoning into deity, hold up God's own promise to God — even at times against God? We must affirm here that faith is not on a continuum with sight, but that thinking is always thinking (like prayer and service) as an expression of faith itself. That God justifies himself as he justifies sinful creatures can be received only by faith and not a strategy of intellectualizing about the inner logic of covenant, election, and the Christ.

Third, for Jüngel, faith is mediated by language, and language mediates experience. Jüngel's concern to situate theology in relation to experience, however, transcends language by means of expressing a meta-experience not so far removed from and comparable to Schleiermacher's "feeling of absolute dependence." Admittedly, for Jüngel, absolute dependence is not the best way by which to gain access to the divine. Rather, "eschatological spiritual presence,"[107] in which the ego is upheld in an encounter with nothingness, resulting in either gratitude or anxiety, better conveys the sense of God's advent. With Jüngel, there is a fundamental ambiguity: is it the word molding experience, or experience molding the word? Undoubtedly, one might not have certain experiences apart from their configuration by certain words. However, the danger in Jüngel's advocating a meta-experience is that quickly it is the meta-experience that configures language rather than vice versa. If we are to be faithful to the gospel, are we not, with Luther, to look to a promise, not an experience? Indeed, is not Jüngel's appeal to experience here similar to a *Schwärmer* approach to faith, as one might likewise construe his "I-Thou" approach to the divine-human relation? With the promise, we hold God to his word. We should never step outside of this word, even when our experience seems so readily to contradict it.

Fourth, in Luther's view, ought faith to be configured with respect to modernity as something private, while the public is secular? Ought Christianity to bless secularity as its "own child"? Or, should not secularity be conceived, ironically, as all too similar to medieval attempts at self-righteousness? Should it not be seen as mediated through alternative, pagan religions, either Epicureanism or Gnosticism? When we can acknowledge that the world is fundamentally God's and that our own creaturely

---

107. GMW 174ff.

activities are, in fact, themselves holy, then with Luther we need not "Christianize" the world, but accept it as God's own moment-by-moment sacrificial gift to us — all for his own good pleasure.

Fifth, from Luther's perspective, is correspondence the best way of construing the divine-human relation on the basis of justification by faith? Ought we not rather to affirm that faith allows us to be the free creatures that we are meant to be? Is it not that grace liberates instead of perfects nature?[108] Correspondence to the divine ought not to be granted the centrality and priority that Jüngel grants it. To his credit, Jüngel powerfully acknowledges that we grow in our humanity. Unlike Athanasius (c. 296–373), it is not a question that God became human so that we might become divine. Rather, with Jüngel, we might say that God became human so that we might actually be able to discern our own humanity, accept it, and even grow in it. For Jüngel, we correspond to God properly in a faith that enables us to live outside ourselves. We have this by grace, while God has it by nature. However, such grace permits us to accept our finitude, including all those things so very unacceptable to the old being that quests for security.

Finally, for Jüngel, the human is threatened not by divine wrath that is operative and pervasive in the world, as it was for Luther, but by chaos. Is it with God that we ultimately contend, or with chaos, overwrought chance? For Jüngel, it is clearly the latter. We are contending against a *Tiamat* with whom we can never get the upper hand. It is God who rescues us. However, is not the devil really God's? While the dualism embedded in Jüngel's position carries the possibility, claimed by theodicists, that God is not to be blamed for much of the world's woe, it is hard to see how God is not implicated. After all, it is he, presumably, who has devised the world with a complex interweaving between order and chance that has given birth to natural laws and their executions, with which the threat of chaos wrestles. Do we not, then, at the deepest level of our inner and social turbulence, ultimately struggle with God?[109]

---

108. Jüngel, *Justification*, p. 90.

109. This is not to deny the devil his own agency; for further discussion, see Chapter Six, pp. 168-69.

Summary and Critical Assessment

In summary, Jüngel's view of the doctrine of justification is one that is highly experiential, in which grace is definitive of the divine being itself, allowing God to be deciphered as the coming One who is not in the world but solely in the word, in which we are saved not from God's wrath but from chaos, and in which the human is fundamentally passive *coram deo*, in opposition to most modern views of anthropology.

A critical assessment of Jüngel's appropriation of the doctrine of justification must naturally ask whether it is licit to move from the event of justification to an ontology of the divine and the human. While the latter is helpful with respect to anthropology, God cannot so easily be unmasked. Does this settle our quest for assurance about God, or do we end up wrestling with other divine masks in the process? Since the real issue is how to deliver the word that justifies, then the emphasis on God's thinkability is off target. Jüngel's apologetic is not credible to the atheist. After all, the atheist is driven by an alternative religious, theological agenda.

The privatization of God adopted by secularism and accepted by Jüngel simply gives permission for the idea that there are no boundaries with respect to human endeavor, since the public realm can be seen to be divested of divine law, thus becoming a fertile field for the uninhibited self-development of the unencumbered, autopoietic self. Instead, we ought to affirm that the public realm is never, this side of the eschaton, divested of its idols of legitimation. Humanity will have some kind of faith. The true faith is that we owe our very being to God.

What can positively be taken from Jüngel's work? First, he has exposed modern self-grounding as a species of incurvation. Second, he offers a unique outlook on the will as bound: we are under the compulsion to establish our worth. Third, he reclaims the theme of mortification and vivification as the effective dimension of the forensically justifying word. Fourth, he grounds human action in a fundamental passivity *coram deo* and acknowledges that true freedom is from incurvation. Fifth, his thinking consistently and powerfully upholds the *coram deo/coram mundo* distinction. Sixth, he maintains the distinction between person and works with impressive consequences, challenging modern works-righteousness. Lastly, he unmasks modern Pelagianism as dehumanizing in the very attempt to secure the human.

What should we disregard in Jüngel's work? First, he tends to intellectualize God and the divine-human relationship. Second, he divests creation of its sacramental nature. He fails to see it as address along with the word. Third, he tends to construe the divine-human relationship as "I-Thou" and ignores that God speaks through physical means. Fourth, he is ambiguous with regard to secularity. On the one hand, it is to be affirmed as offering the kind of freedom that inhibits the human from merely using the divine and vice versa. On the other hand, it is denounced as a manifestation of *ambitio divinitatis*. Fifth, he too closely associates God-for-himself as God-for-us. In this regard, is it God's business to forgive (*pardonner, c'est son métier* [Voltaire])? Sixth, he subverts the linguistic nature of the gospel as promise from the meta-experience it may or may not deliver. We need to affirm that the word remains embodied as word — and is not to be subverted by an experience. Finally, in this regard he makes faith a private matter and thus feeds the illusion of secularism that limits faith's potency in the world.

All in all, no serious contemporary restatement of the doctrine of justification can afford to ignore the remarkable insights and directions that Eberhard Jüngel has offered. However, his theology's ability to serve the church hinges upon the degree to which his thinking heeds the promise. In this regard, his thinking leads to mixed results.

Chapter Three

Wolfhart Pannenberg: Justification in the Theology of the Metaphysical One

With his *Systematic Theology*,[1] Wolfhart Pannenberg, retired from the theological faculty of the University of Munich, has distinguished himself as the foremost Protestant systematician of our time. His work grows out of significant contributions made across several theological fields.[2] Two major com-

---

1. Pannenberg, ST 1, 2, and 3. See also *An Introduction to Systematic Theology* (Grand Rapids: Eerdmans, 1991) and *Theology and the Kingdom of God*, ed. Richard John Neuhaus (Philadelphia: Westminster, 1977). For an assessment of Pannenberg's theology by American theologians, see *The Theology of Wolfhart Pannenberg*, ed. Carl E. Braaten and Philip Clayton (Minneapolis: Augsburg, 1988). For an overview of the *Systematic Theology*, see Mark C. Mattes, "Pannenberg's Achievement: An Analysis and Assessment of His 'Systematic Theology,'" *Currents in Theology and Mission* 26 (1999): 51-60.

2. For Pannenberg's work in fundamental theology, see *Basic Questions in Theology*, 2 vols., trans. George H. Kehm (Philadelphia: Westminster, 1970, 1971); for metaphysics, see *Metaphysics and the Idea of God*, trans. Philip Clayton (Grand Rapids: Eerdmans, 1990). For his work on the relation between theology and science, see *Theology and the Philosophy of Science*, trans. Francis McDonagh (Philadelphia: Westminster, 1976) and *Toward a Theology of Nature: Essays on Science and Faith*, ed. Ted Peters (Louisville: Westminster/John Knox, 1993). For his work in theological anthropology, see *Anthropology in Theological Perspective*, trans. Matthew J. O'Connell (Philadelphia: Westminster, 1985); *The Idea of God and Human Freedom*, trans. R. A. Wilson (Philadelphia: Westminster, 1983); and *Human Nature, Election, and History* (Philadelphia: Westminster, 1977). For his Christology, see *Jesus — God and Man*, trans. Lewis L. Wilkins and Duane A. Priebe (Philadelphia: Westminster, 1977). For his critique of penitential piety, see *Christian Spirituality* (Philadelphia: Westminster, 1983). For his views on ecclesiology, see *The Church*, trans. Keith Crim (Philadelphia: Westminster, 1983) and "Can the Mutual Condemnations between Rome and the Reformation Churches

mitments have influenced his construal of the doctrine of justification in his mature thinking, namely (1) his aim to express a comprehensive metaphysics both compatible with and informative of his systematics, and (2) his loyalty to ecumenism, especially rapprochement between Protestants and Roman Catholics. Pannenberg is guided by the vision that all disparate aspects of reality will be united in the *telos*. This final, ultimate unity can and should now be expressed as visibly as possible, if even in only a provisional way. His metaphysics and ecumenics are substantively, though not formally, commensurable. Given his commitment to ecumenism, he has sought to forge a view of the doctrine of justification that is faithful to Saint Paul and that is compatible with the best of Roman Catholic and Protestant perspectives.

For Pannenberg, the doctrine of justification can be understood when we recognize that Luther simply was not faithful to Saint Paul in specific ways. The categories of law and gospel apply to epochs within salvation history. They do not refer to day-by-day, moment-by-moment ways by which God recreates us to be the people he desires. Additionally, justification is properly an acknowledgment of an ecstatic union between the human and the divine. Employing language from the mystic tradition, Pannenberg notes that faith allows believers to be "raptured" *(raptus)*[3] and live outside themselves, journeying toward union with their ultimate end, the Holy Trinity. Any theory of forensic justification must acknowledge that God's imputative declaration of forgiveness follows and is an acknowledgment of a prior ontic union between believers and God.[4] Indeed, Pannenberg's view of justification is structured by his prior commitment to a metaphysical view of the participation of all finite things in the infinite as the ultimate *telos*. For Pannenberg, the point of theology is to devise a general model of reality applicable to all things, understanding that their concreteness and full efficacy will be manifest only when they reach their ultimate fulfillment. This is true for God as well. God will become more fully himself in the *eschaton,* insofar as finite realities contribute to his life by participating in him.

Be Lifted?" in *Justification by Faith: Do the Sixteenth-Century Condemnations Still Apply?*, ed. Karl Lehmann, Michael Root, and William G. Rusch (New York: Continuum, 1997), pp. 31-43. For his views of ethics, see *Ethics*, trans. Keith Crim (Philadelphia: Westminster, 1981).

    3. Pannenberg, ST 3:178. The reference to Luther is WA 56:303.

    4. For a contemporary restatement of forensic justification, see Gerhard O. Forde, "Christian Life," in *Christian Dogmatics*, vol. 2, ed. Carl E. Braaten and Robert W. Jenson (Philadelphia: Fortress, 1984).

Perhaps for Pannenberg the closest statement that defines the gospel in his *Systematic Theology* can be found in one of his evaluations of Luther's view of forgiveness for the believer. He writes,

> When we evaluate Luther's statements by the way in which the motif of forgiveness occurs in the message of Jesus, in no case must we fail to see that forgiveness there has its basis in the proximity of the divine rule, in the intimation of this rule by Jesus, and in its acceptance by those who believe his message. To those who believe in the proximity of this rule it is present already, and all separation from God is overcome in the fellowship with him thereby opened up.[5]

This is echoed elsewhere: "For Paul, faith itself is the righteousness that counts before God because by faith in Jesus Christ we correspond to the covenant righteousness of God."[6] Clearly, for Pannenberg, the matter of justification cannot be limited to the forgiveness of sins, as he fears is the case in the classical Protestant forensic approach. Rather, the gospel deals with more than forgiveness — namely, the fulfillment of one's whole potential to be united to the Godhead. At the end of the world's historical, cosmic process that God is creating, humans will image God's rule, transformed so as to conform to God's *telos*, to the degree that humans participate in it.[7] The gospel deals not merely with forgiveness. Rather, it deals with overcoming the separation between God and humanity due to finitude and plurality as ontological realities by helping humans achieve their potential for unification with the whole, finding their final place in the infinite's ultimate aim. Forgiveness is ancillary to such ecstatic union. For Pannenberg, faith entails the power to live this union proleptically; the *telos* definitive of life can and should become definitive of life now. Justification is not primarily about God asserting his right over creation by speaking his final decree in the present. Rather, it is the divine recognition that as united to Christ believers live as they grow in their participation in the anticipated ultimate unification that will be both God's and our *telos*.

---

5. Pannenberg, ST 3:82.

6. Pannenberg, ST 3:223.

7. Pannenberg, ST 2:64: "The incarnation is the integrating center of the world's historical order, which is grounded in the Logos and will find its perfect form only in the eschatological future of the world's consummation and transformation into the kingdom of God in his creation."

Justification as imputation, for Pannenberg, is the divine acknowledgment that one shares ontically in Christ's life, the ontology of which is an existence *extra nos*. Faith unites with its object as trust; trust enables the believer to live outside oneself.

Law-Gospel Distinction as Epochal, Not Iterative

Crucial to his argument for revising the traditional Protestant view of forensic justification is the structural separation of the *loci* of law and gospel from that of the doctrine of justification by faith. In the *Systematic Theology,* the discussion of law and gospel follows the relation between the church and the political order within the overall context of the kingdom of God (*Systematic Theology* 3, 12, §3). The discussion of justification, by contrast, follows a presentation of faith, hope, and love as life within the messianic community (*Systematic Theology* 3, 13/II, §4), the basic saving works of the Spirit. Justification is not another way of explaining the relation between law and gospel as a "simultaneous accompaniment"[8] that relates to the re-making of people who trust wholly in God, the question about how the word effectuates faith. Rather, justification implies a historical transition, the epochal succession of Mosaic law to apostolic parenesis within salvation history.[9]

In Pannenberg's perspective, the triune God establishes the divine lordship over the cosmos. This triune life will encompass "all occurrence, and world occurrence can be seen as a whole only in the light of its end, the deity of God in his rule over the world, . . . manifest in Jesus only on the condition that in him the eschaton of history is proleptically present."[10] Hence, the Incarnation is the "integrating center of the world's historical order, which is grounded in the Logos and will find its perfect form only in the eschatological future of the world's consummation and transforma-

---

8. Pannenberg, ST 3:80.

9. Pannenberg, ST 3:79: "Luther did not primarily see the law to which Paul refers in terms of salvation history as the 'old' law that the gospel replaced and that was identical with the Jewish torah. He saw it structurally as law in the absolute. He had before him the fact that phenomena had appeared in the Christian church that to a large extent corresponded structurally to the kind of legalism described by Paul, although in content circumcision and foods were not the issue but pilgrimages and penances. The common denominator was a striving for righteousness by achievements that met accepted norms."

10. Pannenberg, ST 1:229.

tion into the kingdom of God in his creation."[11] That Christ is the "end of the law," as Saint Paul asserts (Rom. 10:4), is to be understood as God's eschatological future already present.[12] Law remains for secular societies, but not for Christians, who instead are motivated by God's love, which triggers "an impulse in us to do what is right."[13] Christians do not need "any law but only the apostolic direction that leads [them] to use the freedom in Christ which is inseparable from sharing in God's love for the world."[14] Hence, Pannenberg notes that the turn from law to gospel has taken place once for all: "The eschatological turn from law to gospel is not something that takes place again and again in the church in the pronouncing of forgiveness. It has taken place definitively in Jesus Christ."[15] The Mosaic law is provisional. Believers are freed from it for following parenesis, laws that are far more relative and context-dependent — binding once again, shall we say, the Christ who had been unbound in his resurrection.

Clearly Pannenberg wants to affirm that two eras are created through the intervention of the gospel: (1) Mosaic law and (2) parenetic love. Yet, how are law and love radically different, particularly when love is seen socially as rendering justice to the neighbor? Surely Pannenberg is not intending to infer that the first gives specific determinate rules while the second suggests *ad hoc* rules that should be applied case by case as based on need. Luther too speaks of two "times."[16] This is entailed in his view that with Christ's death and resurrection the law is "discharged" for faith. However, outside of this unbound Christ, what is there but law for the old being? Pannenberg's perspective is guided by an affirmation of two successive historical phases, the one preparatory to and the other a fulfillment within salvation history moving toward its totality. Luther's affirmation of the simultaneity of law and gospel operating in life would thwart the power of this *telos* that demarcates this division, undermining any contribution we might be able to make *coram deo*. Pannenberg's metaphysical commitment leads him to affirm that opposites must be sublated for the sake of a distinction, not separation, in eternity.

---

11. Pannenberg, ST 2:64.
12. Pannenberg, ST 3:95.
13. Pannenberg, ST 3:95.
14. Pannenberg, ST 3:95.
15. Pannenberg, ST 3:87.
16. See Gerhard Ebeling, *Luther: An Introduction to His Thought,* trans. R. A. Wilson (Philadelphia: Fortress, 1972), p. 147.

But there is the rub: Pannenberg's view of the relation of law and gospel is controlled by his prior commitment to a metaphysics that prioritizes transformation. This metaphysics is inherently Aristotelian, seeing movement as going from potentiality to actuality, an *entelechy* that strives toward an ultimate unity. For Pannenberg, theology ought to be led by an intelligible continuum between the finite and the infinite, time and eternity, rather than refracted through a discontinuity between the old and the new established by the resurrection of Jesus Christ. Thus, faith is situated from the first as an incipient *notitia*,[17] on a continuum with sight. Faith is not primarily a counter-intuitive, ever-contrastive agreement with God's promise in the face of experiences which contradict it, such as affirming that one is just even though one's conscience accuses, or that one belongs to God even when it would seem that the devil has the upper hand. Pannenberg criticizes this "iterative" view, in which law and gospel, from moment to moment, effectuate themselves upon one's life, both in the books of nature and Scripture, accusing the old and resurrecting the new. His preference for an "epochal" view is entailed by his metaphysical commitment to a teleology in which the future is persuasively developing the greatest harmonization possible for all things, manifest in their fullness as eternity. Pannenberg says,

> As concerns the distinction of law and gospel, however, the finality of the turn that for Paul came with Christ's coming did not make its full impact because Luther, unlike Paul, viewed Christian life in the flesh as a life still subject to law. Paul precisely did not say that Christian life "in the flesh" is still under the law. For him believers are already to let their earthly life be determined by the Spirit.[18]

This calls for critique. What becomes of the *simul iustus et peccator*, if law and gospel are epochally sequential? Can Romans 7 be read as if Romans 6 did not immediately precede it? With the law-spirit distinction, Paul is really acknowledging the impact of a new cosmic reality upon an old. The divine Emancipation Proclamation is valid, even in the face of pockets of resistance. Saint Paul is not then referring to a discriminate, non-simultaneous, non-parallel change of epochs, but, like Luther, to an interactive struggle between cosmic epochs that constantly impinge — person-

17. Pannenberg, ST 3:138.
18. Pannenberg, ST 3:86.

ally, socially, and even in nature — upon our lives. Thus, Saint Paul can affirm that as long as one is a sinful person, the law will accuse (Rom. 7:9-12).

For Pannenberg, however, we are free from the (Mosaic) law in the new epoch established in Jesus' resurrection, but not from God's righteous will. Therefore, apostolic parenesis takes the place of Mosaic law. But how is apostolic parenesis not an alternative species of law, a commentary on the double-love commandment? No overt antinomian, Pannenberg smuggles parenesis through the back door as the basis for moral order in the "new" life, in contrast to the rules of Mount Sinai. However, we should keep in mind that for Saint Paul, "the contrast is not between two laws which differ in quality or degree, but between two ways of life, one dominated by its relationship to the legal, and the other by its relation to Christ which puts an end to the necessity of life ordered according to judicial decree."[19] The issue is not primarily replacing one way of life with another. Rather, it is the power of Christ to remake us to be people of faith. Pannenberg fails to understand the element of the totally new in the new life. In Pannenberg, the paradoxes between flesh and spirit, law and gospel, life and death — so important for both Saint Paul and Luther — are flattened out by viewing them as epochally sequential. Might he not affirm parenesis over Mosaic law because it, apparently unlike Mosaic law, is seemingly do-able, at least for the believer? We participate in our transformation toward our final *telos* through these guidelines. Since the law-gospel distinction as epochal, not iterative, is yoked to his metaphysics of cosmic transformation, it is to be taken seriously to the degree that his metaphysics is taken seriously. If the latter falls, so does the former. Similar to Jüngel's ontology, Pannenberg's metaphysics wants to decode the hidden God. Yet, only absolution can assure us in the face of the absolute.

In order to support his view that law and gospel are epochal and not iterative, Pannenberg must affirm that Luther fundamentally misread Saint Paul. The Reformation failed to unfold the "finality"[20] of the eschatological turn in its implications for the theological understanding of law. Luther does not do justice to the breadth of the gospel. He individualizes Paul.[21] While Luther's view of law is to be rejected, his view of baptism is, for Pannenberg, to be affirmed. Pannenberg writes, "In his baptismal the-

---

19. See Roy A. Harrisville, *Romans* (Minneapolis: Augsburg, 1980), p. 103.
20. Pannenberg, ST 3:86.
21. Pannenberg, ST 3:82, 83.

ology Luther in a pioneering way articulated the definitiveness of the eschatological turn for individual Christian lives, and he did this precisely by way of his insight into the relation between baptism and penitence, penitence being understood by him as a daily fulfilling of that which has been done once and for all sacramentally in baptism."[22] When penance is tied to a baptismal theology of daily repentance, and forensic imputation is a response, an analysis of an actual, ontic change in the believer, then the pall of the medieval penitential piety that Luther inherited and furthered — a view which is no longer "relevant" to today's world — will be lifted.[23]

Of course, the preaching of law, as well as its actual encounter in daily experience, is not intended to make us to feel bad about ourselves, but rather to remedy old beings' indifference to their neighbors. If we fail to love our neighbor from the heart, then we will be legally coerced to care for our neighbor — and think of our God — even if we do not wish to. Preaching law is best when it is simply telling the truth,[24] acknowledging our utter dependence upon God and our responsibility to care for our neighbor and the earth. In this regard, law and gospel are not especially to be seen as "iterative," opposed to an epochal view, as if law and gospel were working only in a personalistic fashion upon the isolated individual. Rather, law and gospel operate as mediated socially and even in nature, as enmeshed in the extinguishing of the *ambitio divinitatis* of the old being and the living by faith of the new, a message conveyed in both Scripture *and creation,* insofar as creation too is God's address to us. Baptism, then, is God's concrete claim upon the individual. Its daily gift is the renewal of faith as we cling to God's word. Pannenberg fails to understand that baptismal theology offers the effectual dimension to forensic justification.

Justification by Faith as "Ecstatic Fellowship"

Pannenberg's view of justification is tied to *ecstasis,* the clue to genuine humanity. This *ecstasis* finally has its goal in God as the ultimate *telos* of human

22. Pannenberg, ST 3:86.

23. The criticism of Luther's theology as tethered to medieval penitential piety is long-standing and decisive in Pannenberg's critique of Luther. See Pannenberg, ST 3:83 and *Christian Spirituality,* pp. 24-25.

24. See Timothy J. Wengert, "The Lutheran Confessions: A Handbook for Sharing the Faith," *Lutheran Partners* 17 (2001): 24-29.

endeavor. Thus, his view of justification implies and is implied by a specific anthropological perspective. This anthropology can be summed up in his affirmation that "exocentric self-transcendence, this being present to what is other than the self, constitutes the ego or person."[25] Such an anthropology is wholly compatible with Luther's insight that humans, in Pannenberg's words, "have to trust in something, that our heart must hang and rely on. Here is what we might now call the exocentric form of human life. We have to rest on something outside ourselves. We have no choice. We can choose only on what to rest."[26] As in Luther, this supposition serves as an understanding of religion as "constitutive" of human nature: the universality of religious themes and symbols corresponds to the feature of human behavior described as openness to the world, exocentricity, self-transcendence, or "primal trust."[27] Again, similar to Luther, Pannenberg thinks that the greatest problem for humans is the inability to accept finitude in view of the freedom entailed by the power of thinking, the platform humans share with infinity itself. Hence, Pannenberg writes, "it is our human destiny and the goal of our existence to glorify God by our lives. Our sin is our withholding from God the honor that is due him as Creator (Rom. 1:21)."[28] Again, "but it does not follow that human beings accept their own finitude. They usually live in revolt against it and seek unlimited expansion of their existence. They want to be like God."[29] Even more clearly said:

> We may turn aside from the revelation of deity, from the declaration of the divine will. We have already done so when we do not weigh the possibility of it. But we cannot turn aside so directly from the divine mystery that is most inwardly present to our lives. Nevertheless, there is that turning away from God that we call sin. It takes place indirectly, however, as an implication of our human willing of the self when we put the self in the place that is properly God's.[30]

Given this view of sin as a result of misplaced trust, Pannenberg sees the ministry of Jesus Christ as opening "up access for [people] so that in ac-

---

25. Pannenberg, *Anthropology in Theological Perspective*, p. 85.
26. Pannenberg, ST 1:113.
27. Pannenberg, ST 1:156.
28. Pannenberg, ST 2:56.
29. Pannenberg, ST 2:24.
30. Pannenberg, ST 2:260.

cepting their own finitude like him, and in fellowship with him, they come to share in life from God and can already live this earthly life assured of the eternal fellowship with God that overcomes the limitation of death."[31] Grace thus "elevates"[32] believers outside of themselves, effectuating a wholeness.[33] Believers are moving not only "out" to others in their needs, an "incarnation," shall we say, but also, and significantly, "up" to God. They are lifted ecstatically above their own particularity by means of participation in the Sonship of Christ.[34] This effectuates agency not only *coram mundo* but also *coram deo*. After all, for Pannenberg, the finite not only bears the infinite but also contributes to its overall fulfillment. In this regard, how Pannenberg could avoid, or would even want to avoid, a theology of merit needs explanation.

The Spirit, in this view, is the "pledge of the promise" that the life procured by the Spirit "will finally triumph over death, which is the price paid for the autonomy of creatures in their exorbitant clinging to their existence, in spite of its finitude, and over against its divine origin."[35] Believers are "ecstatically raptured and are outside themselves in Jesus."[36] The basis of such an existence outside itself is faith that "relies on God as the other than itself"[37] and that frees us "from our imprisonment in self."[38] Hence, the verdict of the last judgment "already has been passed for believers." It is one that is, with Karl Holl (1866-1924), "wholly analytical" — "declaring righteous already presupposes righteousness"[39] — and thus is not itself a basis for justification. Hence, "it is a mistake to ground the righteousness of faith in the act of pronouncing righteous."[40]

For Pannenberg, faith necessarily includes love; it is not to be distinguished from an incipient love. It is an ecstatic elevation to God, an upward movement that enables participation in Jesus' filial relation to the Father, a mutual relationship between God and humanity. In such *ecstasis*, we

---

31. Pannenberg, ST 2:434.
32. Pannenberg, ST 3:192.
33. Pannenberg, ST 2:452.
34. Pannenberg, ST 3:130.
35. Pannenberg, ST 3:2.
36. Pannenberg, ST 3:16.
37. Pannenberg, ST 3:153.
38. Pannenberg, ST 3:196.
39. Pannenberg, ST 3:223-25.
40. Pannenberg, ST 3:234.

are not merely recipients *coram deo,* but rather we mutually participate in the inner-Trinitarian life of God, not only passively, but also to a degree actively. In mimetic participation, we enrich the triune life. Pannenberg shares in the widespread rejection of divine *apatheia.* However, the question of God's passion or even real relation with the world is separate from Pannenberg's view that our actions enrich God's life. This latter supposition is a result of his prior Hegelian understanding of God's being as essentially future, the result of a process of self-fulfillment. The merit of human agency here is that it helps the divine fulfill itself. If with Luther we maintain that justification is not a process but a "mathematical point,"[41] then our transformation or growth in the Christian life has no bearing with regard to God, but only with regard to our ability to serve the neighbor and the earth. The content of faith is not the merit of good works, but Christ himself.[42]

For Pannenberg, the ultimate outcome of human existence is to be distinct but not separated from God and all other things. "In the eschatological consummation we do not expect a disappearance of the distinctions that occur in cosmic time, but the separation will cease when creation participates in the eternity of God."[43] Faith allows an existence "outside the self" in order to overcome the egoistic separation between ourselves and God that results from sin. Here, Pannenberg builds on an ecumenical commitment to a view of *theosis* or divinization from the Finnish Luther scholar Tuomo Mannermaa.[44] For Mannermaa, imputation is secondary to the union of the believer with Christ. *Theosis* is wholly compatible with Pannenberg's metaphysical commitment, in which the finite

41. See Werner Elert, *The Structure of Lutheranism,* trans. Walter Hansen (St. Louis: Concordia, 1962), pp. 81-82.

42. LW 26:130 (WA 40/1:229-30).

43. Pannenberg, ST 2:95.

44. See *Der im Glauben gegenwärtiger Christus: Rechtfertigung und Vergottung zum Ökumenischen Dialog* (Hannover: Lutherisches Verlaghaus, 1989). See also *Union with Christ: The New Finnish Interpretation of Luther,* ed. Carl E. Braaten and Robert W. Jenson (Grand Rapids: Eerdmans, 1998). For excellent critiques of this perspective, see Lowell C. Green, "The Question of Theosis in the Perspective of Lutheran Christology," in *All Theology Is Christology: Essays in Honor of David Scaer,* ed. Ean O. Wenthe et al. (Fort Wayne, Ind.: Concordia Theological Seminary Press, 2000), pp. 163-80, and Anssi Simojoki, "Martin Luther at the Mercy of His Interpreters: The New Helsinki School Critically Evaluated," in *A Justification Odyssey: Papers Presented at the Congress on the Lutheran Confessions* (2001), ed. John A. Maxfield (St. Louis: The Luther Academy, 2002), pp. 117-36.

thirsts outside itself for the infinite and can receive the goal of this thirst proleptically. For Pannenberg, Andreas Osiander (1498-1552), with Saint Paul and Luther, understood correctly that God's imputation acknowledges Christ's prior indwelling. Melanchthon and the Protestant Orthodox fathers were wrong to reverse this order.[45] In response to Mannermaa's thinking,[46] Lowell C. Green has helpfully commented that "forensic justification must never be divorced from the person and work of Christ. One should not teach the imputation of the passive righteousness of Christ in such a manner that only a 'legal' procedure is taking place. It is precisely Christ and his gifts which are given in forensic justification."[47] Again, what is problematic for Pannenberg is the efficacy of human agency *coram deo*. Does our agency bear upon the divine? The issue is relevant not just for contesting the apathy axiom — that God has no real relations with the world. Rather, the pertinence of this question can be formulated thus: Are our actions that mimic God, as instantiations of divine goodness, meritorious in that they help fulfill the divine destiny? The question results from Pannenberg's blending a Neoplatonic view of *mimesis* with a Hegelian eudaimonism in the divine's quest for self-fulfillment through cosmic and human history.

Pannenberg's asserted goal is not to rid the doctrine of justification of juridical language but to situate it properly. Pannenberg's view of *ecstasis* is tied to his anthropological convictions. But given his commitments, it is not clear that we primarily and exclusively receive our being from outside of ourselves. In *entelechic* striving for wholeness, it is ambiguous whether the agent is wholly passive *coram deo*, or rather, primarily passive and somewhat active, with respect to God as *omega*. At the very least, this distinction is not clear. How is "striving," a self-potentiation, linked with ecstatic being outside self in another? If union with the divine is the actualization of an *entelechy* which potentiates the self, then how does one ever get outside oneself in God? The quest to fulfill one's *entelechic* potential is an inextricably egocentric perspective, at odds with the altruistic ecstatic existence by which Christ incarnates acts of love through us.

45. Pannenberg, ST 3:227.
46. For further discussion, see Chapter Five.
47. Lowell Green, "The Question of Theosis in the Perspective of Lutheran Christology," p. 171.

Can a theory of participation really solve this dilemma? Admittedly, Pannenberg is deeply indebted to Lutheran insights that believers live *extra nos* and as such can accept their own finitude, but he wants to incorporate these insights into an overall metaphysics of transformation. This latter goal serves to potentiate the self rather than extinguish its self-absorbing desire.[48]

Guided by a view of *telos* as oneness with the infinite, the goal of human striving and endeavor, Pannenberg affirms that believers in the transformation of their empirical existences share in the righteousness that they have in Christ and thus experience a gradual change of their empirical selves,[49] a consequence of and not a precondition for justification. At this point, he follows Luther closely. Like Luther, Pannenberg does not accentuate such progress in the Christian life — growth in one's ability with respect to righteousness. However, unlike Luther, he does see it as an aspect of the overall divine agency in creation, the incorporation of all free creatures into the rich, diverse unity that composes the ultimate kingdom. Construed in a Plotinian way, this kingdom as eternity is "the complete totality of life . . . seen from the standpoint of time only in terms of a fullness that is sought in the future."[50] Human *cooperatio* or synergy, then, is not merely the incarnation of our lives in various forms of service but growth in higher degrees of mimetic participation in the divine, insofar as the divine seeks to incorporate this agency in its fullness. In contrast, Luther's view strongly opposes any soteriological ramifications for our service in the world. But Pannenberg maintains that such *cooperatio* is intimately tied up with soteriology via the union we share with Christ.

It is precisely in this ambiguity with respect to human agency *coram deo* that we must question Pannenberg. Does nature need perfecting instead of liberating through grace? If nature is to be liberated, can the old being escape the cross? The new Finnish "real-ontic"[51] approach to justification cannot help but commit one to a stance in which grace is said to perfect nature, a deification of nature by means of participating in Christ, the prerequisite for justification. With the new Finns, Pannenberg seems to

48. For a discussion of "extinguishing desire," see Gerhard O. Forde, *On Being a Theologian of the Cross: Reflections on Luther's Heidelberg Disputation, 1518* (Grand Rapids: Eerdmans, 1997), p. 17. Forde is referring to thesis 22 of the Heidelberg Disputation.

49. Pannenberg, ST 3:218.

50. Pannenberg, ST 1:408.

51. Pannenberg, ST 3:214.

make law — as the Golden Rule — a means by which we participate in God. Hence, Pannenberg and the new Finns ultimately default to a position hardly distinguishable from that of Aquinas. For Aquinas, faith is the form and love is the substance of the Christian life. However, in Luther's wholly theocentric approach to justification, faith is passive before God. Luther's view rejects all anthropocentric eudaimonism and thus proffers genuinely selfless love for God and neighbor. Christ himself as *donum* is the matter, substance, or content of the Christian life, and love is what Christ produces through us (as good fruit from a good tree). We "participate" in Christ in that he appropriates our sin, and we through faith appropriate his righteousness. It is not that we grow in mimetic instantiation of the true, the beautiful, and the good in all our words, thoughts, and deeds. In faith itself Christ is present *(in ipsa fide Christus adest)*.[52] But this means not that an opportunity is opened for our synergy to be exercised with respect to God, but rather that God does *everything* for us already. As Klaus Schwarzwäller affirms, God "goes it alone" with respect to salvation.[53] He does not need help, and actually makes us to be sinners, unable to help him. Thus, faith alone fulfills the First Commandment. Against the *Schwärmer* view, it is an external word that creates such liberating faith.[54]

---

52. Luther also describes this with the metaphor that we are "cemented" to Christ: "But faith must be taught correctly, namely, that by it you are so cemented to Christ that he and you are as one person, which cannot be separated but remains attached to Him forever and declares: 'I am as Christ.' And Christ, in turn, says: 'I am as that sinner who is attached to Me, and I to him. For by faith we are joined together into one flesh and one bone.'" See *Lectures on Galatians* (1535), LW 26:168 (WA 40/1:285-86).

53. Speaking of Luther's view of predestination, Schwarzwäller writes, "For him [Luther], the doctrine was essential. Why? Because the doctrine is indispensable if we want to keep grace God's heavenly grace and let God be God. For it holds that God does it alone. That is by no means mere theory. It was Hans Joachim Iwand who demonstrated that responsibility and responsible acting are dependent on predestination. Otherwise, he explained, we are unable to carry the burden of responsibility. So he makes clear that Christian ethics presuppose the bondage of the will! For unless God Himself has taken full care of us, we have no liberty to act according to what is necessary to do but, rather, we are always eager to gain something for ourselves, even in acts of charity, and have in mind neither God's glory nor our neighbor's welfare but our own advantage or our — presumed — merits in the eyes of God or men. Thus, without predestination, we end up inevitably with the religion of success, that is, with the attempt to be God ourselves." See "The Lutheran Tradition and Its Obligation," *Lutheran Quarterly* 1 (1987): 182.

54. Compare Luther, *Against the Heavenly Prophets* (1525), who asserts, "Observe carefully, my brother, this order, for everything depends on it. However cleverly this factious

Pannenberg's approach to justification is tied to a view of the Christian life as a pilgrimage, certainly outward in acts of love to the neighbor, but decisively *upward* — finally far beyond our limitations — so that our lives become harmonious within the wholly inclusive divine chorus in which one's life will finally blend with that of the Trinity. While Luther occasionally looks at the Christian life as, in some sense, a journey or movement that includes growth, Luther breaks with the *viator* approach. For Luther, we are moving not from sin to virtue in the Christian life, but rather from virtue to grace.[55] Indeed, we are candidates for justification only because we are completely sinners. Thinking no longer *ad modum Aristoteles* but *ad modum scripturae,* we affirm that it is faith alone that not only makes us righteous but also helps us acknowledge our sinfulness. Hence, the Christian life has revealed to it the absolute simultaneity of sin and righteousness. Imputed righteousness in faith establishes the truth of the *simul* as total states, because the person, in contrast to Pannenberg, cannot be considered a continually existing subject. Before the divine tribunal there are no saints but only sinners, and faith alone makes the guilty to be forgiven for Jesus' sake. The divine imputation makes it true that we are old and new, sinners and righteous at the same time. This is to be understood as total states. It is not that we are half-bound and half-free, but that we live our lives on a battleground of two mutually exclusive totalities. It is this truth to which the great Reformation battle hymn refers: "He breaks the cruel oppressor's rod and wins salvation glorious."

Sanctification, then, is to be seen not as a continuous process of growth in virtue or participation in forms that expand our being in the tri-

---

spirit makes believe that he regards highly the Word and Spirit of God and declaims passionately about love and zeal for the truth and righteousness of God, he nevertheless has as his purpose to reverse this order. His insolence leads him to set up a contrary order and, as we have said, seeks to subordinate God's outward order to an inner spiritual one. Casting this order to the wind with ridicule and scorn, he wants to get to the Spirit first. Will a handful of water, he says, make me clean from sin? The Spirit, the Spirit, the Spirit, must do this inwardly. Can bread and wine profit me? Will breathing over the bread bring Christ in the sacrament? No, no, one must eat the flesh of Christ spiritually. The Wittenbergers are ignorant of this. They make faith depend on the letter. Whoever does not know the devil might be misled by these many splendid words to think that five holy spirits were in the possession of Karlstadt and his followers." See LW 40:146-47 (WA 18:136-37).

55. See Gerhard O. Forde, "Luther's 'Ethics,'" in *A More Radical Gospel: Essays on Eschatology, Authority, Atonement, and Ecumenism,* ed. Mark C. Mattes and Steven Paulson (Grand Rapids: Eerdmans, 2004), p. 140.

une community, but as an oscillation in which the beginning and the end are equally near. All that we are from our old nature is totally enveloped in sin, while all that we are from our new nature, from Christ, is totally claimed as righteous. To be sanctified is to acknowledge God's glory in his imputation. We grow in service as this claim becomes more definitive of our lives. In faith, one is able from the heart *(ex animo)* to hate sin, and even oneself as a sinner *(odium sui)*.[56] Hence, the movement that needs to be discussed as decisively shaping every aspect of the doctrine of justification is not the movement of believers to their ultimate end but the movement of that *telos* toward believers. It is this movement that motivates believers to incarnate their lives in service to others within a plurality of vocations through which God continues his creative work. Hence, sanctification is not the goal of the Christian life but its source. The only movement to be discussed between God and humans is that of God's movement toward us. This too subverts metaphysical speculation, because we can only describe what we received, and not infer it from the giver. Through God's grace, we have already arrived at our goal. To use the old distinction about imputation as analytic (as Pannenberg, with Karl Holl, holds) or synthetic (as was held by Albrecht Ritschl [1882-1889]), we maintain that the judgment is synthetic. The judgment as the offering of God's unconditional promise of commitment to creatures is wholly performative: a word which says what it does and does what it says. The word and the gift are one, a gift-word that effectuates God's claim over those who are God's by his just and legitimate right as creator. Indeed, it is a word that effectuates the strange economics of the kingdom, exchanging divine righteousness for the sinner's unrighteousness. With Hans Joachim Iwand (1899-1960), Pannenberg maintains that faith honors God by asserting that he is in the right especially in his judgment; faith gives supreme honor to God by agreeing with him.[57] However, we must note that Pannenberg's is finally a misinterpretation of Luther's doctrine of baptism. Since Pannenberg's sacramental theology, along with his doctrine of justification, is configured by his metaphysical teleology, in which the finite comes to its fulfillment in the infinite, baptism ("the doctrine of justification in concrete form")[58] is not only an outward voyage into service but also an upward, "raptured" journey of mystic union with the divine.

---

56. See Gerhard O. Forde, "Forensic Justification," in *A More Radical Gospel*, p. 123.

57. Pannenberg, ST 3:140-41.

58. Pannenberg, ST 3:233.

Metaphysical Presuppositions

In sharp contrast to one aspect of the nineteenth century's Kantian-influenced theologies, such as Schleiermacher's, Ritschl's, and Herrmann's (1846-1922), or the twentieth century's no-less-Kantian neo-Orthodox theologies, such as Barth's and Bultmann's, metaphysical concerns are central, not peripheral, for Pannenberg. Metaphysical vocabulary, syntax, and grammar can serve for the theological. We should be skeptical of Pannenberg's appeal to a general metaphysics as the best route to truth, as supposedly offering scientific neutrality. Indeed, it is saturated from the start with soteriological assumptions, which inherently alter the discussion of the doctrine of justification. Pannenberg's metaphysics is not as general as he wants; it is decisively Plotinian and Aristotelian. Undoubtedly, Pannenberg wants to develop a comprehensive metaphysics in order to establish common ground between the academy and the church, for the sake of opening a space in which God's reality would sound credible to contemporary skeptics. Not only theology needs metaphysics, if it is to talk about God's reality (because talk of God can happen only in tandem to a world), but also science needs metaphysics since it, like theology, is not without presuppositions. In this regard, Pannenberg does not overcome the fact-value split that infects contemporary thinking, which tends to see faith as subjective and private, a feeling within the ego, non-threatening to social transactions and economic exchanges. This is because he aligns theology on the side where modernity positions truth as "fact," by providing an intellectual framework for any notion of facticity. Both theology and theoretical science employ models of truth as they go about their tasks, since both are based on drawing inferences about their subject matter and not establishing direct proofs. Indeed, since theoretical science is unable to explain empirically its own empirical method, and thus is unable to justify its own instrumental rationality by its own standard, it needs metaphysics in order to ground its rationality. Pannenberg forgoes any metacriticism of scientific method that would locate its models and proposed experiments within a larger narrative framework, for that would likewise relativize its ability to encompass or measure "reality."

In Pannenberg's view, a congenial rapport must be established between metaphysics and theology, if theology is to share the same scientific rigor for how truth is publicly established in the academy as well as foster a healthy ecumenism. In the latter goal, the church should serve as a "sign" of the coming kingdom. God is the power of the future, for Pannenberg, and the future is the engine that generates the striving of all plural realities toward an inclusive, harmonized, and fulfilled unity. Time is no ahistorical, static "moving picture of eternity," as it was for Plato, because for Pannenberg, the trajectory of history results from the irresistible draw of future fulfillment in the One. Eternity will harmonize the agencies of various contributors to this process. In the final *telos,* proleptically manifest in the resurrection of Jesus, all realities will be harmonized, although their distinctiveness will be preserved. Here the triune life serves both as the transparent map by which to chart all reality and as the consummate goal by which to pattern ecumenism. The church today should seek to manifest ecumenically this metaphysical unity. After all, there is a *communicatio idiomatum* (exchange of properties) between metaphysics and ecumenics: the two are one in the self-unfolding, decipherable triune life.

Similar to the theology of Eberhard Jüngel, as mediated by Hegel's thinking, Pannenberg's theology seeks to demonstrate that the finite and the infinite can be reconciled via historical phases of divine embodiment, since the finite gives concretion to the infinite, and the infinite is instantiated as the finite.[59] This is ironic, since both Jüngel and Pannenberg tend to think that they offer strict methodological alternatives. With Hegel, Pannenberg shares the view that the divine goal is the *entelechy* of the history that God initiates and drives. In contrast to Hegel, Pannenberg affirms that God is independent of the world. Appealing to Scripture, he supports the *contingentia mundi.* Unlike both Hegel and process thinking, he believes that God does not need the world — although, apart from the world, God's life would be significantly different. Of course, Pannenberg, like Jüngel, and Hegel before, misreads the Lutheran doctrine of the *finitum capax infiniti,* which was devised not for the sake of affirming human potential to sleuth the divine, but to affirm that God's promise is so real that it can be tasted on the tongue, even swallowed, because, in Jesus Christ, God is a gift for humanity. For Pannenberg, the *finitum capax infiniti* doctrine is employed not to reassert the concrete tangibility of the promise over against the Reformed position, but falsely to chart the divine.

Given Pannenberg's Hegelian supposition, God is not fully God yet, but will be so at the *telos.* The resurrection is both an affirmation that the *telos* will come to completion and a clue about what that completion will

---

59. See Mark Mattes, "Hegel's Lutheran Claim," *Lutheran Quarterly* 14 (2000): 249-79.

be like. On principle, there can be no "hidden God" *(deus absconditus)*, that shape-shifter who ever thwarts all theologies of glory by bringing us to our knees. Hence, Pannenberg writes,

> But Luther obviously did not want any dualism of a revealed and a hidden God. There is tension between these two aspects of the one divine reality so long as the course and outcome of history are still open. Only at the end of history will the God who is hidden in his overruling of history and in individual destinies finally be universally known to be the same as the God who is revealed in Jesus Christ.[60]

If God should ever hide himself, faith could not at heart be a *notitia* that shares a continuum with sight. Thinking is not to usurp faith, but to help distinguish words of promise from law. Faith is clinging to such promises as "I am the Lord your God. . . . Lo, I am with you always. . . . Your sins are forgiven. . . . I am for you." Nevertheless, for Pannenberg, law and gospel are stages within God's triune history, not ways by which God governs the world so as to bring people to faith. Law and gospel are structured within a complex narrating of inner-Trinitarian dynamics. It is this speculative view of the Trinity that positions law and gospel, not law and gospel that guide the formation of the Trinity (the Trinity as the God of the gospel — the revealed God only as offered in the promise). For Pannenberg, there is no theological problem that cannot be solved by means of developing an adequate ecclesiology; furthermore, there is no ecumenical problem that cannot be solved by means of a proper understanding of the Trinity. In deciphering the triune life, all mysteries are comprehended and, finally, comprehensible.

Given this "exchange of properties" between metaphysics and ecumenics, the believer's action — particularly *coram deo* — is stressed. How do I participate in the divine life? How do I now correspond to or conform to its future fellowship that fulfills my deepest core? Conversely, it might be asked, how does the divine so instantiate itself in earthly life, such as in the community of the church? How might such a sign appropriately instantiate the glory of the divine unity-in-plurality, plurality-in-unity, if not as a "visible unity," at least allowing its future, yet to be manifest unity to become ever more visible? Christ's indwelling initiates a process of

---

60. Pannenberg, ST 1:340.

transformation. God's forensic decree acknowledges this initiation. Admittedly, grace is prior to this transformation that perfects nature. It is the *omega* that draws, activates one. The human is elevated to *cooperatio* within the divine life, and offered finally a *theosis* via participation in God.

Not only do metaphysics and ecumenics become one in Pannenberg's thinking, but so also do metaphysics and soteriology. Soteriological categories are inherently metaphysical and vice versa. This can be shown with respect to five metaphysical categories: unity, intelligibility, the infinite, *telos,* and participation.

First, with respect to unity, salvation for Pannenberg is the order or harmonization of all realities in the *omega.* It is sin, after all, which inhibits or prohibits such harmony and for which we need grace to live outside ourselves for others and in God. "It is not so much the course of history as it is the end of history that is at one with the essence of God."[61] This is the salvific goal: the unity of all — properly distinguished, not separated — from each other. Yet, such salvific unity is tethered to a metaphysical concept. "And because the unity of the real, understood as world or cosmos, is a unity that consists in the order of the many (i.e., of the many individual things), the unity of the world raises the question of a ground, a foundation, that is able to order the many and hold it together as a unity."[62]

Second, with respect to the intelligibility of soteriological assertions, Pannenberg is ever driven by the Enlightenment fear of fideism, in which the object of faith supposedly is finally in nothing other than the act of faith itself. If we are to surmount such fideism — either in science (since science is not in a position to ground itself on its own terms) or theology, we must appeal to a metaphysics that links our thinking about reality with the ultimate reality as the source of all other realities. Why do we need metaphysics? Talk of God is dependent on a concept of the world! Indeed, the Christological and sacramental doctrine of the *finitum capax infiniti,* mentioned earlier, is yoked to metaphysical convictions. Hence,

> The concept of the whole as the all-inclusive whole of all finite reality, a notion that in the human sciences otherwise remains nebulously in the background, therefore becomes an explicit theme for theology whether one wishes it or not. . . . The totality of the world is certainly

61. Pannenberg, *Revelation as History,* with Rolf Rendtorff, Trutz Rendtorff, and Ulrich Wilkens, trans. David Granskov (New York: Macmillan, 1968), p. 133.
62. Pannenberg, *Metaphysics and the Idea of God,* p. 22.

not the real theme for theology, but only the correlate of its real theme, the idea of God. God is not the whole of what exists finitely, and the concept of the whole does not include God within it as one of its parts.[63]

Dogmas, then, as "eschatological" are provisional;[64] they are statements about God, anticipations of the totality of the world. The metaphor of "ascent" particularly links soteriology and metaphysics. "Ascent" points us toward a heavenly journey. Yet, it is also how the "multiplicity of what is given in the consciousness of worldly objects and one's own ego"[65] can be unified with the One.

Third, the concept of the infinite, which "is already in truth a mode of the presence of God"[66] as prethematically at the basis of all human consciousness, is inextricably and simultaneously both soteriological and metaphysical. Most specifically, the Hegelian dynamic of the infinite's ability to overcome its opposition to finite things proffers a kind of salvation. Pannenberg notes that in order truly to be conceived as infinite, the infinite must not only be set in opposition to the finite, but must also overcome the opposition. "It must be conceived both as transcendent in relation to the finite and as immanent to it."[67] Here also the metaphor of ascent reappears: "Metaphysics attempts to rise above the multiplicity of the finite toward the idea of the One, a One that grounds the unity of the world and provides the unifying context for the multitude of things within the world."[68] Metaphysically defined, God is "the unifying unity of the totality of the finite."[69] Likewise, the Logos "is not a timeless universal structure like natural law or a theoretical system of order in terms of natural law. It is the principle of the concrete, historically unfolded order of the world, the principle of the unity of its history."[70] Insofar as soteriology makes our lives meaningful, Pannenberg notes that "the meaning that we ascribe to the data of our own individual histories and to the events of so-

---

63. Pannenberg, *Metaphysics and the Idea of God*, p. 142.
64. Pannenberg, ST 1:16.
65. Pannenberg, *Metaphysics and the Idea of God*, p. 17.
66. Pannenberg, *Metaphysics and the Idea of God*, p. 29.
67. Pannenberg, *Metaphysics and the Idea of God*, p. 36.
68. Pannenberg, *Metaphysics and the Idea of God*, p. 42.
69. Pannenberg, *Metaphysics and the Idea of God*, p. 143.
70. Pannenberg, ST 2:63.

cial history depends on anticipation of the totality which is developing in history. . . ."[71]

Fourth, we most clearly see how metaphysics and soteriology are one with the concept of the *telos*. Every conception of the One must recognize that it is the "constitutive ground and highest good of subjectivity." As such, it "becomes only the future goal of all striving within the realm of the finite."[72] Pannenberg points out that it was Plotinus (205-270), not Heidegger, who first maintained the primacy of the future in the understanding of time.[73] Thus, he can affirm that it is the eschaton that is the creative beginning of the cosmic process. Since all creatures desire this totality of life that they do not yet possess, they will find their ultimate fulfillment — their salvation — in it.

Finally, participation, a metaphysical way of describing how the finite relates to the infinite, also carries soteriological import. Pannenberg notes, "Only a future of our lives' completion in distinction from the future of death that breaks off life, a future, then, beyond death, can actualize this totality that will manifest the identity of our existence in full correspondence with the will of God as Creator by unbroken participation in the eternal life of God insofar as this is compatible with creaturely finitude."[74] Our salvation is in our *entelechic* self-fulfillment in the metaphysical one. Overall, the mirror imaging of metaphysics in soteriology and vice versa may not be a unique observation. However, given both Pannenberg's metaphysics and ecumenics and how both structure his view of salvation, he must configure justification as due to an indwelling, based on an ultimate union of the human with the divine, and a human transformation in virtue. He must underplay those themes in Luther's thinking that would stand in stark contrast.

Strategies of Ecumenism

Is it Pannenberg's metaphysics that directs his ecumenism, or his ecumenism that directs his metaphysics, or — what is most likely — both? A di-

71. Pannenberg, ST 1:55.
72. Pannenberg, *Metaphysics and the Idea of God*, p. 62.
73. Pannenberg, *Metaphysics and the Idea of God*, p. 77.
74. Pannenberg, ST 3:601.

vided church fails to reflect adequately the anticipated metaphysical unity. Furthermore, it is a travesty to the world; it lacks the resources to withstand secular assaults in both politics and the academy. As an ecumenist, Pannenberg provides a seminal paradigm for ecumenical strategies, some of which are obvious and some less so: (1) establish similarities between theological traditions, (2) de-center confessional distinctives and displace them as peripheral, and (3) show the deficiencies within each confessional position.

These three strategies can be outlined point by point. First, it is with Mannermaa's interpretation of the Christ-present-in-faith that he believes he can find a point of contact between Luther and the divinization and *theosis* traditions of Roman Catholicism and Eastern Orthodoxy. Indeed, Pannenberg wants to see the gospel as compatible with "new law." The Reformation does not surrender the obligatory nature of God's righteous demands; "instead, pronouncement of the forgiveness of sins enables us to do the will of God freely. . . . In fact, however, this is also the intention of the doctrine of the gospel as new law that is characterized by the work of the Spirit and grace."[75] For Pannenberg, the Reformers' opposition to new-law teaching is much less than is often supposed. Luther replaced love with faith alone in opposition to the scholastic *fides caritate formata. Caritas,* for Luther, meant love of neighbor and thus was different from justifying faith.[76] Yet, Pannenberg contends, Luther could agree to the scholastic formula when he identified faith as that which fulfills the First Commandment, including fear, *love,* and trust. Conversely, the Council of Trent's affirmation of justification as a process of inner change by means of grace was decisively anti-Pelagian.[77] Sinners are unable to restore fellowship with God. Not only does grace incorporate creaturely reality apart from Jesus Christ, but free will also cooperates with grace and does not act independently of or supplementary to it. Hence, for Pannenberg, the real differences between Roman Catholic and Reformation soteriologies are (1) the significance of faith and (2) the sacramental mediation of incorporation.[78] He cautions that we must be careful how we interpret the concept of transformation: there is no exegetical support for the view that faith is

75. Pannenberg, ST 3:75.
76. Pannenberg, ST 3:190.
77. Pannenberg, ST 3:221.
78. Pannenberg, ST 3:221.

only linked to the beginning of justification and then completed by the infusion of love into believers' hearts.

Second, for Pannenberg, confessional distinctives between Catholicism and Protestantism are peripheral. After all, justification is but one of many ways of expounding salvation. It is not the center of Paul's theology; this center is Jesus Christ himself. Nevertheless, justification is misunderstood if it is seen as only an anti-Jewish polemic. Rather, it is a Christian's present expectation of future salvation. Even a Catholic distinctive such as the Petrine office might be appropriated as a "visible sign" for the unity of the whole church, if it could appropriately be restructured as "subordinated to the primacy of the gospel."[79]

Third, Pannenberg contends that neither Reformation nor Roman Catholic views on justification wholly square with Saint Paul. The Council of Trent "did not pay adequate attention to the decisive significance of faith for the relation of those born again by baptism to God. The Reformation side, Luther apart, does not give due attention to the relation between justification and baptism but attempts, contrary to Paul, to ground the righteousness of faith in the act of pronouncing righteous."[80] Hence, the two views should be relativized and not be church-dividing. They are "the antitheses of two theological schools, both of which are trying to describe fellowship with Jesus Christ as decisive for partaking of salvation."[81]

In response, we must note that a major disagreement at the time of the Reformation was the nature of catholicity itself — just as it had been in the polemics between the Eastern and the Western churches. At stake, given one's confessional loyalty, is the catholicity of papal primacy, a celibate clergy, a specific historical episcopate, or the doctrine of transubstantiation. Recently, even an ecumenist has been arguing on the basis of patristic texts that justification by grace alone through faith alone is indeed the authentic and genuine apostolic — and thus catholic — faith.[82] Given these concerns, one can rightly although quite ironically ask, How "catholic" is the Roman Catholic Church? Is it not, in its own way, quite sectarian, quite *Roman?* Obviously, that has always been the position of Eastern Orthodoxy. However, it was a question newly raised, for the West, at the time of the Reformation.

---

79. Pannenberg, ST 3:421.
80. Pannenberg, ST 3:234.
81. Pannenberg, ST 3:234-35.
82. Thomas Oden, *The Justification Reader* (Grand Rapids: Eerdmans, 2002).

Pannenberg's ecumenism is driven by the fear that an increasingly secularized society will "divide and conquer" the public forum by marginalizing the church. He favors the ecumenics of visible unity both because of a metaphysical commitment that such visible unity is the best sign of the final *telos,* and because a visibly unified church offers the best apologetic for Christianity in a world rampant with a resurrected Gnosticism (Sheilaism)[83] and Epicureanism.[84] In public life, this secular world has the upper hand; it polices the Christian community by relegating its truth claims to the realm of private feelings, not allowing such claims to affect politics and economics. Only a church can save us now, it would seem. However, is this not a reversal of truth? Is it not the gospel alone that can save us now, not the church that the gospel creates?

Pannenberg and Luther

The differences between Pannenberg and Luther would be hard to miss. These differences result from and are activated by Pannenberg's metaphysical and ecumenical commitments. From the perspective of Luther, four issues must be raised with regard to Pannenberg's theology.

First, for Pannenberg, it is God that is the object of theology,[85] in contrast to Luther's view, in which it is the sinful human and the justifying God.[86] This point of departure already positions Pannenberg for a highly theoretical approach to theology, one largely governed by a "speculative Good Friday,"[87] instead of a theology of the cross *(theologia crucis).* Again,

83. See Robert Bellah et al., *Habits of the Heart: Individualism and Commitment in American Life* (Berkeley and Los Angeles: University of California Press, 1985), pp. 221, 235.

84. See Benjamin Wiker, *Moral Darwinism: How We Became Hedonists* (Downers Grove, Ill.: InterVarsity Press, 2002).

85. See Pannenberg, *Theology and the Philosophy of Science,* pp. 299, 361.

86. See Oswald Bayer, "Martin Luther," in *The Reformation Theologians,* ed. Carter Lindberg (Oxford: Blackwell, 2002), pp. 53-54.

87. With respect to the significance of Jesus' crucifixion, Hegel maintains, "Indeed, within this history as spirit comprehends it, there is the very presentation of the process of what humanity, what spirit is — implicitly both God and dead. This is the mediation whereby the human is stripped away and, on the other hand, what-subsists-in-itself returns to itself, first coming to be spirit thereby." See *Lectures on the Philosophy of Religion,* One-Volume Edition (1827), ed. Peter C. Hodgson (Berkeley and Los Angeles : University of California Press, 1988), pp. 468-69.

Pannenberg's aim is to map reality so as to show how God fits on this map. For Pannenberg, God is the *alpha* as the *omega,* the source that creates from the future in order to draw all reality into his life. Theology is primarily for the sake of speculation, not proclamation. As we noted, law and gospel are absorbed as dispensations within the divine history seeking its own self-fulfillment. Thereby, the gospel is eclipsed for the sake of law. The question for the intelligible transparency of all in the triune life, including the historicity of that life itself, is the fateful condemnation that accuses humans of *ambitio divinitatis* in both their "thinking" and "doing," heedless of the gift of creation and preservation, in which the source of life is received moment by moment. In contrast to Pannenberg, we need to reaffirm that the only solution to the threat of the absolute is not the route of domesticating transcendence,[88] leveling God's power by making it decipherable, but rather the rite of confession and absolution that releases us of our *ambitio divinitatis.* Accepting our finitude *coram deo* can never be a purely theoretical affair, but only a result of encountering God's backside *(posteriora dei)*[89] in lived experience.

Second, if faith becomes supplanted by theory, as it does for Pannenberg, what then becomes of the promise? Surely the test for theology, the proper *discretio spirituum* (1 John 4:1), is whether it helps us to deliver the promise. If the word we share as gospel is an appeal, deeds will be evoked. If it explains something, understanding will be aroused. If it is a statement, knowledge is given. Only if the word is promise is faith born.[90] This is not to say that our thinking and doing are irrelevant. If we were never to think speculatively, questioning from whence we have come and to where we will go, we would fail to think adequately. Never to do anything would be to fail to walk in those "good works" that God has prepared for us (Eph. 2:10-11). Only the gospel liberates us from the incurvation that misplaces our knowledge and ethics and exchanges their appropriate roles as service for that of salvation. Reason has its limits; it is no monarch! There is no reason, only reasons![91] In this regard, the proper task of the

---

88. This term is taken, of course, from William C. Placher, *The Domestication of Transcendence: How Modern Thinking about God Went Wrong* (Louisville: Westminster/John Knox Press, 1996).

89. Compare LW 31:52 (WA 1:362, 1f.).

90. See Theologie, C, 4, p. 454.

91. *"Keine Vernunft, nur vernünfte."* See Oswald Bayer, "Schriftautorität und Vernunft — ein ekklesiologisches Problem," in LWRNK, 166-67.

theologian is not to decipher God but to deliver Christ. Christ alone bears the office that establishes assurance with respect to God.[92]

Third, against Pannenberg's positioning of science as definitive for truth (as if science is contextless, devoid of past and future, or poetry and history), we must with Luther affirm that science is a form of law operative as providential grace. In addition to affirming the natural wonder and curiosity that is a part of our creaturely existence, science helps tame the forces of chaos by comprehending them. Science deals with power over the world in order to help make this world more livable. Thereby, however, science is inherently theodic. It is appropriate to develop conflict-laden conversations with the natural and social sciences. We cannot ignore the deeply religious subterranean aspects of their methods. When, however, these disciplines aim to provide a soteriology, it is the proper task of Christian theology to demythologize them. When properly de-mythed, science is best seen as a form of wisdom as law.[93]

Fourth, the hiddenness of the true church needs stressing today as never before.[94] The visibility that Pannenberg seeks is nothing other, for the likes of Luther, than the attempt to walk by sight apart from faith. Given the ubiquity of secularism, an apologetic retreat into the church is attractive, particularly as idealized as a medieval romance in which church and state were one. A host of groups quest for this ideal unity: members of the Hauerwasian-inspired *Ekklesia* Project, the Radically Orthodox, and various stripes of Evangelical Catholics. Given the ruins of the contemporary church — its divided confessional stances, its accommodations to ideologies of both the left and the right, the permission that many in the church give themselves to behave boorishly and uncivilly — one is tempted to think that the gates of hell have indeed prevailed against the church. Like Elijah, many who despair over such matters need to hear God's affirmation that seven thousand in Israel have not bowed to Baal (1 Kings 19:18). With Luther, we must maintain that it is the church that is accountable to the gospel and not vice versa. Likewise, we must affirm that in its present state, composed of both wheat and tares (Matt. 13:24-30), the church is in God's hands, and that he has the upper hand with respect to

92. Bayer, "Martin Luther," p. 54.

93. Theologie, C, 2.3.4, p. 435.

94. In "On the Councils and the Church," Luther speaks of seven signs of the church (LW 41:148-68 [WA 50:628ff.]). This visibility, however, testifies to God's action in the church, and not our ethics or theory.

the church's enemies both within and without its fold. Pannenberg seeks less a retreat of the church from the world and more an *imperium* of the church over the world. However, theology is not about integration but disputation. In light of church unity, we *believe* in the one, holy, catholic, and apostolic church. It is not available for empirical scrutiny.

Summary and Critical Assessment

In essence, Pannenberg's view of the doctrine of justification is one that is bound to his views of ecumenics and metaphysics, in which grace is definitive of the divine being itself: God's being-for-self is one with God's being-for-us, allowing God to be thought. God is deciphered in terms of a general metaphysics as the infinite that draws all things into its own life. God does not primarily save us from wrath, as Luther maintained, but from ontological limitation and separation. Law and gospel, for Pannenberg, are epochal and not daily experiences impinging upon sinners. Justification is primarily union with Christ and derivatively forensic. Humans are passive *coram deo* as receivers. However, humans also contribute to the overall good of the infinite and thus carry (meritorious?) potency *coram deo*.

What is useful in Pannenberg's work? First, with regard to anthropology, his affirmation of human exocentricity offers great insight not only for theology but also for liberal studies. One accords with human nature via primal trust. Second, salvation as involving the ongoing acceptance of one's finitude by entrusting limitations, responsibilities, and guilt into God's hands is also helpful. Third, Pannenberg's view of sin as a result of misplaced trust is insightful.

What is not useful in Pannenberg's work? First, his view of law and gospel as epochal misconstrues the unavoidable, though often denied, encounter of all people with God as accusing and hidden in daily experience when people are driven to potentiate the self. Second, his affirmation of the imputative judgment as analytic, not synthetic, sidesteps the performative aspect to the words of promise uttered in the present. The proclamation "Your sins are forgiven for Jesus' sake" grants life and salvation — delivering us from God's wrath expressed in the conscience and in creation, promising a hopeful, reconciled future, not only with God but with others. Our union with Christ depends on the word which delivers it, not vice versa! Third, there is transformation — even progress to a degree —

in the Christian life. But it is not one "upward," as Pannenberg maintains, but one outward — an incarnation as service. Finally, his view of *theosis* fails to acknowledge the very acceptance of finitude that he wants to affirm. Again, *theosis* construed as a future elevation is precisely a form of the *ambitio divinitatis* that should be avoided. Union with Christ does nothing other than take everything out of our hands spiritually and place it in God's — where it belongs.

If the point of theology is to help Christians discern the gospel, both for its proclaiming and its hearing, Pannenberg raises important questions. However, he fails to help us develop justification as a *discrimen* that is needed today. The gospel is lost in a *contemplatio* by which to ground both metaphysics and ecumenics.

Chapter Four

Jürgen Moltmann:
Justification in the
Theology of Liberation

For the last half-century Jürgen Moltmann, retired from the Protestant faculty of theology at Tübingen, has been recognized as one of the most important of contemporary Protestant theologians. He is not confessionally a Lutheran, nor has he distinguished himself as an interpreter of the doctrine of justification. However, given his prominence in the academy and the church, the importance of his theological method, his appeal to Reformation theology, and his reputation as the "pastor's theologian," a thorough study of contemporary views of justification must analyze the role that the doctrine plays in his thinking, or at least how his method situates the doctrine. The key concept that guides Moltmann's work is "liberation,"[1] specifically being set free from various kinds of social and personal oppression for the sake of just and humane politics, existential meaningfulness, ecumenical openness, and the affirmation of the earth.[2] His view of justification is influenced both by the social ethics of the Radical Reformers that sought an egalitarian social system, and by a Calvinism that seeks a Christian transformation of culture. While justification is not a hub that configures all of his theology, it is foundational for his work.

---

1. Moltmann, *The Future of Creation: Collected Essays,* trans. Margaret Kohl (Philadelphia: Fortress, 1979), pp. 99, 105, 110.
2. See Geiko Müller-Fahrenholz, *The Kingdom and the Power: The Theology of Jürgen Moltmann* (Minneapolis: Fortress, 2001).

85

The early Moltmann believed that modern atheists, particularly those inspired by Marx, such as Ernst Bloch (1885-1977), who focused on hope for a just society, helped lead the way for theologians to deal again with truth. For Moltmann, it is primarily hope for a coming new world, not faith, which gives credibility to Christianity. Hence, eschatology is "not one element of Christianity, but it is the medium of Christian faith as such, the key in which everything in it is set, the glow that suffuses everything here in the dawn of an expected new day. For Christian faith lives from the raising of the crucified Christ, and strains after the promises of the universal future of Christ."[3] Because Christianity "is eschatology, is hope, forward looking and forward moving," it "revolutionizes and transforms the present."[4] As seen in Moltmann's future-oriented perspective, faith implies that our present behaviors should conform to this very specific future. In a sense, the church's task is to make the invisible future as visible as possible in society. Eschatology impinges upon and involves ethics, specifically that of the kingdom's *telos* engaging world history, giving meaning to all specific historical events as preparatory.

The kingdom's politics, as described in Scripture, is that of preferential treatment for the socially marginalized, victims, and the poor. Our solidarity with those now marginalized by economic and political systems, our sympathy and commitment to them, is a foretaste, a making visible[5] of that future in which injustice will not prevail. Indeed, in Jesus' cross, God identifies with both the godless and the god-forsaken.[6] The task of theology is not merely to express truth in relation to a definitive meta-experience, like that of an "experience with experience," as with Eberhard Jüngel, or the theoretical positing of a grand, unified theory of reality, in which God as the *omega* is the creator of all things, as with

3. TH 16.

4. TH 16.

5. Moltmann writes, "Everywhere in the New Testament the Christian hope is directed towards what is not yet visible; it is consequently a 'hoping against hope' and thereby brands the visible realm of present experience as a god-forsaken, transient reality that is to be left behind. . . . Christian hope is resurrection hope, and it proves its truth in the contradiction of the future prospects thereby offered and guaranteed for righteousness as opposed to sin, life as opposed to death, glory as opposed to suffering, peace as opposed to dissension." See TH 18.

6. Moltmann, *The Crucified God,* trans. R. A. Wilson and John Bowden (New York: Harper & Row, 1974).

Pannenberg. Rather, its task is thoroughly saturated in the discernment of how to rectify current injustices in light of a future just society. The point is to make the politics of the present world correspond to that of the future kingdom as much as possible. For Pannenberg, the focus on the future offers a comprehensive theory of the divine. For Moltmann, it offers a comprehensive ethics. In either case, though, theory suggests ethics, and ethics suggests theory.

Echoing Marx (1818-1883), Moltmann repeatedly affirms that we are not to interpret the world, but to change it.[7] This theme, established early in *The Theology of Hope* (1964) and *The Crucified God* (1972), both theological best-sellers, was reworked in *The Church in the Power of the Spirit* (1975), which appeals to the Spirit as the agent of this new order. Similar to the views of the Radical Reformers, with their attack on sixteenth-century feudalism, Moltmann's view sees the church as (1) a provisional anticipation of the coming kingdom, (2) the messianic fellowship of committed believers, and (3) a free society of equals who identify with the socially marginalized. Indeed, the church is "the source of continual new impulses towards the realization of righteousness, freedom and humanity here in the light of the promised future that is to come."[8] The church is not, then, as in the *Augsburg Confession*, "the assembly of saints in which the gospel is taught purely and the sacraments are administered rightly."[9] The *Augsburg Confession* presents an insufficient definition of the church because it fails to acknowledge the agency that the church should have in transforming culture. Moltmann focuses on activity: the church is the unique body that bonds with those marginalized, in contrast to the wider culture, which ignores and abuses them. In contrast, the *Augsburg Confession* sees the church primarily as a recipient of God's work. However, we need to acknowledge that Moltmann fully agrees with Luther's "seventh mark" of the church, in "On Councils and the Church," as cross and trial.[10]

For Moltmann, the ultimate, ideal goal for the world gives it potential for its self-fulfillment. Christianity's mission is to help the world real-

---

7. TH 84; see also *The Trinity and the Kingdom,* trans. Margaret Kohl (New York: Harper & Row, 1981).

8. Richard Bauckham, "Jürgen Moltmann," in *The Blackwell Encyclopedia of Modern Christian Thought,* ed. Alister E. McGrath (Oxford: Blackwell, 1993), p. 387.

9. BC 43:1 (BSELK 61:1).

10. See Luther's discussion on the marks of the church in "On Councils and the Church," LW 41:148-68 (WA 50:628ff.).

ize that potential. The powers that be in our current culture oppose the threat that this future egalitarian world has for them. Counterculture then becomes the Spirit's vehicle for this new world. Moltmann has formulated these views with the aim of reshaping traditional dogmatic *loci*. He offers volumes on the Trinity, creation, Christology, and the Spirit, as well as numerous other books and essays.[11]

Justification within the Matrix of Hope

For Moltmann, faith is insufficient without hope. "In the contradiction between the word of promise and the experiential reality of suffering and death, faith takes its stand on hope and 'hastens behind this word,' said Calvin."[12] Indeed, following Calvin (1509-1564), without the perspective of hope, faith "falls to pieces, becomes a fainthearted and ultimately a dead faith. It is through faith that man finds the path of true life, but it is only hope that keeps him on that path. Thus it is that faith in Christ gives hope its assurance. Thus it is that hope gives faith in Christ its breadth and leads it into life."[13] Hope fulfills and gives body to faith. It protects faith from compromising with the wider culture, which is established upon unfair exchanges between exploitative "masters" who dominate the economic arena over others as "slaves." "For the loss of eschatology — not merely as an appendix to dogmatics, but as the medium of theological thinking as such — has always been the condition that makes possible the adaptation of Christianity to its environment and, as a result of this, the self-surrender of faith."[14] For Moltmann, the future is a free gift, neither earned nor deserved. However, it offers itself as a pattern by which we should model our behavior analogously to it. The future is an ellipse that impacts on the present as gift,[15] but it simultaneously offers itself in the present as the im-

---

11. See the following volumes by Moltmann, all published by Fortress (Minneapolis): *Experiences in Theology: Ways and Forms of Christian Theology* (2000); *God in Creation: A New Theology of Creation and the Spirit of God* (1993); *The Coming of God: Christian Eschatology* (1996); *The Spirit of Life: A Universal Affirmation* (2001); and *Christ: Christology in Messianic Dimensions* (1995).

    12. TH 19.

    13. TH 20.

    14. TH 41.

    15. TH 53.

perative of task.[16] Hence, the indicative of faith leads to the imperative inspired by hope.

Task — indeed, duty[17] — follows on the heels of gift, not as life given and promised, but as demanded and required. We must help society conform to this coming future. This includes both the task of changing social structures so that they are harmonious with it and the task of bringing ourselves personally into synchronicity with it.[18] The kingdom announced by Jesus is primarily an ethical or political state, of which counterculture is currently a trace. Politics has soteriological import for Moltmann. The kingdom will save us. Moltmann does not hold to Luther's view of keeping salvation to the promise, trusting that it liberates us from incurvation and returns us to creation. Political orders belong to the realm of law; they should serve people and not themselves. In Luther's view, the kingdom is promised. It is Jesus Christ in action. Its power subverts that of human

---

16. Moltmann, *Creating a Just Future: The Politics of Peace and the Ethics of Creation in a Threatened World,* trans. John Bowden (London: SCM Press, 1989), p. 6: "However, out of each gift there arises a corresponding task. If the church, if Christians, are the work of the action of God which creates justice and makes peace, then they are also and equally seriously the instrument of this divine action in this world. From the justification of the unjust there follows their mission with a commitment to better justice in society. From the reconciliation of those who are not at peace there grows a mission to create peace in the conflicts of this society. There cannot be any other response by Christians to their experience of God. The creative action of God and the action of human beings in response to that are indeed not on the same level, since God is God and human beings are human beings. But no one may separate these two levels which God himself has brought together. As human beings wholly owe their justice to God, so God is utterly concerned with just human action. When God justifies men and women he puts the hunger and thirst for righteousness in their hearts. God gives us his peace in order to make us peacemakers. Anyone who is personally satisfied with the peace of God for his or her own person and does not become a peacemaker does not know the dynamics of the Spirit of God."

17. Here with Moltmann, we are reminded of Kant's ode to duty: "Duty! Thou sublime and mighty name that dost embrace nothing charming or insinuating but requirest submission and yet seekest not to move the will by threatening aught that would arouse natural aversion or terror, but only holdest forth a law which of itself finds entrance into the mind and yet gains reluctant reverence (though not always obedience) — a law before which all inclinations are dumb even though they secretly work against it: what origin is there worthy of thee, and where is to be found the root of thy noble descent which proudly rejects all kinship with the inclinations and from which to be descended is the indispensable condition of the only worth which men can give themselves?" See *Critique of Practical Reason,* trans. Lewis White Beck (Indianapolis: Bobbs-Merrill, 1956), p. 89.

18. Moltmann, *The Crucified God,* p. 23.

agency. For Luther, "The coming of God's kingdom to us takes place in two ways: first, it comes here, in time, through the Word and faith, and second, in eternity, it comes through the final revelation."[19]

For Luther, the kingdom is realized linguistically, not existentially, metaphysically, or politically, in the gift-word of the gospel as sheer promise. Increasingly, against Ernst Troeltsch (1865-1923), scholars have emphasized that Luther's opposition to establishing the kingdom through the sword, as if the world could be saved through violence, is not tantamount to quietism.[20] Indeed, when the integrity of the gospel is at stake, Lutheranism is known for active resistance. The social transformations effectuated by Lutheranism led to greater recognition of individual freedom of conscience and thought, the need for education for all, and the dignity of the individual.[21] Marx had insight: the social outcome of Luther's reform entailed that priests became laity and laity became priests.[22] This entirely upset medieval power structures. Also, Luther acknowledged that the incipient capitalism of his time legitimated greed.[23] Still true, this social discernment ought to bear on preaching, teaching, and involvement in social welfare.

For Moltmann, by contrast, the kingdom is an alternative to the future envisioned by the status quo. Here, as with Barth, law is the form of the gospel.[24] Along with Engels and Bloch, who maintained that commu-

---

19. Luther, "The Large Catechism," in BC 447:53-55 (BSELK 674:53-54).

20. For instance, with respect to the Peasants' War, Uwe Siemon-Netto notes, "Luther supported many of the peasants' demands. But when they resorted to violence, when they set out to kill the lords and ransack their estates, they rebelled against a divinely established order which existed 'since the beginning of the world,' and thus Luther opposed their tactics." See *The Fabricated Luther: The Rise and Fall of the Shirer Myth* (St. Louis: Concordia Publishing House, 1993), pp. 78-79. David Whitford likewise points out that "Luther felt that to compel reform undermined preaching and transformed the Gospel into Law. Ministry in the kingdom of Christ, then, is always focused on proclamation, not coercion." Unlike Müntzer, who sought a theocracy, Lutherans tend not to sanction events as God's will, as if the latter were transparent. See *Tyranny and Resistance: The Magdeburg Confession and the Lutheran Tradition* (St. Louis: Concordia Publishing House, 2001), pp. 95-97.

21. See Wilfried Härle, "Zur Gegenwartsbedeutung der 'Rechtfertigungs'-Lehre: Eine Problemskizze," in *Zeitschrift für Theologie und Kirche*, Beiheft 10 (1998): 135-37.

22. See *Selected Writings*, ed. David McLellen (Oxford: Oxford University Press, 1977), p. 69.

23. See Carter Lindberg, *Beyond Charity: Reformation Initiatives for the Poor* (Minneapolis: Fortress, 1993), p. 111.

24. See "Gospel and Law," in *Community, State, and Church*, trans. Will Herberg (Gloucester, Mass.: Peter Smith, 1968), pp. 71-100.

nism was indebted to Müntzer (1490-1525),[25] Moltmann believes that the human is always an agent *(homo semper agens)*,[26] not a recipient. The governing idea is correspondence, not so much of faith to thought, as one might see with Jüngel and Pannenberg, but of human social behavior to the coming ideal political order. The paradoxes that help preserve faith, described by Luther (that one is simultaneously lord and servant, sinful and righteous, that God is hidden and revealed, and that Jesus Christ is human and divine), are flattened out into a "Christ transforming culture" perspective, effected, strangely enough, by means of a counterculture — "Christ against culture," to use the helpful typology of H. Richard Niebuhr (1894-1962).[27] Moltmann wants both Calvin's view of reshaping communal life in light of the future kingdom, albeit from the Christian "left,"[28] and the *Schwärmer* view that mainstream culture is only able to further and defend its own aggressive dominance, and is thus wholly corrupt in its indifference to the poor. The church as a little flock needs to be a beacon for the marginalized. Faith is transfigured by hope. Hope, stirring us to transformative agency, is the pivotal mode in which we relate to God. Here, the gospel is given within the matrix of law. The real point of Christian identity is to change the world; secondarily, it is to enjoy the world, a theme that sometimes gives balance to the moral rigorism of Moltmann's work.[29] In contrast to Moltmann's view, the gospel recognizes that God does his work on all humans — breaking down their quest for self-recognition through domination and building them up in the confidence that God will provide for them, together with all creatures *(samt allen kreaturen)*.

When Moltmann speaks about the justification of the godless, he can do so in appropriate and powerful terms. The problem is that he does not

---

25. See Eric Gritsch, *Thomas Muentzer: A Tragedy of Errors* (Minneapolis: Fortress, 1989), p. 122.

26. See Theologie, B, 2.3.2.1, p. 359.

27. See H. Richard Niebuhr, *Christ and Culture* (New York: Harper, 1951).

28. See Hans Schwarz, "Eschatology," in *Christian Dogmatics*, vol. 2 (Philadelphia: Fortress, 1984), p. 526, where he writes that Moltmann's "almost exclusively sociopolitical emphasis bears so much resemblance to the Calvinistic idea of establishing a theocracy on earth that we hesitate to agree with it without first expressing a loud and clear eschatological caveat to all such too-human endeavors."

29. See, for example, *The Passion for Life: A Messianic Lifestyle,* trans. M. Douglas Meeks (Philadelphia: Fortress, 1978).

permit this understanding to filter through and alter his entire theological framework. The gospel is, then, trumped by an overarching system of ethics. Moltmann can speak the gospel with remarkable clarity: "Through the raising of Christ from the dead, God makes real his claim upon people in that he justifies them (Rom. 4:25). Through the outpouring of his Spirit on all flesh (Acts 2), God renews his likeness on earth, unites a divided humanity, and liberates his creation from the shadow of evil. In the coming of his kingdom, God will ultimately glorify his right, justify human beings, and transfigure creation."[30] One could hardly think of a more accurate description of the evangelical doctrine of justification. However, he just as quickly situates this affirmation of evangelical faith in an ethical matrix: "Because the divine right of grace is proclaimed to all people through this gospel, the God-given dignity of each and every person is proclaimed in conjunction with it. But where this human dignity is revealed, fundamental human rights are also made to come in force."[31] At stake is not the question of human dignity and its corresponding rights, attributes attested to by both creation and justification.[32] Rather, it is that the indicative of faith is insufficient for producing new life apart from the imperative of meeting the social, ethical, and legal entitlements demanded by these rights.

Moltmann fails to realize that justification as law and gospel unmasks political systems as based on *false beliefs* used to legitimate their power. They are grounded in the idolatry of mammon. Ultimately, ethics cannot solve ethical problems. The root of these problems is outside ethics in misplaced trust. People trust their own power by trusting the things used to secure their power. That their neighbors are sacrificed in this process is a consequence they can easily ignore, similar to the priest and the Levite in the parable of the Good Samaritan (Luke 10:31-32). Ethics helps diagnose social inequities, and it can help toward some social improvement, albeit stingily as duty. However, it is unable to get at the heart of these problems, which is theological: matters of misplaced trust. We can give freely only when we are aware that in creation and renewal God has generously given and will continue to lavish treasures upon us. The notion

---

30. Moltmann, *On Human Dignity: Political Theology and Ethics,* trans. M. Douglas Meeks (Philadelphia: Fortress, 1984), p. 31.

31. Moltmann, *On Human Dignity,* p. 31.

32. See Wilfried Härle, "Zur Gegenwartsbedeutung der 'Rechtfertigungs'-Lehre," pp. 135-37.

of "limited resources" is a faulty perception. There is enough to provide for everyone's needs. The question is, Will we share?

Ironically, given his affinity to Marxist thinking, Moltmann separates the personal and the political, which has likewise become paradigmatic in mainline Protestant theology. His only way to stand with the victim is to modify politics; otherwise the gospel only helps people personally cope with violent social systems. In Reformation thinking, the liberated conscience can stand with and seek to serve the neighbor, especially when neighbors suffer. It can do this because it leaves the politics of the kingdom in God's hands. The personal and the political need not be dichotomized.

Moltmann is never able to penetrate far enough to the victim to see that the victim is, in alternative environments, often a victimizer. That is, the violence received by the victim is projected onto others by that victim. "For God has imprisoned all to disobedience so that he may be merciful to all" (Rom. 11:32). Victims in turn victimize and thus contribute to a world characterized not only by the "death God works" but also the "death God finds,"[33] a world of wrath. Such interchangeability, while never an excuse for acts of violence or ignoring justice, certainly tends to equalize the ethical playing field. The compassion for victims spontaneously unleashed by the gospel permits solidarity with them free of co-dependently valorizing, even idolizing them. To name a victim fails to wipe away moral ambiguity, such that faith can give way to ethical sight by virtue of meritorious deeds with respect to the victim.

A Christian conscience will strive to meet the needs of the neighbor, especially the need to recognize another's rights. Yet this quest is always marked with ambiguity. Faith, not social engineering by moral sight, opens new horizons. The problem with Moltmann is that the message that justifies is seemingly a prelude for the real action, which is maintaining human autonomy. Hence, in the language of the old indicative-imperative distinction (similar to Bultmann's), Moltmann writes,

> The imperative of the Pauline call to new obedience is accordingly not to be understood merely as a summons to demonstrate the indicative of the new being in Christ, but it has also its eschatological presupposition in the future that has been promised and is to be expected — the

---

33. See Martin Luther, *The Bondage of the Will*, trans. J. I. Packer and O. R. Johnston (New York: Fleming H. Revell, 1957), p. 170 (WA 18:685).

coming of the Lord to judge and to reign. Hence it ought not to be rendered merely by saying: "Become what you are!," but emphatically also by saying: "Become what you will be!"[34]

Moltmann fails to recognize that God's forensic word is also creative, impacting the social order. In his word and the various orders in creation, God is sanctifying the world through sin-laden social contexts in which he does people-making, the three estates identified by Luther as the church, the home, and the state *(ecclesia, oeconomia, politia)*.

More than anything else, both Moltmann's political view of the gospel and his emphasis on the third use of the law are set within a Müntzerian vision of the kingdom. The manifestation of this kingdom, it would seem, is quite indebted to Kant's "kingdom of ends," an ideal moral community in which human dignity and autonomy would always be secured.[35] Admittedly, Moltmann claims that "the righteousness of God then refers not merely to a new order for the existing world, but provides creation as a whole with a new ground of existence and a new right to life."[36] However, such giftedness is always developed within a process that will be completed only at the *parousia* of Christ. It is this linearity, this framework of potentiality and actuality, expectation and fulfillment, which feeds an anthropology in which humans are seen primarily as agents, not recipients, seemingly even *coram deo*, since our energies contribute to the very fulfillment of that final kingdom. It is this anthropology which does not square with the truth that, *coram deo*, humans are fundamentally receivers, completely passive with respect to the gifts of life and new life. In this latter view, agency is properly understood as service to creation, neighbor, and the earth, liberated from the attempt to save the earth and human society. Ethics is fundamentally a human task shared between Christians and non-Christians. Christians have no privileged political or ethical insights. It is not as if non-Christians are incapable of thinking ethically or as if people are incapable of rectifying immorality apart from Christian intervention.

The Reformation concept of promise *(promissio)*, so prominent in Luther and the Confessions, is likewise reconfigured in light of Molt-

---

34. TH 162.

35. Immanuel Kant, *Groundwork of the Metaphysic of Morals*, trans. H. J. Paton (New York: Harper, 1953), pp. 100-101.

36. TH 204.

mann's Müntzerian eschatology, which sees the kingdom as an anticipated goal. As Moltmann describes it in *The Theology of Hope,* promise is composed of several features. First, it is a declaration that announces the coming of a reality that does not yet exist. It sets one's heart on a future history in which the fulfillment of the promise is to be expected. Second, it binds one to the future and gives one a sense of history. Third, its history does not consist in a cyclic recurrence but has a definite trend toward fulfillment. Fourth, its word that is seeking fulfillment is not congruous with present reality but contradicts it. Fifth, it permits an interval of tension between the uttering and the redeeming of the promise. Sixth, it offers elements of newness and surprise with its fulfillment. Finally, it helped Israel find new and wider interpretations of experience.[37] As noted, the future for Moltmann is indeed an eschatological gift. However, the task that it analogously evokes for revamping moral order is to make this invisible future visible in human society. If the future will offer the vindication of the victim, then we must presently side with victims and seek to grant them that status for which they are destined in the new world. One's own self-recognition *coram deo* is dependent upon identification with others in their victimization. Again, since the status quo fails to recognize this, it is the church as countercultural community that should identify with the oppressed. Thereby, conflict between the forces of good, which sympathize with the outcast, and the forces of evil, which gain their power at the outcast's expense, is inevitable.

Such conflict is not total. For Moltmann, we should assume an overall progress in human transformation for both the oppressed and the oppressors, who will grow toward a perfected totality,[38] since the final kingdom is secure in the resurrection of Jesus Christ. In a sense, if we were to describe this by employing designations of North American fundamentalist dispensationalism, we could say that Moltmann is a post-tribulation premillenialist of the "left": there will be no "rapture" of the church but a clear vindication of the oppressed and those who sympathize with them, after they undergo trial, prior to Christ's millennial reign. Moltmann's view is quite different from that of Luther, for whom the promise is a word that says what it does and does what it says. For Luther, the promise is not defined from the future, because the future is instead birthed from God's

37. TH 103-4.
38. TH 207.

promise in the present.[39] The present includes the future as gift, a diachronic extension of life both granted by and granting the promise of God's fidelity to us. It can be seen as a "speech act" that holds the promiser accountable to his word.[40] It delivers the word of assurance that gives us certainty in the midst of the ambiguity of experience with which we must daily wrestle.

What, then, is the Christian's hope? It is that God will be true to his word. That God will be true is vouchsafed in the good gifts received now, the Spirit to comfort (Eph. 1:13), the fruits of creation to sustain, and, most importantly, this word that, in Jesus Christ, God is for us (Rom. 8:1), even in the face of law that accuses, human untrustworthiness due to deceit, betrayal, and sloth, and the very uncertainty of life itself.

In contrast to some existentialist readings that have dominated twentieth-century understandings of justification, Moltmann offers a perspective that counters such "personalism," an "I-Thou" relation abstracted from language, culture, and history. Justification is mediated through creation, thus unleashing a cosmic dimension to justification. "The cosmic ideas of Christian eschatology are therefore not by any means mythological, but reach forward into the open realm of possibilities ahead of all reality, give expression to the 'expectation of the creature' for a *nova* creation, and provide a prelude for eternal life, peace and the haven of the reconciliation of all things."[41] With Moltmann, we agree: the creation groans and sighs in travail for the future world (Rom. 8:22). However, God's promise is not merely or solely forward-looking, but primarily focused on what he is doing right now, in his unfinished, even tormented creation, which too bears the mark of punishment (Gen. 3:17-18). The issue, then, is to deliver the gift-word.

In this light, what could be more important than the preaching office? Moltmann affirms earthly existence in opposition to Platonism's and penitential piety's flight from the world. Yet, his affirmation is tethered to a moralism anxious that we can never trust the powers that be, that their self-interest will always thwart their ability to deliver social good. Nor can one trust the power of the word alone to actually change the world apart

39. See Oswald Bayer, "Rupture of Times: Luther's Relevance for Today," *Lutheran Quarterly* 13 (1999): 45.

40. See Oswald Bayer, LBF 43 (AGL 50); for Bayer, forensic justification is effective, and effective justification is forensic.

41. TH 215.

from specifying the goal to make the raw materials of life correspond to the blueprint of the future kingdom.[42] Hence, one needs to be vigilant with regard to the corrupt power of the status quo. For Moltmann, the Bible is a blueprint for society, offering patterns for social order and freedom that accord primarily to the political "left," not the "right" (unlike many others who likewise look to the Bible as a blueprint for society). For Moltmann, the promise finally delivers a theodicy, an explanation for evil:

> It is neither that history swallows up eschatology (Albert Schweitzer) nor does eschatology swallow up history (Rudolf Bultmann). The *logos* of the eschaton is promise of that which is not yet, and for that reason it makes history. The promise which announces the eschaton, and in which the eschaton announces itself, is the motive power, the mainspring, the driving force, and the torture of history.[43]

The whole explains and makes sense of the parts, the "slaughter bench" of history, as Hegel put it.[44] For that reason, history is moving toward such totalization.[45]

Not law and gospel, but gospel and law, indicative and imperative, expectation and fulfillment are on a trajectory toward a unity, that of the kingdom in which the ideals of the High Enlightenment (liberty, equality, and fraternity) are honored, but now no longer for white males alone, as in the High Enlightenment, but for all. Such a totality is inherently theodic. Pain is not meaningless; it is the birth pangs of future liberation. However, is Moltmann's strategy not also the attempt to supplant faith with sight? The true moral order, when achieved, will be able to justify God's ways with humans and make sense of current ambiguities, since it will validate the educative import of the suffering which humanity has had to endure. Indeed, as Moltmann explains, liberation theology will see all individual suffering and failure against the backdrop of God's patient suffering. "It

---

42. Moltmann writes, "The righteousness of God which reveals itself in the gospel to the godless is therefore both gift and power, assurance and promise, obedience and liberty. It does not as yet set man down at his goal, but only puts him on the road to it. It makes him part of the process through which God establishes his divinity, his justice and his glory, and brings the whole creation into his own liberty." See *The Future of Creation*, pp. 166-67.

43. TH 165.

44. See G. W. F. Hegel, *The Philosophy of History*, trans. J. Sibree (New York: Dover, 1956), p. 21.

45. TH 207.

therefore sees all partial movements towards liberation against the horizon of God's own perfect and final history of liberation."[46] For Moltmann, as for Thomas Aquinas, grace perfects rather than liberates nature. Such perfection of nature is envisioned in the purity of the social relations of the coming kingdom.

While Moltmann acknowledges the paradox and ambiguity attendant upon a *coincidentia oppositorum* in *The Crucified God*, his overall quest aims for omnipresent visible justice on earth. This goal has difficulty abiding paradox and ambiguity, which seem to be part and parcel attendant with the gospel itself: God hidden in inextricable evil and suffering, lordship simultaneous with service, righteousness inseparable from sinfulness. For him, these paradoxes must be seen as the rude initial steps in the unfolding of the transparent matrix of an unambiguous ethical future. Therefore, law follows gospel, mopping up the social messiness that the gospel can withstand. The new life in Christ is not a comprehensive, receptive "aesthetic," inclusive of ethics, as grounded in a promised freedom, but primarily a morality in which the indicative drives to the imperative. Here the analogy between God and humanity, human correspondence to God, viewed existentially by Jüngel and theoretically by Pannenberg, is seen ethically by Moltmann. We correspond to God primarily in action and secondarily in thought. Either way, the pall of Barthianism hangs over these theologians. When law is the form of the gospel, the gospel is lost. Faith is subverted by sight. Driving these theologies is an apologetic: The gospel itself will be justified to (Schleiermacher's) "cultured despisers" of religion when it delivers the new moral world.

Human Praxis as the Clue That Makes Divine Agency Transparent

If Jüngel's tendency is to liken the gospel to a meta-experience, a "feeling," and Pannenberg's is to refine it into a grand, unified theory, a "knowing," Moltmann's tendency is to translate the gospel into a *praxis*, a "doing." For Moltmann, the aim of theology is not merely "to understand the world differently; it wants to change the world as well. It sees itself as one component in the process through which the world is liberated. That is

46. Moltmann, *The Future of Creation*, p. 99.

the fundamental idea underlying the new theology of liberation."[47] Liberation is the context in which to understand the cross. The cross is not simultaneously Jesus' crucifixion and that of the old, incurvated being. Instead, one attempts to forego this latter crucifixion for the sake of developing an overarching, theoretical *praxis* of liberation. "But the theology of the cross is a critical and liberating theory of God and man. Christian life is a form of practice which consists in following the crucified Christ, and it changes both man himself and the circumstances in which he lives. To this extent, a theology of the cross is a practical theory."[48] Christian *praxis*, in Moltmann, is opposed to the irredeemable current social structures that have compromised Christianity's true ideals. A Ritschlian Calvinism "of the right" rebaptized its age as the "Christian world," church one with culture. In contrast, the goal of Moltmann's *praxis* is to identify with another's suffering, become a *homo sympatheticus*. In this way, we would fulfill that possibility of a "concrete utopianism which strives not after things that have no place, but after things that have 'no place as yet' but can acquire one. It is the realism, skeptical of such goals, that truly has 'no place.' Thereby we actually conform to the deity of God itself."[49] Through doing those culture-challenging practices born from sympathy for the downtrodden, we correspond to God's very deity, which is no longer hidden but disclosed via its impinging future. Whereas God's coming was, for Jüngel, mediated by a "word event," evoking a meta-experience "with experience," God's "advent,"[50] for Moltmann, evokes a corresponding human practice of political subversion. All this is for the sake of unmasking the hidden God, making God transparent and comprehensible. Finally, it also makes God intolerable insofar as his visibility is gained at the expense of the gift as sold over to task, the vigilance of conforming to the future kingdom in all that we do, the condemning coercion to fulfill our potential as caring people. Thus, the hidden God

---

47. Moltmann, *The Trinity and the Kingdom*, p. 7.

48. Moltmann, *The Crucified God*, p. 25.

49. TH 30: "The God of the exodus and of the resurrection 'is' not eternal presence, but he promises his presence and nearness to him who follows the path on which he is sent into the future. YHWH, as the name of the God who first of all promises his presence and his kingdom and makes them prospects for the future, is a God 'with future as his essential nature,' a God of promise and of leaving the present to face the future, a God whose freedom is the source of new things that are to come."

50. TH 31.

returns. In contrast, the gospel would open a life of service within the all-too-messy world that actually exists.

As with Jüngel and Pannenberg, we have, with Moltmann, a making finite of the infinite and a making infinite of the finite, no longer primarily within the schema of *theoria,* as in the latent Hegelianism of Pannenberg and Jüngel, but primarily within the schema of *praxis,* as with the left-wing Hegelian Marx, and behind this, Kant. Compassionate solidarity with the victim is the characteristic mark of true discipleship, whereby one's siding with God's future is decisive. With penetrating insight, Gerhard Forde has named this type of moralizing a "negative theology of glory," in which we can at least offer our sympathy for the victim as a good work.[51] Moltmann is not content with the sharp division between faith and love on which Luther insists, in which faith alone is appropriate *coram deo,* while love is spontaneously generated *coram mundo.*[52] Since, for Moltmann, the kingdom is both gift *and* task, gospel *and* law, we are agents aiding its arrival. Undoubtedly, Moltmann fears a passive, indifferent, conforming Christianity. He knows firsthand the evils of a compromised Christianity from his own upbringing in Nazi Germany. But, finally, must we not contend that it is only God who can change the incurvated human heart, opening it to genuine care? Moltmann's *Schwärmer* view of the kingdom makes the proper distinction between law and gospel impossible, because it moralizes the gospel and makes the law the impetus for the self-realization of our compassion. Love here becomes a sign of the kingdom's advent. Consciences are wrongly directed to look at their compassion. This inflates the foolish, who actually magnify their prowess as compassionate, and manhandles the sensitive, who are all too much aware of their shortcomings. It is true: *Victimization calls for justice and compassion.* Indeed, through the victim God calls us to care.[53] This is all the more reason to distinguish law and gospel in both preaching and theology. Only the gospel can liberate a compassion free of self-righteousness. That said, this is no reason to seek to unify law and gospel as Moltmann's work tends to do.

51. Forde, *On Being a Theologian of the Cross: Reflections on Luther's Heidelberg Disputation, 1518* (Grand Rapids: Eerdmans, 1997), p. 84.

52. LW 26:161 (WA 40/1:274).

53. Despite the fact that all too many claim victim status in our culture (see Charles J. Sykes, *A Nation of Victims: The Decay of the American Character* [New York: St. Martin's, 1992]), we are still called to discern real victims from pretenders and to stand with the former. That all too many cry wolf is no reason to deny that there really are wolves afoot.

Given the unprecedented horror of the depths of human violence seen in the last century — events such as the Holocaust, Hiroshima, and various forms of ethnic cleansing — it is victimizers, not victims, who demonstrate that all are "imprisoned to disobedience" (Rom. 11:32), because they, especially in their incurvation, are defiant of the altruism that their liberated nature could offer. Victimizers feed off victims and in such vampirism are less than human.

Admittedly, Moltmann offers the insight that many legitimate their lives on the basis of wealth, power, and status, often gained at the expense of others and the earth. That said, does he move us beyond the quest for autonomy that fosters these standards? In the perspective of the autonomy affirmed by the political "right," an individual's personal liberties are limited for the sake of social order, while the economy is allowed to run libertine. In the very same perspective of autonomy, the political "left" argues for the maximal liberalization of personal freedoms, provided no harm accrues to others, while the economy is to be tamed, lest it run roughshod over individuals.[54] For the left, social order stymies individual liberty, while for the right, a tamed economy would do so.[55] Christian theology ought to challenge the very notion of autonomy at the heart of these formulations, not because it fails to acknowledge that automomy is at odds with our participation in God as our highest good, as Robert Jenson teaches, but because genuine freedom is freedom from self-centeredness *(homo incurvatus in se)* and because no one experiences freedom apart from an identity established within community. The purpose of the government ought not to be to secure the individual autonomy of a "sacred self" (as we can sense in the portrait of Sheila that Robert Bellah so famously renders),[56] as both the political right and the political left insist, but to curb sin and provide a healthy framework for service in all of its pluriform modes. Justice is a profoundly human task — so much so that it is hard for many in the church to entrust it to the hands of the world, including the agency of Christians in their daily vocations in the world, over which God too has oversight.

54. We might call this the "inverted golden rule": Do not infringe upon another's autonomy even as you would not want others to infringe upon your own. In its Epicurean form, the inverted golden rule would read thus: Do not infringe upon others' self-pleasuring, even as you would not want others to infringe upon your own.

55. See Jean Bethke Elshtain, *Democracy on Trial* (New York: Basic Books, 1995), p. 4.

56. See Robert Bellah et al., *Habits of the Heart: Individualism and Commitment in American Life* (Berkeley and Los Angeles: University of California Press, 1985), p. 221.

As for Pannenberg and Jüngel, there is for Moltmann a transparency between history and historicity. The cross is an event between the Father and the Son: the Father abandons the Son into death, and the Son suffers abandonment. Like Jüngel and Pannenberg, Moltmann utilizes the vocabulary and syntax of German Idealism to develop his view of the Trinity: "God loves the world — God's self-communication to the world by virtue of his self-differentiation and his self-identification. God is love: he is in eternity this process of self-differentiation and self-identification, a process which contains the whole pain of the negative in itself."[57] Moltmann opposes those views, such as the early Jüngel's, that favor the perception of God as a self-unfolding subject via self-differentiation into otherness. Rather, God is a social essence. His unity is an abstraction of the concrete mutual interrelationships between the triune persons. The doctrine of the Trinity is employed in order to decipher the reality of the divine. Since Platonism is not in the ascendancy, and modernity's favoring of the isolated, unencumbered subject is under critique, Moltmann apologetically appeals to a social model of the Trinity as most apt to capture contemporary imaginations and to ward off the anxieties created by atheism. However, as also must be asked of Jüngel and Pannenberg, was the doctrine of the Trinity originally intended as a way to map God, now serving, for Moltmann, as a model for the ideal human community? Was it not rather intended to guarantee the proper use of theological grammar for the promising God as well as to be faithful to Scripture?

For Moltmann, God has identified with a specific victim, Jesus of Nazareth, and in this way the depth of God's being is rendered transparent; we are invoked to imitate it. That we are accused as the victimizers is not our end *(finis)* as old beings. Rather, it is the invitation that we, like God, should identify with victims as well, and fulfill our potential *coram deo,* by standing on behalf of victims. Victims so one with God by God's own choice have a favored, even sacral status. However, the cross does not offer us an ability to correspond ethically to it. It is our death. Ethical correspondence to the divine is not the believer's goal. Rather, it is service to the neighbor.

For Moltmann, culture worships God as monarch. Counterculture perceives the true God, who is one with the socially marginalized. Even so, Moltmann offers the one clue by which the totalization of all the world's

---

57. Moltmann, *The Trinity and the Kingdom,* p. 57.

experiences can be accomplished. Counterculture imitates the divine to which culture is blind. Thereby, it offers the one true meaning to reality. It is the means whereby culture can be transformed in light of the kingdom. However, is an alternative culture the answer to the problems of culture? The best response to social problems is not replacing one culture with another but discerning judgment and grace within any culture. Only that *discrimen* can set boundaries to that culture, forbidding it to take God's name in vain by using God to legitimate its power or by securing for itself a scapegoat on which to project its anxiety. All cultures and countercultures are prone to such false self-legitimation. Social problems are finally best understood as the result not of faulty ethics but of false doctrine. The church's responsibility to the world is to expose and confront such false doctrine. It is the gospel that liberates and grants assurance, such that we can affirm culture without deifying it.

In Moltmann, we are servants not concretely subject to all real people, but instead abstractly subject to a general duty. Such clear and transparent legitimating of behavior — solidarity with the victim for the sake of liberation — offers one the sweet possibility of never sinning boldly or acting uncertainly because all action is a result of the sublime duty of standing with the victim. Thereby, one has an advantage with respect to the majority, who mindlessly conform to those power structures indifferent to victims.

Justice without Liberation

As noted by Moltmann, the point of theology ought not to be to interpret but to change the world. Hence, he carefully nuances this affirmation with the claim that "political theology does not reduce everything to politics (C. Schmitt) nor does it submit theology and the Church to the terms and requirements of state policy. . . . Political theology denotes rather the field, the milieu, the realm, and the stage on which Christian theology should be explicitly carried on today. . . . There can be no apolitical theology."[58] Perhaps Moltmann is right. To be human is to be inescapably thrust into a social milieu defined in terms of exchanges of power and is thus inevitably

---

58. *Religion and Political Society,* ed. Jürgen Moltmann (New York: Harper & Row, 1974), p. 19.

political. However, because we inevitably and decisively seek an ultimate sanction for the legitimation of our political decisions, it would be more on the mark to say that *all politics, as they are currently engaged, are inherently and inescapably theological.* Ultimately an individual or a people will appeal to a "higher power," however it is named, in order to justify their behavior.[59] All too often such calling upon gods or God to sanction, legitimate, and justify behavior simply violates the First and Second Commandments. If a war, for instance, is about the acquisition of a resource such as oil, then it would be a rare country that would sanction that war solely on the basis of the acquisition of this resource. Rather, the war will be fought in the name of "freedom," even the God who legitimates this "freedom." What nation or community would admonish its youth to fight, kill, or even die for oil and not some "higher cause," such as autonomy? It makes far greater sense to affirm that politics is inescapably theological rather than that theology is political, since to get at the heart of the political agenda is to ferret out the ultimate, or theological, sanctions for social directives or justifications. Here Moltmann can help us: current Marxist-inspired secularizations of theology need to come clean. There really is no privileged secular space that positions theology. All human endeavors are, at some fundamental level, inherently theological.

The great experiment to secularize the political realm has only resulted in furthering superstitions. Theology now has the important social role of decoding and even demythologizing these sanctions. Penultimate matters are made ultimate when theology is privatized as the musings of the individual's assumptions about one's own *summum bonum.* Moderns are apt to believe that some mode of politics could itself save, such as making the world safe for democracy, liberating the proletariat, or furthering the master race. Admittedly, some politics are more useful than others for advancing human well-being. However, even these should not be rendered soteriologically.

Our current problem is not that the public realm is irreligious but that it is all too superstitious. Much foreign and domestic social policy is

59. Hence, Ernest Becker writes, "Society itself is a codified hero system, which means that society everywhere is a living myth of the significance of human life, a defiant creation of meaning. Every society thus is a 'religion' whether it thinks so or not: Soviet 'religion' and Maoist 'religion' are as truly religious as are scientific and consumer 'religion,' no matter how much they may try to disguise themselves by omitting religious and spiritual ideas from their lives." See *The Denial of Death* (New York: Free Press, 1973), p. 7.

structured by contemporary Gnostics who affirm that the self is sacred, or Epicureans who affirm that the good is a result of pleasure within moderation. Social conservatives offer economic agendas that are mythically scripted in terms of a premillennialism, while many social liberals offer economic agendas that are mythically scripted in terms of a postmillennialism.[60] Either way, the deception of the "scientific" nature of both politics and economics inhibits their ability to meta-critique their own worldviews, codified by some ultimate, legitimating sanction. A healthy view of secular society could be obtained if we, like Luther, would not make the penultimate ultimate, but instead acknowledge the estates of family, government, and the church as venues by which God does people-making. In other words, the political realm could really be seen as worldly if we could accept that it is not an instrument for human salvation. There is no politics, either of the right or of the left, that will save us. Only God can save us. When the ultimate is secured for people, the penultimate is free from being made into an idol. It is opened as an arena for service. Politics would lose its all-too-anxious status of importance. However, with its more humble and limited focus, it could offer ways of evaluating the health of social structures on the basis of service as the criterion of goodness. If that were to happen, then we would have to reject the soteriological status that Moltmann accords politics. We would have to give up his hopes for a "concrete utopia" and recognize that this side of the eschaton, politics will always be ambiguous. Quests for justice will be tainted with bold sinning and mixed results.

Undoubtedly, Moltmann's concern that theology not primarily interpret but change the world is born from an apologetic that Christianity not be an "opiate" of the people, drugging them into a passive acceptance of the status quo. Realistically, though, we should affirm that it is not religion, if it ever was, by which the masses drug themselves, but rather entertainment, film, television, the Internet, sports, gambling, nightclubs and taverns, electronic gizmos and toys, and other forms of "amusement." This is not said in order to return to a killjoy Pietism. Life as such is indeed a gift we are permitted to treasure and enjoy (Eccles. 7:14). However, it is said to expose the misuse of this gift.

The purpose of theology is not so much to change, decipher, or help

60. See Robert H. Nelson, *Economics as Religion* (University Park, Pa.: Pennsylvania State University Press, 2001), p. 31.

us cope with the world, but to deliver the promise, God's claim upon the world. The purpose of theology is not to do the world's work for it, but to honor the world when it legitimately does its proper work. The quest for justice belongs to the order of creation, not salvation. This is not because justification is a personal instead of a political matter, but because it deals with a passive righteousness as distinct from the active righteousness that is to be socially practiced. The church is to bear witness to the establishing of just relations in society; but finally, it is society as a realm of God's creativity that needs to affirm justice, whether as urged by Christians or non-Christians. The church is obliged to promote freedom, pluralism, and the cause of the downtrodden in the wider society. It does so not as uniquely the church, as Moltmann thinks, but simply as concerned citizens of the world. In this regard, the Roman Catholic ethicist George Weigel rightly points out that Christians can "relax a bit" with respect to politics:

> Knowing that the Son, the first-born of many brethren (Rom. 8:29), has been raised to glory, and knowing that he, not we, will build the City of God, we can relax a bit about the world and its politics — not to the point of indifference or insouciance or irresponsibility, but in the firm conviction that, in the extremity of the world's agony and at the summit of its glories, Jesus remains Lord. And our primary responsibility, as Christian disciples, is to remain faithful to the bold proclamation of *that* great truth. For *that* is the truth the world most urgently needs to hear — 2,000 years ago, today, and until God's Kingdom comes, in God's time and by God's gracious initiative.[61]

We must be equally wary of conservatives who idealize the past and liberals who fantasize about the future as a golden age. Our hope is placed in the gospel alone.

While Moltmann is critical of theologians promoting the status quo, ironically he is markedly similar in content to the nineteenth-century bourgeois systematician Albrecht Ritschl. For Ritschl, theology was accountable for delivering both justification *and* reconciliation (again, the pattern of gift *and* task, gospel *and* law), the former offering an inner reorientation for the believer, the latter contributing to the social good,

---

61. Weigel, "The Church's Political Hopes for the World," in *The Two Cities of God: The Church's Responsibility for the Earthly City,* ed. Carl E. Braaten and Robert W. Jenson (Grand Rapids: Eerdmans, 1997), p. 63.

progress toward the development of the kingdom of God. Ritschl, of course, was optimistic that culture could serve as the proper venue for the kingdom's manifestation.[62] Moltmann is skeptical of this, but he is not skeptical that the church's mission is twofold, as the following quotation shows:

> Today, for the church to make the kingdom of God its lodestone means evangelization and liberation. The church's divine mission is to proclaim the gospel of God's kingdom to all human beings, the poor of this world first of all, so as to awaken the faith which consoles and strengthens us here and gives the certainty of eternal life. And at the same time the church's divine mission is to bring liberty to the oppressed, human dignity to the humiliated, and the justice which is their due to people without rights. Evangelization and liberation complement one another, like the raising up through faith of the soul that is bowed down and the healing of the tormented body.[63]

One wonders how God could possibly continue with his creation were the church not to fulfill this twofold task. Can one really trust God with the world, or is the world not so filled with evil that the church must carry its load? Can we trust the word that the church is charged to proclaim as not only necessary but also sufficient for its task? Can we trust the laity to do justice in their vocations and seek to change unjust social structures? We must question the false "no third path" between either a transparent activism or a morally numb escapism that Moltmann assumes. What drives the liberation that he seeks is a rephrasing of Enlightenment autonomy, mediated not by capitalism (enhancing autonomy with a "trickle down" of wealth), but by socialism (enhancing autonomy by redistributing wealth). Yet, such autonomy, when construed eudaimonistically in High Enlightenment fashion, is disclosed finally as a species of incurvation. One can affirm the appropriateness of democratic government without affirming Enlightenment autonomy. As procedural, democracy need not depend on

---

62. See Claude Welch, *Protestant Thought in the Nineteenth Century,* vol. 2 (New Haven: Yale, 1985), 3. In Ritschl's famous discussion, the gospel entails an ellipse determined by two *foci:* justification or reconciliation and the kingdom of God, or faith and love, or the religious and the ethical.

63. Moltmann, *Jesus Christ for Today's World,* trans. Margaret Kohl (Minneapolis: Fortress, 1994), p. 28.

the individualism of the "modern Narcissus"[64] for identity and power. Indeed, it would be even more empowered if it would hold itself to a common good. Perhaps the sympathy of Moltmann's *homo sympatheticus* is, all too often, prone to self-righteousness: "I'm better since I care and you don't" — a pharisaical intolerance that fails to recognize both the mixed motives of one's own heart and the multiple ways of distributing justice. By contrast, the redeemed as agents in creation will say, "Lord, when was it that we saw you hungry and gave you food, or thirsty and gave you something to drink?" (Matt. 25:37). Yet, with Moltmann, we can maintain that Christians will seek an economics that serves humanity and not vice versa.

In light of the hidden autonomy at the heart of Moltmann's theology, what needs to be said about freedom? Freedom has been the great goal of the modern world. But, among the many potential candidates for genuine freedom, which are we to accept? Whose freedom? Which liberation? Is freedom that of the Stoics — to change one's inner life and accept the world when one can do little or nothing about imposing social circumstances? Or is it Epicurean freedom — to seek pleasure in moderation? Is it a utilitarian freedom in which one should have the maximal autonomy possible, provided no harm is done to others? Is it a Kantian freedom in which one needs to honor autonomy in oneself and others and thus embody the kingdom of ends? Or is it a Hegelian freedom in which Spirit is working itself out in and through us? Perhaps it is the Marxist freedom of the liberation of the proletariat, seemingly closest to Moltmann's view. Or is it the Lockean freedom of self-ownership? Or perhaps it is a nihilistic freedom in which one exercises one's power as a god unto oneself in the fray in which all are unmasked as competitive power plays apart from any *summum bonum*. Or, finally, is it not freedom from the wrath that actually engulfs all these other purported freedoms, the tyranny that drives us to establish our worth?

This freedom accepts the paradox that lordship and service are compatible and, in fact, require each other if their integrity is to be preserved: we are free lords subject to none and dutiful servants subject to all. Or again, as Luther put it, we live outside ourselves with our neighbor due to a word that remains ever alien but allows genuine care spontaneously to flow for the other; this is the liberation of human nature from the damnation of the quest for self-recognition. Such unleashed power is never, as

---

64. See Oswald Bayer, "The Modern Narcissus," *Lutheran Quarterly* 9 (1995): 301-14.

Troeltsch wished to argue, largely in response to politically conservative Lutherans (such as Frederick J. Stahl [1802-1861]), passive and submissive to the state. In particular, its action is unleashed when the gospel is at stake. Given that justice is the form that love takes in society,[65] social structures must be accountable to people, not vice versa. Nevertheless, the most important social contribution that the church can make is to do the task required of it: distinguish (not separate) law and gospel, for the sake of the purity of the gospel, in the confidence that God is transforming the world as he sees fit. What saves is not ethics, theory, or feeling, but a word. In a sense, we need liberation from liberation theology. We need justice, within the orders of creation, without "liberation," with its inherent political soteriology, if the *coram deo–coram mundo* distinction is to be honored.

The promise of a perfect political realm of peace and justice is a draw for many, particularly among many mainline Protestants and some Roman Catholics. It can sustain a sense of vocation and piety. However, it is largely a Müntzerian view of the Reformation. We need to maintain that the answer to an existentialist read of the gospel is not to be found in politicizing it but in recognizing that God's promise is always embodied, and that humans, as that species on which God is currently doing work,[66] are restored to life that honors the neighbor. The best answer to bad politics is good theology.

Moltmann and Luther

In comparing Luther and Moltmann, we will focus on the differences between them over the role of law in politics and the Christian life and the relation between nature and grace. Clearly, a third use of the law predominates in Moltmann's thinking. For the Lutheran Confessions, the second use of the law is always the most important, though it is true that the "Formula of Concord" affirms a third. Seeking fidelity to Luther's critique of antinomianism, the "Formula of Concord" recognizes that the believer has a twofold nature. The confessors do not affirm that the believer as such

---

65. See Carl E. Braaten, *Principles of Lutheran Theology* (Philadelphia: Fortress, 1984), p. 132.

66. See Eberhard Jüngel, *The Freedom of a Christian: Luther's Significance for Contemporary Theology* (Minneapolis: Fortress, 1988), p. 46.

needs the law, but in opposition to the charges of antinomianism, they affirm that the old nature will always need the law both to order its life and to accuse it of sinful behavior. We are not "under the law [as new beings] but in the law [as old]."[67] Nomianism is not an option for believers as such. They are free in Christ. Hence, we must always deal with the paradox that, in Christ, the law is both at its *telos* and its *finis*. The old being hears the imperative that we should fear, love, and trust in God above all things, but is unable to fulfill this. Only the gospel is able to call forth the new being who fulfills the First Commandment in faith. In contrast to Moltmann, we must affirm that to leave the future entirely in God's hands allows one the freedom to do something for someone else here and now. Our hope is not primarily in a future state but in God's commitment to us to be for us in our need.

The social dimension of human life is likewise primarily a gift. God's creation is *creatio continua*,[68] unfolding life as thoroughly upheld in social relations. Yes, freedom is promised. In our various "tasks" in life, we can cooperate with God in his creative work. We are even unwittingly his instruments and tools in his creation. Yet, such engagement with God's ongoing creativity is indeed *poietic*, not redemptive. In this regard, eschatology ought not to be a source of political self-potentiation for the sake of realizing the kingdom but a reception of God's promise to provide. We pray that God's kingdom comes among us as well, for it is *sure to come.* Moltmann's view of the kingdom is all too much like an "anti-Pelagian

---

67. "Formula of Concord, Solid Declaration," in BC 590:18 (BSELK 967:18). Of the many works that treat the question of the third use of the law, Scott R. Murray has offered an important study, *Law, Life, and the Living God: The Third Use of the Law in Modern American Lutheranism* (St. Louis: Concordia, 2002). Murray tends to see Gerhard Forde as an existentialist, despite the fact that Forde has always cautiously distanced his work from that of Bultmann. Murray also tends to see Forde as an antinomian, despite the fact that Forde has always affirmed the need for the law with respect to the old being even after faith. Murray uncritically endorses the work of David Yeago, who takes Lutheranism outside of a confessional framework and into an ecumenical, quasi-Thomistic one. For a critique of this latter view, see Mark C. Mattes, "The Thomistic Turn in Evangelical Catholic Ethics," *Lutheran Quarterly* 16 (2002): 65-100. For a thorough, critical response to Murray, see Matthew Becker, "Review of *Law, Life, and the Living God* by Scott Murray," www.day-star (Internet). See also Mark C. Mattes, "Review of *Law, Life, and the Living God* by Scott Murray," *Journal of Lutheran Ethics* (2003), http://www.elca.org/scriptlib/dcs/jle/ (Internet).

68. See William Lazareth, *Luther, the Bible, and Social Ethics* (Minneapolis: Fortress, 2001), p. 66.

codicil,"[69] in which one needs to work for the kingdom's coming, but when it finally arrives, one can see that it was all a gift. If the cross permeates all experience, then it too is an end to our self-potentiation. There is no *entelechy* to the coming of the kingdom, even for counterculture. Rather, the eschatological last judgment and creation itself coalesce now in the delivering of the promise. The human is not properly *homo agens semper,* as for Barth, Marx, and Moltmann. Rather, we must ask with Saint Paul, What do you have that you have not received? (1 Cor. 4:7).

In order to honor the truth that nature is liberated, not perfected by grace, we must allow politics and the economy to belong to the orders of creation, not be a means of salvation, in opposition to modern superstitions. The genuine theological task is to challenge pagan or heretical theologies within current politics and economics, instead of offering culturally entrenched "countercultural" political salvations that are often simply forms of syncretism and have yet to impact concretely those who are suffering. Neither capitalism nor socialism saves — any more than Baalism was a legitimate alternative to Yahwism. Both views fail to recognize that one is not a self-owner and that property is a gift to be used for the neighbor,[70] not an entitlement guaranteed as a result of labor. Since God's gifts are generous, it is wrong to believe that we need to hoard them.[71] Political fidelity for Christians requires demythologizing the belief that politics can save. The most important stance that the church can bring to the political realm is the truth that the political realm is never ultimate.

Furthermore, the purity that Moltmann seeks will never square with

---

69. See Eric W. Gritsch and Robert W. Jenson, *Lutheranism: The Theological Movement and Its Confessional Writings* (Philadelphia: Fortress, 1976), p. 39.

70. Carter Lindberg, *Beyond Charity: Reformation Initiatives for the Poor* (Minneapolis: Fortress, 1993), p. 111.

71. In the "Treatise on Good Works" (LW 44:108 [WA 6:272]), Luther notes, "If the heart expects and puts its trust in divine favor, how can a man be greedy and anxious? Such a man is absolutely certain that he is acceptable to God: therefore, he does not cling to money; he uses his money cheerfully and freely for the benefit of his neighbor. He knows full well that he will have enough no matter how much he gives away. His God, whom he trusts, will neither lie to him nor forsake him, as it is written in Psalm 37 [:25], 'I have been young, and now I am old, yet have I never seen a man of faith who trusts God (that is, a righteous man) forsaken, or his child begging bread.' The Apostle calls no other sin idolatry except covetousness [Col. 3:5], because this sin shows most starkly that a man does not trust God for anything, but expects more benefit from his money than from God. It is by confidence that God is truly honored or dishonored, as I have just said."

the experience with evil with which Christians must daily wrestle. This side of eternity there is no other choice but to accept God's creativity, in which he produces infinite good through finitely bad situations. Even so, this truth we can affirm by faith alone. While Moltmann fears Christianity presented as a Platonism for the masses, his answer of looking to a future pure world of righteous social transactions is no less escapist. The Bible urges social justice but offers no blueprint for social perfection. God's action in the world is always veiled. In all social transactions, we must seek a just cause but also, unlike Müntzer, a just means. However, similar to Luther, Moltmann recognizes *ambitio divinitatis* and our inherent self-justification.[72]

Luther offers a view of politics free of securing ultimate matters, either as a participation in the highest good or as offering a salvific dimension. We are called to do justice in our vocations and challenge those systems that threaten injustice. Recognizing the inability to unify law and gospel this side of the *eschaton,* we must avoid the totalization that Moltmann seeks. Instead of accommodating to secular politics with their hidden religious agendas, and instead of Christianizing politics, we must allow politics to be worldly, not as self-serving but as other-serving, the very energy of creation itself. We must also recognize that in a world plagued with much evil and moral ambiguity, God continues to work infinite good, providing for daily needs, sustaining people by his Spirit, offering vocations for daily service, and empowering people to care. As originally given, human nature is compassionate. It is incurvation that dams up this energy, and faith alone can unleash this power. The freedom to leave the politics of the kingdom in God's hands allows us all the more energy to care for our neighbor and creation.

---

72. "The knowledge of the cross brings a conflict of interest between God who has become man and man who wishes to become God. It destroys the destruction of man. It alienates alienated man. And in this way it restores the humanity of dehumanized man. Just as Paul contrasted the wisdom of this world and the folly of the cross, and in parallel with this, contrasted righteousness by the works of the law and the scandal of the cross, so Luther brought together the religious way to knowledge through the contemplation of the works of God, and the moral way of self-affirmation through one's own works, and directed the *theologia crucis* polemically against both." See Moltmann, *The Crucified God*, p. 71.

Summary and Critical Assessment

What then can be taken from Moltmann, and what should be left for our constructive work? We can honor Moltmann's concern for the neighbor in need, and recognize that Luther teaches us that property is not finally our own but given for the sake of the neighbor's well-being.[73] Moltmann's naming of *ambitio divinitatis* as the source of human sin is also helpful. Moltmann is on target: you can expect good fruit from a good tree. Also, power structures as the divine sanction for right are to be challenged when they claim an ultimacy.

However, Moltmann's anthropology, in which the human is always an agent and not properly a recipient *coram deo,* his tendency to see the kingdom as primarily task and not gift, the church as solely a focus for ethics, his quest for a pure society, and his failure to distinguish law and gospel are all grave matters of concern with respect to the constructive adequacy of his theology for justification.[74]

73. Hence, Carter Lindberg notes that the "Christian life is not governed by the demand to move from vice to virtue but rather lives from grace. This stands against the transformation of any social agenda, regardless of its merit, into a pseudo-gospel, an ersatz liturgy." See *Beyond Charity,* p. 167.

74. Walter Altmann's attempt to link Luther to liberation theology is far more successful and insightful than Moltmann's work. Altmann notes that "in Latin America, a context of domination and dependence, the term 'liberation' is particularly well suited to express the 'wholeness' of salvation and its character as a process as well as its personal and its historical dimension. 'Liberation' also communicates the biblical dialectic of being free from (a slavery) and free for (a service), weaving God's gratuitous action together with our human ethical commitment." See *Luther and Liberation,* trans. Mary Solberg (Minneapolis: Fortress, 1992), p. 41.

However, as can be seen from the study outlined above, liberation is a notion entrenched in the mythology of the High Enlightenment. Is it really needed? Can one not merely agree with Carl Braaten that justice is a form of love in society? (See *Principles of Lutheran Theology,* p. 132.) Might that quest for justice, free of "liberation," serve as our criterion by which to evaluate political systems and theories, despite their congenital ambiguity and intractable messiness? Such systems and theories are never able to produce the purity that Moltmann seeks, and when such purity is remotely established, it becomes itself tyrannical and monstrous.

PART TWO

THE ROLE OF JUSTIFICATION IN NON-ACCOMMODATING THEOLOGICAL STRATEGIES

Chapter Five

Robert Jenson:
Justification in the Theology
of the Perfected Church

With his *Systematic Theology*,[1] Robert Jenson, until recently the senior scholar at the Center for Theological Inquiry in Princeton, has distinguished himself as one of America's foremost theologians. In addition, Jenson has established himself as an authority in several theological fields.[2] Of the theologians presented in this book, he alone has evidenced a significant change of mind about the doctrine of justification. Midway through his career, Jenson offered a robust interpretation of the doctrine of justifi-

1. See Jenson, ST 1 and ST 2. For evaluations of this work, see George Hunsinger, "Robert Jenson's *Systematic Theology*: A Review Essay," *Scottish Journal of Theology* 55 (2002): 161-200; Francis Watson, "'America's Theologian': An Appreciation of Robert Jenson's *Systematic Theology*, with Some Remarks about the Bible," *Scottish Journal of Theology* 55 (2002): 201-23; and Mark Mattes, "An Analysis and Assessment of Robert Jenson's *Systematic Theology*," *Lutheran Quarterly* 14 (2000): 463-94.

2. Jenson established himself early as a Barth scholar. See *Alpha and Omega: A Study in the Theology of Karl Barth* (New York: Nelson, 1963) and *God after God: The God of the Past and the God of the Future, Seen in the Work of Karl Barth* (Indianapolis: Bobbs-Merrill, 1969). However, he is also an Edwards scholar; see *America's Theologian: A Recommendation of Jonathan Edwards* (New York: Oxford University Press, 1988). He is an expert on the doctrine of the Trinity — see *The Triune Identity: God According to the Gospel* (Philadelphia: Fortress, 1982) — and the sacraments: *Visible Words: The Interpretation and Practice of Christian Sacraments* (Philadelphia: Fortress, 1978). He thoroughly knows the Lutheran confessional tradition; he authored, with Eric Gritsch, *Lutheranism: The Theological Movement and Its Confessional Writings* (Philadelphia: Fortress, 1976). His work in ecumenics is *Unbaptized God: The Basic Flow in Ecumenical Theology* (Minneapolis: Fortress, 1992).

cation as rightly distinguishing law from gospel: "So speak of Christ that you 'rightly divide law and gospel.'"[3] With more nuance, he wrote, "Make the subject of your discourse those points in your and your hearers' life where its value is challenged, and interpret the challenge by the story about Christ, remembering that when this is rightly done your words will be an unconditional promise of value."[4] In a word, the doctrine of justification is to function "meta-linguistically,"[5] discerning word as promise in order to deliver it in distinction from all other discourse.

In his later writings, by contrast, Jenson commits himself to (1) an ecumenism that anticipates a future, visibly unified church undivided by confessional oppositions,[6] (2) the church's organic unity in the "total Christ" *(totus Christus)*,[7] as inclusive of his body, the church, and (3) a vigorous Trinitarianism similar to that of Karl Rahner (1904-1989), where the immanent trinity is the economic trinity and vice versa.[8] Here, justification is no longer primarily seen in forensic terms but rather in ontological terms. Unlike traditional Roman Catholics, Jenson does not regard faith as a theological virtue. However, he does consider faith a prerequisite for the ultimate unification of the soul with God by means of greater degrees of imitative or mimetic participation in the Trinity through the Spirit's agency.[9] The point of justification is to describe how we participate eschatologically in God, the "triumph of community,"[10] through the perfection

3. Jenson and Gritsch, *Lutheranism*, p. 43.

4. Jenson and Gritsch, *Lutheranism*, p. 43.

5. Jenson and Gritsch, *Lutheranism*, p. 43.

6. For an ecumenical theology similarly driven by an institutionally unified church, see Ephraim Radner, *The End of the Church: A Pneumatology of Christian Division in the West* (Grand Rapids: Eerdmans, 1998).

7. The image of *"totus Christus"* for the church is important especially for Cardinal Joseph Ratzinger. See Miroslav Volf's discussion of Ratzinger's work in *After Our Likeness: The Church as the Image of the Trinity* (Grand Rapids: Eerdmans, 1993), pp. 29-72. Among the Fathers, Jenson appeals (Jenson, ST 1:81), for instance, to Augustine's reference to the "total Christ" in *In Johannem*, XXI, 8: "Let us rejoice, then, and give thanks that we are made not only Christians, but Christ. Do ye understand, brethren, and apprehend the grace of God upon us? Marvel, be glad, we are made Christ. For if He is the Head, we are the members: the whole man is He and we."

8. See Rahner, *The Trinity* (New York: Herder & Herder, 1970), pp. 21-22.

9. In this respect David Yeago and Reinhard Hütter follow Jenson's lead. For a critique of their theologies, see Mark C. Mattes, "The Thomistic Turn in Evangelical Catholic Ethics," *Lutheran Quarterly* 16 (2002): 65-100.

10. Jenson, ST 2:126.

of ecclesial existence in the completed triune life. For Jenson, the heart of theology should now no longer be the attempt to distinguish law and gospel properly, but to speak on behalf of the church for the sake of its future visible unity, narrating the life of that one organic body as it increasingly grows into its proper place within God. The life of the church contrasts with that of the world, which is, in Augustinian terms, the "city of man." When justification is conceived largely in forensic terms, it becomes a sectarian doctrine, unable to achieve the goal of a visibly unified church, an antidote to contemporary culture's pervasive nihilism.

If we compare Jenson to the previous theologians investigated, we see marked similarities in content and marked differences in form. First, with respect to content, Jenson, like Jüngel, Pannenberg, and Moltmann, affirms a view of God in which God is fully deity only at the end of the process that is his life. For Jenson, as for these other thinkers, God is seemingly de-Platonized. God is not an atemporal Being-as-such in contrast to time. Rather, God is in time, which both participates in and instantiates this eternity. Jenson shares in the Hegelizing tendencies of these thinkers.[11] Similar to Hegel's Platonic assumption of the triumph of reason over sense is Jenson's idea that participation in God is no longer tantamount to the instantiation of an eternal form in a temporal reality, but rather a vehicle of the eternal divine life in its self-development toward its own *telos*, in which we are graciously permitted to share. Time is no longer a Platonically inspired "moving picture of eternity" but the very stuff of eternity's life. Like Moltmann, Jenson focuses on the church as a countercultural community participating in this divine quest. However, unlike Moltmann, whose counterculture is shaped by Kantianism, seeking full autonomy for individuals within a "kingdom of ends," and Marxists, who seek liberation from oppressive power structures, Jenson wants the church to offer an alternative city to the human city now covered by the pall of nihilism — a world that has "lost its story."[12] Unlike the radical individualism that contours and distorts life, the church as a Catholic counterculture should be guided by a common goal manifest in the *reditus* of the divine life. The unity of the Trinity is a result of social transactions within the tri-

11. See Hunsinger, "Robert Jenson's *Systematic Theology*," pp. 176-79, and Mattes, "An Analysis and Assessment of Robert Jenson's *Systematic Theology*," p. 484.

12. See Robert Jenson, "How the World Lost Its Story," *First Things* 36 (1993): 19-24. Or, would it be closer to the mark to say that the world exchanged the biblical story for the Epicurean or Gnostic stories?

une social community, its economic missions. Its unity is not found in the life of the *personae* who share a logically prior, atemporal common life, as in Augustine, nor found in the Father holding a logically prior position in relation to the other two persons, as in the Cappadocians. The reality of God, then, is in cosmic and human histories, not in a Platonic view of Being. The life of God is defined by its outcome, whose realization has been assured and whose foretaste is offered in history in Jesus' resurrection.

However, Jenson markedly differs from Pannenberg, Jüngel, and Moltmann by eschewing any epistemological foundationalist strategy. For Jenson, there is no universal reason independent of culture or tradition that would encyclopedically encapsulate reality as such. Instead of leaning on general epistemological strategies, Jenson is markedly more true to Hegel than is Pannenberg, since the logic of the resurrection and the church is fundamentally presuppositionless.[13] Knowledge is tied to communal practices. One must already be a part of the community in order to have internalized its way of self-understanding and share in its *ethos*.

The three previous thinkers find strategies of accommodating to the Weberian-inspired "fact-value split"[14] of the modern academy, in which reason is seen as instrumental while the final purpose of life is deemed to be wholly subjective. Via accommodation, they also "Weberianize" the church in the process. In a Weberian mode, mainline Protestantism tends to manage bureaucratically the confessional diversity that it fosters. When it seeks a "public" voice, it does so under the conditions of modernity, transforming the promise into ethics, feeling, or theory. In a Weberian mode, Christian mission establishes a specific ethics of human potential for the world (like Kant), or involves a transcendental depth dimension to life (like Schleiermacher), or offers a better cartography of the cosmos in league with the natural sciences (like Hegel). For Pannenberg, truth conforms to scientific method as offering models of reality and experience. For Moltmann, truth is to be found in establishing an ideal just society. For Jüngel, truth is conveyed by a unique experience "with experience" indifferent to science. In contrast, Jenson wholly disavows this fact-value split. For Jenson, much of what is called "science" is linguistically, culturally, and

13. See Rolf Ahlers, *The Community of Freedom: Barth and Presuppositionless Theology* (New York: Peter Lang, 1999).

14. To this day, the single best response to this split remains Wayne C. Booth, *Modern Dogma and the Rhetoric of Assent* (Chicago: University of Chicago Press, 1974).

mythically codified and structured, even though these codes have long been submerged or ignored.[15] Ethics is seen as subjective, since the common good, as the objective beatific vision, has been sidestepped for the individual's own autopoiesis. Hence, Jenson appeals to narrative identity, not metaphysics, for presenting the reality of God. This narrative identity is culturally and linguistically mediated in the church as the non-nihilistic, purposeful *civitas dei*.

Trinity as Abbreviated Church; Church as Extended Trinity

Jenson sees theology as pre-eminently an ecclesial task in which the gospel, as the message of the church, and the church, as the social, historical embodiment of the gospel, mutually determine each other.[16] Here, Jenson is clearly criticizing the Protestant supposition that the church is a "creature of the word."[17] Given the current divisions between the many confessional identities which all claim, in different ways, to be the "church," it is not clear that Jenson adequately defines and justifies what criteria should be used to discern exactly what constitutes a "church." Jenson wants to identify the church as the community organically united to the Trinity. Similar to Pannenberg, Jenson sees the Trinity as an abbreviated church, since all members of the church participate to varying degrees in the triune life, thus ultimately becoming constitutive of the narrative identity of God. Conversely, this ontological participation likewise makes the church an extension of the Trinity.

The church about which Jenson speculates is one that is largely hypothetical, since it does not seemingly correspond to any actual, present ecclesial community. Nevertheless, he uses the claim that the gospel and the

---

15. Jenson criticizes our tendency to continue the Enlightenment's elevation of the Greek element of our thinking to the position of unilateral judge or criterion for knowledge. He is highly skeptical of "the qualification of truth taught by Plato or Aristotle as more 'natural' or 'rational' than truth taught by Isaiah or Paul" (Jenson, ST 1:9). Not surprisingly, then, he criticizes metaphysical language games as somehow more scientific than other metaphors. He claims, "There is no apriori reason why, for example, 'substance' — which after all simply meant 'what holds something up' — should be apt for conscription into metaphysical service and, for example, 'tune' should not" (Jenson, ST 2:39).

16. Jenson, ST 1:5.

17. GMW 312.

church mutually determine each other in order to argue that there is no reason for theology to appeal to extra-ecclesial sources for discerning theological truth, such as has been attempted by theology's historic quest to discover a universal theological discourse, a "natural theology," shared by both believers and nonbelievers. For Jenson, "natural theologies" and much of "secular," Western philosophy can be unmasked as particular faiths, variants of the pagan Mediterranean Olympian-Parmenidean religion. The appropriate Christian posture toward such alternative theologies is not to adopt them, but as Thomas Aquinas did with Aristotle, to converse with them.[18] Also, since the gospel is tied to a specific God as its determinate object, the gospel therefore should not be misconstrued as whatever humans might find to be personally salvific.[19] The gospel should not be thought to be apart from its communal, historical embodiment in the church.

For Jenson, the theological norms are a trio of Scripture, creed, and the church's teaching office.[20] Only this "Catholic" understanding of authority adequately grasps the alleged diachronic implications of the gospel (as a historic episcopate). In direct opposition to a Protestant view of apostolicity as (diachronic) fidelity to the apostles' message, Jenson locates the preservation of the gospel as dependent upon an institutional succession of messengers endowed with a special charism from the Holy Spirit that enables them to perpetuate the gospel's truth through history.[21] To this proposal, must it not be countered that the historic episcopate has been woefully inadequate to the task of preserving the gospel's truth? Also, must we not ask, Is such coercive authority of the old era actually required for the effectiveness of the gospel's authority in the new? The gospel undoubtedly carries with it an office that is authoritative for those ambassadors who deliver its message (2 Cor. 5:20). However, Jenson's problem is that he conflates gospel with church, particularly the church discerned as a hierarchical teaching office, and thus jeopardizes the gospel's eschatological limit.

The doctrine of justification for Jenson is situated by the quest for a

---

18. Jenson, ST 1:21.

19. Jenson, ST 1:12.

20. Jenson, ST 1:23.

21. Jenson, ST 1:40: "Through the teaching office, the church speaks as one diachronically communal reality and is guarded in this unity precisely by so speaking; therefore the teaching office must itself be essentially characterized by diachronic unity. In the church's traditional language, this is called 'succession': those are to teach who make one community with former teachers."

unified church. The true church re-unified in the future will complete the triune life. The inner logic of the biblical and theological narratives that have led Christians to affirm their faith in a triune God is grounded not in a general metaphysics, as Pannenberg claims, but in a specific story. Jenson claims, "Since the biblical God can truly be identified by narrative, his hypostatic being, his self-identity is constituted in *dramatic coherence*."[22] This implies that the being of God must be conceived in terms of a goal that sums up and specifies the character of the divine life, since dramas are emplotted with their resolution in mind. Jenson's conception of God radically departs from the traditional Parmenidean bias that the essence of divinity is free of temporality.[23]

Eternity is not timelessness, for Jenson, but God's inexhaustible ability to anticipate the future. The story of God is to be interpreted primarily from the *eschatos,* and not merely from the *arche,* as has traditionally been done. The future, here, is a window to deity that unmasks the hidden God. God is rendered intelligible from the inside out and thus is transparent to human understanding. Again, this can be seen as another form of "domesticating transcendence."[24] Jenson notes, "God is not hidden because we can see only some of him though at metaphysical distances. He is hidden because his very presence is such as at once altogether to reveal and altogether to hide him."[25] However, it is not the case, as for Thomas Aquinas, that what is known is known on the basis of the knower, but rather that the incurvated human can never see God's face and live. It is God in his mercy

---

22. Jenson, ST 1:64.

23. To capture Jenson's perspective, it is worthwhile to quote his logic in full: "Since the Lord's self-identity is constituted in dramatic coherence, it is established not from the beginning but from the end, not at birth but at death, not in *persistence* but in *anticipation.* The biblical God is not eternally himself in that he persistently instantiates a beginning in which he already is all he ever will be; he is eternally himself in that he unrestrictedly anticipates an end in which he will be all he ever could be. It holds also — or, rather, primally — with God: a story is constituted by the outcome of the narrated events. Within the sequence of events a specific opening future liberates each successive specious present from mere predictability, from being only the result of what has gone before, and just so opens each such present to its own content, given precisely as what it does not yet encompass." See Jenson, ST 1:66.

24. The phrase is taken from William C. Placher, *The Domestication of Transcendence: How Modern Thinking about God Went Wrong* (Louisville: Westminster John/Knox Press, 1996).

25. Jenson, ST 2:161.

who turns his back on us so that we might look to him in faith and not sight. A better alternative to Jenson's Trinitarianism would be that the Trinity should be understood not as a way to decode God's deity, but rather as the concrete assurance that God in his being is committed to the promise.

The divine social ontology that Jenson develops is to make God "roomy" — to include a people who will be deified, the ultimate significance of the doctrine of justification. The church is not a means to an end, but insofar as it is on the route to deification in the triune life, it becomes an end in itself. Seeing God as personal, however, is not best understood as a correlation of identity and personality, a move that cannot help but construe selfhood as "monadic entity, a self-possessed, closed unity."[26] Rather, following Karl Barth, the triune self-unfolding should be seen as the dynamics of a "self-*revealing*" and not "a self-*containing*" subject.[27] Hence, Jenson claims, "God is not personal in that he is triunely self-sufficient; he is personal in that he triunely opens himself."[28]

Deification results from the fact that not only God is social by nature, but so also is humanity. This feature shared by both God and humanity is the basis for the church as a social organism that is to be deified. Agreeing with many contemporary theological anthropologists, Jenson affirms that human nature is characterized by transcendence. For Jenson, this contention is expressed by the idea "I am the object of the subject I am," where such self-objectification never encapsulates the "I" but always carries it further.[29] The human's ability to transcend itself (an Augustinian supposition) implies that humanity's proper home, the goal of its restlessness, should be God. Carrying this line of inquiry further, in light of the theories of human agency of Maurice Blondel (1861-1949) and Henri de Lubac (1896-1991), Jenson believes that the significance of any act transcends that particular act. Focusing as it does on an infinite self-transcendence implicit in all action, this theory of human action implies a continuum between the natural and the supernatural, a "supernaturalizing the natural," as John Milbank has interpreted Blondel's and de Lubac's work.[30] The natural order is not a "double" of the supernatural order. Rather, from within itself via the tran-

---

26. Jenson, ST 1:123.

27. Jenson, ST 1:124.

28. Jenson, ST 1:124.

29. Jenson, ST 2:64.

30. See Milbank, *Theology and Social Theory* (Oxford: Blackwell, 1990), p. 207. Jenson himself, however, does not use this phrase.

scendence indicated by human agency (every act implies more than the achievement of its intention), the human can be seen as open to, though as not having an aptitude for, grace.

The weakness here is not that humanity can live "externally," outside itself, but that such externality is configured within a transcendence dominated by the metaphor of "ascent." This implies that our agency has bearing *coram deo*. It ignores the truth that before God, we are fundamentally passive — solely receivers. Before God, our life is best understood, with Luther, as a passive life *(vita passiva)*. The moral life that accords with such passivity is active service to the neighbor,[31] and the appropriate metaphor for the Christian life is "descent" in charity toward others. It is faith that opens the horizon of love. Only in this sense would our agency "participate" in that of Christ. We must be liberated from our incurvation before we can live externally. Such liberation is to be seen not as an "ascent" to God, as if we could offer merit, but as a "descent" toward others in service. Freedom from incurvation liberates spontaneous and creative agency on behalf of others — witness the Good Samaritan — in one's vocation.

In a radical departure from the Lutheran affirmation that the church is an assembly of people shaped by the gospel's message and sacraments, Jenson believes that God expresses his identity to the world as a creature, the body of the church. Jenson claims,

> The body of the *totus Christus* is a creature, that creature that makes sense of the rest. This body is in the created heaven a self-possessed conscious creature. And this creature speaks through the phenomena Thomas observed, of creatures' dependence, inferiority, and comparability to — something. It is thus that God reveals himself through our experience of creatures.[32]

Nevertheless, with Luther, Jenson believes that creation likewise "masks" God, not fully revealing him. Unlike Luther, however, Jenson consistently fails to associate the dynamics of God's hiddenness and revealedness with God's "being preached" or "not preached."

As we have seen, ecclesiological issues have been anticipated throughout Jenson's work. This feature is due to the fact that Jenson sees the *totus Christus* as definitive for both God's and humanity's life to-

31. See Theologie, C, 2.2, pp. 42-49.
32. Jenson, ST 2:159.

gether. With his in-depth analysis of the church, Jenson investigates the founding, polity, sacramental nature, ministry, and message of the church. Not surprisingly, Jenson's ecclesiology is molded by distinctly Roman Catholic themes. He chides Protestantism for failing to appreciate that the church, as an institution, shares an organic unity with God. Nevertheless, he also faults Catholicism for failing to appreciate the Spirit's agency in the church as calling it toward a future, instead focusing solely on the past as the genuine venue of spiritual authority. He seeks to mediate an ecclesiological path between the extremes of a spiritless Catholic institutionalism and an untethered Protestant enthusiasm. In contrast to the Protestants who confess that the church is a "creature" of the gospel,[33] Jenson sees the establishing of the church as a new event of the Spirit in the overall history of salvation rather than as an order of creation. Hence, "God institutes the church by not letting Jesus' Resurrection be itself the end, by appointing 'the delay of the Parousia.'"[34] The church then is neither an institution of the old age nor a realization of the new. Rather, "she is precisely an event within the event of the new age's advent."[35] Pentecost is a peer of Easter because the Spirit liberates Jesus from the bonds of death, not only through Jesus' resurrection but also by the liberation of a community that can receive and be Jesus' "actuality within the present time of this age."[36] As a vehicle of the Spirit, the church's role in relation to society is clearly prophetic, "a single communal prophet,"[37] which continues the ministry of Jesus. Indeed, even the legitimating of earthly politics ought to be openness to such prophecy.

Justification as Real-Ontic Bond

In the *Systematic Theology*, Jenson concludes his discussion of the church under the rubric *"Anima Ecclesiastica,"*[38] in which he offers an interpreta-

---

33. Jenson, ST 2:168.
34. Jenson, ST 2:170.
35. Jenson, ST 2:171.
36. Jenson, ST 2:181.
37. Jenson, ST 2:199.
38. This term is a favorite of Cardinal Joseph Ratzinger's. See, for example, his *Church, Ecumenism, and Politics: New Essays in Ecclesiology*, trans. Robert Nowell (New York: Crossroad, 1988), p. 130.

tion of the doctrine of justification that is particularly indebted to the thinking of Tuomo Mannermaa and the new Finnish school of Luther Research,[39] which we also encountered in Pannenberg. While Jenson may have arrived at his conclusions independently of Mannermaa's work, it is, at this point, hard to separate his perspective on Luther from that of Mannermaa, since he has incorporated Mannermaa's work into his theology. Mannermaa's reading of Luther was undertaken to establish a view of *theosis* in Luther that could serve as a platform for ecumenical dialogue between the Evangelical Lutheran Church of Finland and Eastern Orthodox churches. The new Finnish school has insisted that most modern Luther research has missed the theme of divinization in Luther's thinking because it has been biased by neo-Kantian philosophical presuppositions that eclipse a "real-ontic"[40] relation between Christ and the Christian. For the neo-Kantians, relations can only be construed in terms of the effects of things on one another, and not as the participation of things in each other. In response to the alleged neo-Kantian misreading of Luther and in dialogue with Mannermaa, Jenson claims that an adequate account of the doctrine of justification must incorporate three viewpoints: (1) Augustine's view of justification as an accurate account of the Christian *transitus* from sin to righteousness, (2) Luther's view of justification as a hermeneutical key that guarantees that the gospel will be expressed as promise and not law, and (3) Saint Paul's theological concern that God establishes his faithfulness even in spite of human unfaithfulness. The question here is

---

39. The most important text of the new Finnish school of Luther research is clearly Tuomo Mannermaa, *Der im Glauben gegenwärtige Christus,* trans. from Finnish into German by Hans Christian Daniel and Juhani Forsberg (Hannover: Lutherisches Verlaghaus, 1989). A partial translation of this text can be found in "The Doctrine of Justification and Christology, Chapter A, Section One of *The Christ Present in Faith,*" trans. Thomas F. Obersat, *Concordia Theological Quarterly* 64 (2000): 182-239. Under the auspices of the Center for Catholic and Evangelical Theology, a collection of essays by students of Mannermaa along with North American responders has been published as *Union with Christ: The New Finnish Interpretation of Luther,* ed. Carl E. Braaten and Robert Jenson (Grand Rapids: Eerdmans, 1998). Also, see Risto Saarinen, *Gottes Wirken auf Uns: Die Transzendentale Deutung des Gegenwart-Christi-Motivs in der Lutherforschung* (Stuttgart: Franz Steiner Verlag, 1989), which argues that German Luther scholars failed to see the "real-ontic" bond of participation of humanity in God by means of grace because they read Luther through the eyes of the neo-Kantian philosophy that Nominalistically affirmed an external relationality but not an organic union between various entities.

40. See Mannermaa, *Der im Glauben gegenwärtige Christus,* p. 48.

whether Jenson can accomplish such a synthesis or whether the second and third viewpoints are incompatible with the first.

Jenson believes that the traditional Lutheran or "forensic" approach to justification as an unconditional declaration of pardon to the sinner should be affirmed because when construed as a "word event," it has the power to break through human incurvation and re-orient its hearer so as to honor God, and not use God for one's own self-justification. Jenson jeopardizes this theme, however, when he interprets it in light of the new Finnish school. The position of the new Finns, in contrast to the Lutheran confessional writings, is that such a forensic interpretation of justification must itself be grounded in an "effective" view, in which the sinner is united with Christ by means of a "real-ontic" bond. This bond exchanges the believer's sinfulness for Christ's righteousness and vice versa, such that the believer is formed by the theological virtues of faith, hope, and love. In this way, the new Finns contend that God's forensic declaration is one of fact, not fiction. Quoting Luther's phrase "*in ipse fide Christus adest* [in faith itself Christ is present],"[41] Jenson, in league with the new Finns, argues that justification is properly a "mode of deification."[42] Christ, with whom the believer is one, unifies the believer likewise with the life of God, since Christ is fully human *and divine.*

In contrast to the Roman Catholic tendency to emphasize sight as the proper metaphor that adequately describes the ultimate union of the believer to God, the "beatific vision," Jenson appropriates Luther's preference for hearing. He affirms that the mind becomes what it hears.[43] Hence, Jenson claims that for the believer, God becomes one's "living ego."[44] However, Jenson also appropriates, in a rather attenuated, unparadoxical

---

41. Luther writes, "Therefore Christian faith is not an idle quality or an empty husk in the heart, which may exist in a state of mortal sin until love comes along to make it alive. But if it is true faith, it is a sure trust and firm acceptance in the heart. It takes hold of Christ in such a way that Christ is the object of faith, or rather not the object but, so to speak, the One who is present in the faith itself. Thus faith is a sort of knowledge or darkness that nothing can see. Yet the Christ of whom faith takes hold is sitting in this darkness as God sat in the midst of darkness on Sinai and in the temple. Therefore our 'formal righteousness' is not a love that informs faith; but it is faith itself, a cloud in our hearts, that is, trust in a thing we do not see, in Christ, who is present especially when He cannot be seen." See *Lectures on Galatians* (1535), in LW 26:129-30 (WA 40/1:228-29).

42. Jenson, ST 2:296.

43. Jenson, ST 2:295.

44. Jenson, ST 2:299.

fashion, the Lutheran insight that humans can be simultaneously saints and sinners. As one with Christ, one is a saint; however, outside of Christ, as belonging to other publics, one is a sinner.[45] If Jenson's discussion of "effective" justification were to obtain, then we would have the "Catholic Luther" for which ecumenists have been looking for decades.[46] Nevertheless, decisive *Lutheran* features mark Jenson's construal of the Christian life that might raise concerns for Roman Catholics or the Eastern Orthodox. For instance, Jenson is skeptical of any kind of empirical confirmation of progress in the Christian life. Instead, the Christian life is a daily return to baptism, which itself offers all we could ever hope for in this life.[47]

Many will find Jenson's appropriation of Mannermaa's view of justification as deification problematic. Departing from the view espoused in the Confessions,[48] Mannermaa holds that the indwelling Christ is the basis for the declaration of righteousness, and not vice versa. This new Finnish view jeopardizes the centrality and objectivity of the "external word" *(verbum externum)*, God's means to comfort anxious consciences threatened by the accusatory function of the law. Luther's view of the indwelling Christ and the happy exchange are grounded in this external word, which comes to humans from *outside* of themselves. Christians are directed to trust this external word that defines their very being, and not their own intuitions about this new being. Only by clinging to the external word of the promise is the sinner liberated from incurvation and allowed selflessly to

---

45. Jenson notes, "Short of the Kingdom, more than enough room remains for the commandments to rebuke and direct us and for new hearing of the gospel promise. Nor is there any opportunity for moral quietism. So long as I and my neighbors are not in the Kingdom, we live with each other in the conditions of this world; and the Christ who does all for me and lives in me will do all for them also, in part by way of me. Moreover, if I am to be a fit instrument of this divine work, Christ must curb my remaining egocentric longings, and again he will do this through my own agency, through my self-discipline and resolve." See Jenson, ST 2:297.

46. For a discussion of the "Catholic Luther," see Peter Manns, "The Validity and Theological-Ecumenical Usefulness of the Lortzian Position on the 'Catholic Luther,'" in *Luther's Ecumenical Significance: An Interconfessional Consultation*, ed. Peter Manns and Harding Meyer (Philadelphia: Fortress, 1984), pp. 3-26; and David C. Yeago, "The Catholic Luther," *First Things* 61 (1996): 37-41.

47. Jenson, ST 2:297.

48. See the "Formula of Concord," Epitome, Art. III, antitheses 6-8, "Righteousness" [BC 497:16-20; BSELK 785:16-20], which makes it clear that the indwelling Christ and sanctification are not logically prior to but a result of justification.

serve the neighbor. While Jenson and the new Finns are apt to emphasize a reciprocity between the justifying word and the indwelling Christ, only the logical and rhetorical prioritizing of forensic over effective justification (which may both be temporally simultaneous) can address Luther's chief pastoral concern to console the anxious conscience in his formulation of the doctrine of justification.

If, for Jenson, the church is the community that is to be deified as a participant in the eternal triune life, then this deification will happen only as it continues to be properly ordered by grace. Why should Jenson, whose theology for decades was configured in terms of properly distinguishing law and gospel, have come to this point of distorting their relationship? Undoubtedly, the inability of mainline Protestantism to counter accommodation to the wider culture's revamping of faith as therapeutic, political, or theoretical was a factor.[49] However, Jenson himself was early on a significant player in the reshaping of North American Lutheran identity into the accommodating structures of mainline Protestantism that he now eschews. In the midst of an antinomianism that Jenson mistook as inherent to Protestant identity, he turned to a nomianism of a Catholic conception of Christianity as the answer to such accommodation. Ironically, it was his reading of the American Calvinist Jonathan Edwards (1703-1758) that brought this move to the fore. Jenson notes that for Edwards there can be no community apart from law.[50] Only law can order communal life. If the gospel is conceived in the narrow sense as opposed to law this side of the *eschaton*, then, Jenson reasons, it offers no bearing upon communal living. Yet, if the extended community of the church is to be transformed ultimately by deification, then law must apply to its life as the standard of its proper ordering to God. The *lex aeterna*, not the "eternal gospel" (Rev. 14:6), prevails

---

49. That mainline Protestantism tends to accommodate to social forces that are at best indifferent to it and at worst downright hostile to it, and that this harms its ability to gain ground in the North American religious landscape is strikingly argued by Thomas C. Reeves, *The Empty Church: The Suicide of Liberal Christianity* (New York: Free Press, 1996). Similarly, for an outstanding study, see John Leith, *Crisis in the Church: The Plight of Theological Education* (Louisville: Westminster John/Knox Press, 1997). A potent exposé of the mainline malady can be found in Thomas C. Oden, *Requiem: A Lament in Three Movements* (Nashville: Abingdon, 1995).

50. "For now so much may suffice: when the Christian gospel is made into a mitigation of the law, it is a spiritual poison of unequalled virulence. A community whose law allows in advance for its own breaking, is dissolving itself." See *America's Theologian*, 60.

for Jenson. If deification is to transpire through higher degrees of mimetic participation, a transformation through both human *theoria* and *praxis,* conforming in ever-increasing degrees of godliness in the ecclesial community destined for deification, then gospel must serve law.

Could God establish a community without rules? For Jenson, a community without rules has no way to restrain evil. Without restraint, all would be chaos. In fact, this has become the destiny of unchurched and anti-churched Western culture. However, we must concur with Gerhard Forde: "That good works do not make a good person is too pessimistic for most; but that a good person does good works is too optimistic!"[51] More than anything, community is established first in promise and trust; order does not take precedence over this. In opposition to neo-Kantian misreadings of Luther on justification, Jenson, with Mannermaa, can claim that God is not imputing a fiction when declaring sinners righteous, but acknowledging a reality insofar as they ontologically participate in divine grace. Unlike the renewed nihilistic Epicureanism of the modern West, the church offers a narrative identity and a distinctive *praxis* which are themselves salvific; they specifically save us from this pervasive nihilism. However, while Jenson's concern about contemporary Epicureanism is legitimate, its antidote is not catholic analogy or degrees of participation in the ultimate *telos.*[52] This is because this *telos* has arrived, is operative now, in word and sacrament. It opens a new horizon of experience that allows us to "participate" in our neighbor's need, free of the bondage of calculating the degree to which our behavior is meritoriously analogous to the divine. Does not Jenson finally offer us only a Catholicism "lite," an episcopate without poverty, chastity, or obedience?

For Jenson, only law sustains community, because law orders life. However, cannot community also be seen as providential grace, God creating us through nature and society? The gospel is to be distinguished, not separated, from the law. Yet, ironically, only faith, not works, can actually "fulfill" the law. Jenson fails to see that we are properly "ordered" to God by faith alone, because it is faith that foregoes any merit and thus is able to give God the glory that is his due. Jenson fails to acknowledge an eschatological limit to law. Law does its good when we are led to Christ. Law may

---

51. See Gerhard Forde, "Luther's 'Ethics,'" in *A More Radical Gospel,* ed. Mark C. Mattes and Steven Paulson (Grand Rapids: Eerdmans, 2004), p. 151.

52. See Milbank, *Theology and Social Theory,* p. 318.

very well be necessary for ordering Christian community this side of the *eschaton*, but it is not sufficient. Only the gospel can create the new life that allows us to forgive others from the heart and to enlarge our communities by welcoming outsiders. Law is not for ordering our lives in higher degrees of mimetic participation in the divine, but for protecting our neighbors so that they can share their gifts. Faith is sufficient to break incurvation and allows us to partake of the divine life — fully as sinful! Christ is the end of the law, both as its *telos* and its *finis;* otherwise there would be no righteousness for anyone (Rom. 10:4).

Baptizing God as the Route to Ecumenism

Jenson has developed his systematics with a constant eye to ecclesiology. This is due to his understanding of the church as *totus Christus* and his view of the *totus Christus* as definitive for the fulfillment of the triune life. He has sought to construct an ecclesiology that avoids what he contends is the Protestant pitfall of viewing the church as an assembly of the charismatic word, not an institution, and the Catholic pitfall of viewing the church as an institution but ignoring the Spirit's agency in reforming this institution. Building on his earlier attempts to bridge Catholic and Protestant ecclesiologies in *Unbaptized God*,[53] Jenson contends that both Catholic and Protestant ecclesiologies misconstrue the relation between "being" and "time." Both see "being" in pagan Parmenidean fashion as atemporal; hence, God remains "unbaptized" — that is, the economic trinity as the temporal involvement of God in the world is never definitive of the immanent trinity, which remains defined in his core by divine "simplicity."[54]

---

53. Jenson, *Unbaptized God*, pp. 107-47.

54. Hence, Jenson writes as follows in *Unbaptized God*, p. 139: "It is the chief residual paganism of the way in which the churches descended from the mission in Mediterranean antiquity have thought of God, that all the derivations run one way, from the Father through the Son to the Spirit: the Father begets the Son and the Son is begotten; the Father breathes the Spirit and the Spirit is breathed. All active-voice relations run from origin to goal; the relations from goal to origin are but their passive voice. Therein unbaptized Hellenism's celebration of beginning over ending, of persistence over openness, of security over freedom, maintains itself even within the doctrine of Trinity. The God whose eternity is immunity to time lurks even within the church's vision of the God whose eternity is faithful adventure in and through time."

With such a view of God behind a Protestant ecclesiology, eternity is never seen as diachronically extended, and ministry can only be construed as a charismatic intrusion into time. With the *same* view of God behind a Catholic ecclesiology, eternity is seen as a sanction that legitimates past configurations of the church and ministry; it thus can never take ownership of reformation that might be demanded in light of discerning God's future. With Protestantism, Jenson might contend, a Lockean definition of the church as a "voluntary society,"[55] and not an organic body united to Christ as the Head, inevitably prevails. Hence, Jenson believes that with Protestantism, the church's identity is vulnerable to dissipating because its identity need not come from Christ alone; it is also shaped by a "club mentality." However, with Catholicism, the church might remain stagnant and not open to the Spirit's drive for renewal and redirection.[56]

Jenson believes that he has overcome the antithesis between institution and freedom falsely created by the "unbaptized" relationship between eternity and time. Contrary to Protestant views, Jenson holds that institution can be a mode of the Spirit, since eternity can be extended diachronically. Contrary to Catholic views, Jenson holds that the institution of the church must be accountable to the Spirit, who remains a free agent with respect to the church. What Jenson misunderstands is that a Protestant view of the church will not succumb to a "club mentality" or depend on an unshaped charisma when it is understood — as defined by *Confessio Augustana* VII — as a gathering *shaped* by the proclamation of gospel and not current fads. It is the gift of the gospel as a linguistic reality, not its deliverers, that defines the church's life.[57] The church can be free from delusions of grandeur about its abilities; its whole identity is to be found in its living from the gospel alone. Jenson is right that mainline Protestantism fails as an adequate vehicle for the gospel. Mainline Protestantism tends to

---

55. See *A Letter Concerning Toleration* (Amherst, N.Y.: Prometheus Books, 1990), p. 22.

56. See *Unbaptized God*, p. 128, where Jenson writes, "Thus what the church does is done by Christ the Logos; and yet he is free over against his church and, indeed, so long as the church is in the flesh, must often reform his church. Here space opens in which Catholic theology may out of its own deepest insight share the Reformation's concern for the unmitigated lordship of Christ over the church, and in which that Reformation concern can be effective without separating the church's agency from God's or pretending it could be merely passive."

57. For further discussion of this matter, see Gerhard Forde, *Theology Is for Proclamation* (Minneapolis: Fortress, 1990), pp. 186-90.

configure denominational life by managing theological and confessional diversity,[58] honoring confessionalism along with revivalism, charismaticism, self-help therapy, and "progressive" politics as salvific. However, the answer to mainline fragmentation is not to Catholicize the church but to accentuate Christ alone as sufficient.

Similar to Pannenberg, Jüngel, and Moltmann, Jenson wants to excise Plato's view of an atemporal eternal life from the heart of God's deity. Instead, God's life is found as realized in history. While Jenson rejects this Platonic view of time and eternity, he retains a Platonic view of "participation." The reality of various entities is to be found in the various shapes that they embody, which, as more inclusive, can be more concrete and potent than those entities themselves. Furthering this Platonism, the view of participation accepted by Jenson is also, and ironically, quite Hegelian. Being and time relate to each other in that Being participates in time in order to achieve its potential and realize its goal of self-fulfillment. The "lower" manifestations of experience through which it must traverse are included in "higher" levels via an *Aufhebung* — the power of the negative[59] — in

58. Jenson's student, David Yeago, has seen this: "Despite a certain amount of radical posturing, such scholarship is quite conservative within the mainline denominations in which it is most devoutly practiced. In those denominations, 'diversity' is the existing status quo; indeed, mainline denominations are perhaps best described as institutional vessels designed to enclose extreme religious plurality. In such settings, criticism that privileges difference and diversity protects denominational institutions from disruptive normative claims that might upset their fragile containment of highly centrifugal actions. If no coherent appeal can be made to a shared norm of scriptural faithfulness, we are all allowed to continue on our parallel tracks, doing and saying the different and incompatible things — conservative, liberal, or centrist — with which we feel comfortable. Every party within the church is thus reduced to a club, boosters of a favorite style or commodity, and therefore to a phenomenon that mainline denominationalism is equipped to manage." See "The Spirit, the Church, and the Scriptures: Biblical Inspiration and Interpretation Revisited," in *Knowing the Triune God: The Work of the Spirit in the Practices of the Church*, ed. James J. Buckley and David S. Yeago (Grand Rapids: Eerdmans, 2001), p. 78.

59. In the preface to *The Phenomenology of Spirit*, trans. A. V. Miller (New York: Oxford University Press, 1977), Hegel writes, "The scepticism that ends up with the bare abstraction of nothingness or emptiness cannot get any further from there, but must wait to see whether something new comes along and what it is, in order to throw it too into the same empty abyss. But when, on the other hand, the result is conceived as it is in truth, namely, as a *determinate* negation, a new form has thereby arisen, and in the negation the transition is made through which the progress through the complete series of forms comes about of itself" (p. 51).

which their lives are simultaneously negated as inadequate for the entirety of self-conscious experience, while simultaneously preserved as appropriate for the role they play in the concretization of the divine historicity. In the Hegelian view, eternity achieves its fullness not atemporally but only at the end of its quest for self-fulfillment. It is the driving force of the temporal, which is not a "moving picture" of eternity but its vehicle, participating in ever widening and more concrete forms of spiritual enrichment. For all that, the eternal Spirit simply uses the shapes through which it traverses, and is not sacramentally united to them.

Embedded deeply in Jenson's theology, due to his indebtedness to Hegel, is a "natural theology of the cross" *(theologia crucis naturalis)*[60] in which the cross's power to effectuate the end of the old being is trumped for the sake of our quest to map encyclopedically all experience by means of unmasking the hidden God. When the cross is so theorized, made a prelude to the resurrection, then its accusation of sinners — who pillage God's good gifts, scapegoat members of God's creation, and attribute their power to their own autopoiesis — is marginalized. The church is robbed of its greatest force for exposing contemporary culture's current idolatries and violence. Jenson's theology does not give the cross its full due.

Jenson posits that the Parmenidean inheritance in Catholicism is a legitimator of the past, inhibiting needed reform urged by the Spirit. This is in contrast to Protestantism's inability, as charismatic, to authorize ministry. Jenson fails to understand that for Protestantism, the church belongs to the orders of creation. Church, family, state: these are the three institutions whereby the *Spiritus Creator* is engaged in people-making. Its institutionalization cannot be ignored or dreamed away. Jenson assumes a personalism as governing a configuration of the church's agency. The answer to a Protestant misreading of ministry as inherently enthusiastic, charismatic, or Montanistic is not to retreat into Catholic hierarchy but to acknowledge that God's address is mediated tri-figurally through earthly institutions, and not only as an "I-Thou" personalism. More than anything else, ministry is to deliver Jesus Christ as sheer gift in word and sacrament for the security of the anxious conscience or the insecure soul. A genuine understanding of Protestant views of ministry affirms its institutional nature and its diachronicity. The word takes effect in the world through time, offering providential grace in creation. As such, the Protestant view avoids

60. Theologie, C, 6.3, p. 514.

a Catholic *Schwärmer* perspective in which the Spirit *arbitrarily* speaks through the papacy, the head of the hierarchy, independently of word or world.

The Primary Mission of the Church

Jenson's theology, in its present form, stands or falls with his "organic" model of the relationship between Christ and the church. His prioritization of the metaphor "body of Christ" configures every aspect of his theology. However, he misreads this metaphor so as to infer that the tension is overcome between the old age of sin, law, and death, and the new age of righteousness, freedom, and life. Jenson's ecclesiology confuses this age with the next. He misconstrues the church's purpose when he contends that it is the seed of the new era, an "event within the event of the new age's advent."[61] The church is, rather, an assembly, which *as* Christ's body in the cruciform existence of service to the neighbor, witnesses to the end of this old age by proclaiming Christ's new age. We should understand that the church, unlike the world, experiences and witnesses to the tension between two ages. For this reason, Christians need, on a continuing basis, to hear the external word that drowns the old being and raises the new. An important result of Jenson's flattening out the paradox of ecclesial existence between two ages is that God's "right hand" or direct rule over humans through the life-giving gospel in the human heart and God's "left hand" or indirect rule over humans through various social structures become divorced. Human politics is too quickly disassociated from God's work, and thus it evaporates into a "city of man," construed as largely demonic. Unlike Jenson, Lutherans affirm that we *believe* in the holy catholic church because we infer it by faith.

Jenson misreads the entire nature of the church in a way that would see the delivery people themselves as the goods. The point of the church's ministry is to deliver the goods that God gives, to open the world as gift, to allow humanity to live in the Spirit that gives life. Like the Helsinki Assembly of the Lutheran World Federation (1963),[62] Jenson sees humanity not

---

61. Jenson, ST 2:171.

62. *Justification Today,* Lutheran World Federation Studies and Reports, 1 (1965 [Supplement]).

as suffering under God's economy of death ("the death God works," not just "the death God finds"[63]), but as infected with nihilistic meaninglessness. We no longer deal with "anxious consciences" but with meaninglessness, disguising itself in various forms of hedonism. What Jenson and the Helsinki LWF assembly fail(ed) to realize is that this meaninglessness is itself an expression of divine wrath. That one no longer fears God's wrath but rather one's own cosmic triviality is no less an operation of law. One reaps what one sows (Gal. 6:7). Epicureans are dealing with God — in God's hiddenness — even if they are unaware of it. Such men and women also need to hear God's word as both judgment and grace. Their own sense of purposelessness is no less an indication that God is operative in their lives — if only as a void that no power, status, or pleasure can finally fill and that indicates impotency with respect to ultimate matters. The answer is not to conflate the gospel with the church, as Jenson does, and turn one's back on, or insulate the church from, the world.

Where then is the church? In our chapter on Pannenberg, we emphasized its invisibility. This truth needs to be accented in our time. Nevertheless, the question about how the church is "visible" can be asked. Luther, we might remember, listed seven signs of its presence: (1) the preaching of God's word, (2) baptism, (3) the sacrament of the altar, (4) the office of the keys, (5) the calling of pastors, (6) the offering of psalms, prayer, and thanksgiving, and (7) sharing in the cross and trial.[64] Such "visibility" (for all these marks testify to the fundamental hiddenness of God's grace)[65] contrasts to Jenson's view that the church is the countercultural organism that partakes in deified life. Here, in contrast to Jenson's institutionalism, a functionalism ought to prevail. The church is to deliver the goods. It is not itself to be conflated with the goods. What are these goods? The seven signs indicate that they are the forgiveness of sins, life, and salvation; it is these goods that are to be delivered within institutions of the world. That the devil holds much turf is never a reason to turn one's back on the world. The church, "mother of Christians,"[66] including both the ungodly who are Christian in name only and the godly who share both the Christian name

---

63. Martin Luther, *The Bondage of the Will*, trans. J. I. Packer and O. R. Johnston (New York: Fleming H. Revell, 1957), p. 170 (WA 18:685).

64. See "On the Councils and the Church," in LW 41:148-68 (WA 50:628ff.).

65. Forde rightly argues that the pairing of hiddenness and revealedness ought to prevail over that of invisible and visible. See *Theology Is for Proclamation*, p. 189.

66. "The Large Catechism," in BC 436:42 (BSELK 655:5).

and the Spirit, will remain a body "hidden under the cross" until the end of time.[67] And yet, the promise is that the gates of Hell will never prevail against her (Matt. 16:18). There was no ideal church in the past — including the apostolic, patristic, and medieval eras — and there will be no ideal church in the future. If, as the noted Bavarian missional pastor Wilhelm Löhe (1808-1872) taught, we are to make the invisible church as visible as possible[68] — through proclamation of the gospel, faithful liturgy, exercising appropriate discipline, building life-nourishing community, and reaching out to those suffering and in need — it will not be in an attempt to surmount this invisibility, this hiddenness. Seek simplicity and distrust it, said Whitehead. Likewise, seek for the church to be iconic of the kingdom — and at the same time distrust its apparent iconicity. Our confidence is to be placed in the gospel alone. The hearing of faith is not directly discernible to this age. Hence, the body of Christ exists in the eyes of faith alone.

Jenson and Luther

Jenson appeals to Luther's theology as mediated by the new Finns to support his view of justification as not primarily forensic but ontological, a change in the human soul that allows its full transformation toward deification. Luther indeed speaks of the efficacy of the word in human interiority. From his monastic background, Luther employs the metaphor of the soul as a "bride" of Christ and married to Christ. This talk is pivotal for his discussion of the "happy exchange."[69] Since the soul is wed to Christ, Christ's gifts belong to the soul, and the soul's liabilities belong to Christ. There is an exchange of liabilities for Christ's treasures — all as a generous gift. Yet, Christ's alien righteousness remains alien. His "interior" righteousness, effectuated by a word that transgresses the boundaries of "one's" interiority, remains *other*. God's promises, Luther notes, "saturate" and "intoxicate" the soul.[70] We are all, even more than Spinoza, God-intoxicated through faith in this promise that shapes our identity. Surely

---

67. "Apology," in BC 176:18 (BSELK 238:4).

68. See Todd Nichol, "Wilhelm Löhe, the Iowa Synod, and the Ordained Ministry," *Lutheran Quarterly* 4 (1990): 12 (quoting Siegfried Hiebart).

69. Luther, *The Freedom of a Christian*, in LW 31:351 (WA 7:53).

70. LW 31:349 (WA 7:53).

the diachronicity of the promise is its speech act so as to establish new identities through time, in those "baked" as "one cake" with Christ.[71] We are absorbed into Christ's story; his story becomes one with our lives. As our interiority is so altered by this efficacious word — the delivery of its forensic judgment of forgiveness for Jesus' sake — God establishes and continues to nurture new beings, who are restored to creation as God intends it. It is not that God offers an analytic judgment by evaluating an ontological righteousness provided by a prior union of the soul with Christ, but that God synthetically evaluates "whores" as his "bride." Through such excessive generosity, God allows our energy to be channeled as love for him and also for our neighbors, heedless of reward.

We are not only righteous but also sinful by faith alone. Sinfulness is not empirically measurable any more than works-righteousness. It is by faith that we acknowledge that we do not fear, love, and trust in God above all things, but look to other gods, other powers, even our own selves to provide for our needs. It offers the "solemn exchange"[72] of attributing to God wisdom in exercising his right over his own. It also rejoices in the "happy exchange" in which, through the word, one receives a closeness between oneself and Christ like the unity of heat and iron in a heated iron.[73] With Jenson, the possibility arises that grace provides transformation *coram deo* in higher degrees of mimetic participation in God through a greater harmonization within ecclesial life, like a musical harmony that knows no minor notes or lack of syncopation. Such "ascent" sidesteps the *pathos* of the cross whereby God is ever regenerative, eliciting an enjoyment of a beauty that can only be discerned along with dissonance and ambiguity.

Jenson fails to understand that the forensic imputation is effective. The new being in Christ is daily remade, a fresh dying and rising with Christ. The word ends an old, incurvated identity and establishes a new one — altering the spiral of incurvation and allowing a spontaneous, natural urge for truthfully attributing the source of one's energy to God alone and service to those in need. We "participate" in God not as we are elevated in higher, seemingly more inclusive patterns of triune sociability (like Plato

---

71. See William H. Lazareth, *Christians in Society: Luther, the Bible, and Social Ethics* (Minneapolis: Fortress, 2001), p. 185.

72. See Eberhard Jüngel, *The Freedom of a Christian: Luther's Significance for Contemporary Theology,* trans. Roy A. Harrisville (Minneapolis: Augsburg, 1988), p. 62.

73. LW 31:349.

and Hegel), but as incarnated in concrete acts of service to others (like Saint Paul). Such spontaneous love opened by faith allows one to "rejoice with those who rejoice and weep with those who weep" (Rom. 12:15). To find ways to help those weeping and share with those rejoicing takes appropriate venues of creativity, all of which contribute to God's ongoing creative work *(creatio continua).*[74] Such human creativity is an outgrowth of the passivity that we experience from God's creation, redemption, and sanctification of our lives in the agencies of the church, the home, and the state.

Jenson's conflation of gospel and church would likewise be problematic for Luther. The world has possibly lost its story. More likely, it has substituted Enlightenment mythologies of progress for that of ancient Epicurean *Fortuna.* The church, in response, needs to be clear about its story. Its story provides it an identity and is coupled with appropriate practices (through which God's service is offered to us), which contribute to and sustain this ecclesial life. However, Jenson's work tends to demonize the world as impure, and falsely establishes the church as empirically capable of social purity. Jenson's route is problematic for both world and church. Admittedly, the world is a *locus* for demonic activity. Jenson's identifying the church as having lost its narrative identity is on target. Yet, it is in this wounded cosmos in which the world bears the mark of its curse and yearns for its renewal that God is working, not least to limit the devil's power. Even the devil, for all his evil and woe, is God's devil; the devil's power is limited. If the "heavens" continue "to declare God's glory" and if the "earth shows forth his handiwork" (Ps. 19), then this world — despite its false self-identifications — reflects God's power and creativity. Nihilism is an expression of divine wrath operative in a human world that will not honor God. It offers a life that is a living hell, an "eternal recurrence" of the same (Nietzsche). However, even nihilism is a symbol that God has not abandoned his world, insofar as his wrath is an alien work expressed for the sake of his care. However, the church is best seen not as a counterculture that could serve as an end in itself. Rather, the church — particularly its leadership, but all are included — is the aegis of the "delivery people." The point of the church is to deliver Jesus Christ as primarily sacrament *(sacramentum),* and only secondarily as example *(exemplum).* The first task is gospel in its pure form. The church lives from the gospel and likewise fosters the gospel.

74. Lazareth, *Christians in Society,* p. 66.

Part of Jenson's ecumenical quest is to reclaim an authority for the church that mainline Protestantism has been unable to assert. Jenson's quest for such authority is not misguided. It is not the affirmation of an appropriate authority in the church that is off-target, but the grounding of gospel authority solely in the legal authority of a historic episcopate. Even in a time in which authority is chronically undermined,[75] preachers will find that the divine word is sufficient to sustain them. The word as law and gospel creates the communal leadership that can give the social support, wise diplomacy, and healthy community needed for its proclamation. The authority of the gospel is unconditional because the promise is unconditional. We need not look to Jenson's trio of Scripture, creed, and teaching office to support authority. *Sola scriptura* must prevail. Undoubtedly, the gospel is embedded in the creeds and teaching office. However, these latter two receive life from the gospel insofar as they convey gospel. Jenson fails to understand that both world and church remain ambiguous. The goodness of creation is often hidden, and the purity of the church is likewise hidden.

Finally, where is the cross for Jenson? It is lost in the *pathos* of the church. The delivery system is substituted for the message itself! This should not surprise us, given his dependence on Hegelian *Aufhebung*. The focus of theology should be not on an alleged *theosis* of the church but on the cross for the world. What then becomes of Jesus Christ? George Hunsinger names the Christ that we lose in Jenson's theology:

> As authorized by scripture, constitutive of tradition, and enshrined in every eucharistic liturgy worthy of the name, he [Jesus Christ] is the Lamb of God that takes away the sin of the world. He has borne our sin on the cross and borne it away. He has suffered what sinners rightly deserved — the divine judgment, curse, condemnation and wrath — in order that they might be spared. While they were yet sinners, he died in their place, despite their enmity toward his person and work, that by his love they might themselves be made new.[76]

If we are to have the gospel, it is this crucified Christ who must be proclaimed. Roses, then, are not to be put on the cross of Jesus. It is both law and gospel. It is law as accusation:

75. See Eugene Kennedy and Sara C. Charles, *Authority: The Most Misunderstood Idea in America* (New York: Free Press, 1997).

76. Hunsinger, "Robert Jenson's *Systematic Theology*," p. 163.

Who was the guilty?
Who brought this upon thee?
Alas, my treason, Jesus, hath undone thee.
'Twas I, Lord Jesus, I it was denied thee.
I crucified thee![77]

As law, the cross cannot be negated and preserved by a higher vision of the true, the beautiful, and the good. It is one's end. *CRUX sola est nostra theologia!* (The cross alone is our theology!)[78]

However, the cross is also gospel. It is God's gift of exchanging sinfulness, incurvation, and self-centeredness for Christ's life, righteousness, and love. It takes away wrath and assures that God is for me because God has claimed the crucified, who bears Peter the denier, Magdalene the prostitute, and Paul the murderer as his own. The cross is God's affirmation of his claim over me the sinner in opposition to any other claimant. Luther sings,

To me he [Christ] said: "Stay close to me,
I am your rock and castle.
Your ransom I myself will be;
For you I strive and wrestle;
For I am yours, and you are mine,
And where I am you may remain;
The foe shall not divide us."[79]

Christ alone can expiate this evil, not the *totus Christus*. This latter concept seeks a transparency with respect to our relation to God that is not afforded us this side of the *eschaton*.

Summary and Critical Assessment

✓ Why did Jenson disavow confessional Lutheranism? The confessionalism that he, early in his career, represented wanted to package itself as mainline Protestantism. However, this mainline Protestantism that he then helped

77. Johann Heermann, LBW #123.
78. WA 5:176, 32.
79. Martin Luther, LBW #299.

to create was too accommodating to the wider culture. Many of its leaders increasingly saw their roles as those of therapists, managers, or social workers. Their first confessional loyalty was to creeds concocted by Freud, Friedman, or Marx, and had little bearing on the classical education that had nurtured Jenson and that he still tried to foster. With an increasing democratization of the church, in which theologians and conscientious clergy had less say, and where voting at national conventions was swayed by the theologically uninformed, Jenson sought an alternative to such accommodation. He turned to an "evangelical" catholicity. However, this meant not just that he accepted the need for a reform movement in the church catholic, but that he would reject the law-gospel distinction as the basis and boundary of theology.

Ironically, the content of Jenson's views of God remained mainline Protestant — as mediated through Hegel. Hence, the future as God's *entelechy,* as well as the model of Trinity-as-society, not Trinity-as-subject, became operative in his thinking. With respect to content, his view of the Trinity and the church is markedly similar to that of Pannenberg and Moltmann. Admittedly, Pannenberg's chief strategy is to subordinate the church to the kingdom as a more inclusive theological category, while it could be argued that Jenson's strategy is just the opposite. However, the overall sentiment is the same. For all these thinkers, the end has already happened in the resurrection of Jesus Christ, and now all cosmic and human history is moving toward its divine *telos,* offering a fulfillment of the divine ambition itself.

Yet, Jenson's rejection of mainline Protestantism as an adequate vehicle of the church's identity gets at the core of accommodationist strategies. Pannenberg, Jüngel, and Moltmann, each in their own ways, seek a foundation for Christian faith shared by non-Christians — a quest for totality, or for a unique, life-giving experience, or for an ideal, completely fair society. Jenson shares no such commonality, no such foundation, with the world. Instead, he offers the church as a clear alternative to the world; the world has no story, while the church's story is guided by the *telos* of God. What makes his view most problematic of all is that it asks us to accept this as good news instead of the promise itself. However, since the promise is ultimate, the community it creates and sustains is penultimate.

What is negative with respect to Jenson's theology for our constructive purposes? As with Pannenberg, Jüngel, and Moltmann, we can list the following: (1) his tendency to map deity on the basis of futurity, (2) his seeing the cross as the *locus* of making the finite infinite and vice versa (as opposed to our *finis*), (3) his affirmation of the *totus Christus* as a potential basis for synergy *coram deo*, (4) his subordination of a forensic to an ontological view of justification, and (5) his claim that sanctification is imitative participation in the divine life. These five features, insofar as they are paralleled in the previous three thinkers, reflect the contemporary natural theology of the cross as it must be addressed today. The transformation of faith into theory, ethics, or a unique feeling has resulted in new orthodoxies in both church and academy. They need to be challenged.

What can we learn from Jenson? With respect to modernity, Jenson wants a non-accommodating, though non-sectarian, strategy. Instead of letting the fact-value split position his theology, as do Pannenberg, Jüngel, and Moltmann, he critiques modernity's rejection of Platonism and Aristotelianism. In this regard he should be affirmed. He is particularly sensitive to the rampant individualism and nihilism that continue to guide Western economics and *ethos,* as well as a lack of appropriate authority in the office of ministry. While his answers to these problems are to be rejected, his raising the appropriate questions certainly is not.

Chapter Six

Oswald Bayer:
Justification and the
Theology of the Speech Act

While not as widely known in the English-speaking world as the three other German theologians examined here, Tübingen systematician Oswald Bayer has distinguished himself as one of the foremost interpreters of both Luther[1] and Johann Georg Hamann (1730-1788),[2] as well as the doctrine of justification,[3] and as a theorist of the task of systematic theology.[4] This work has been done in tandem with other important theological disciplines.[5] My critique of the previous thinkers is significantly indebted to Bayer's insights. It is difficult, if not impossible, to separate the doctrine of justification from Bayer's thinking at virtually any point in his theology. Few contemporary systematicians focus as consistently or adamantly as Bayer on justification *sola fide* as the "basis" and "boundary" of

---

1. Bayer, *Promissio: Geschichte der reformatorischen Wende in Luthers Theologie,* 2d ed. (Darmstadt: Wissenschaftliche Buchgesellschaft, 1989).

2. Bayer, *Zeitgenosse im Widerspruch: Johann Georg Hamann als radikaler Aufklärer* (Munich: Piper Verlag, 1988) and *Vernunft ist Sprache: Hamanns Metakritik Kants* (Stuttgart: Frommann-Holzboog, 2002).

3. AGL (LBF).

4. See Theologie. See also *Gott als Autor: Zu einer poietologischen Theologie* (Tübingen: Mohr Siebeck, 1999) and *Was ist das: Theologie? Eine Skizze* (Stuttgart: Calwer Verlag, 1973).

5. For his work in hermeneutics, see AK; for his theology of creation, see SA; for essays in historical theology, see LWRNK; and for his work in ethics, see *Freiheit als Antwort: Zur theologischen Ethik* (Tübingen: Mohr Siebeck, 1999) and *Zugesagte Freiheit: Zur Grundlegung theologischer Ethik* (Gütersloh: Gütersloher Verlaghaus, 1980).

theology.[6] To that end, he offers important correctives to the accommodations to or rejections of modernity that have been operative in the work of the four previous theorists.

For Bayer, truth is to be found not in a comprehensive knowing (Pannenberg), or in doing (Moltmann), or as attested by a meta-experience (Jüngel), or in a Catholic community (Jenson), or in hybrid combinations of these, but rather in a performative word (akin to J. L. Austin's [1911-1960] theory of the speech act)[7] in which the promise *(promissio)* of the gospel is efficacious. The promise delivers the goods of the forgiveness of sins, life, and salvation. Given the rigor and wide-ranging scope of his thinking, Bayer's theology deserves wide recognition, not only for the purposes of offering the church a responsible ecumenics or articulating a robust theology of mission, but also for its implications for how the academy conducts its research and configures theological method. Bayer's thinking has profound implications for challenging the university's Weberian tendency to dichotomize instrumental reason, with its bias toward subject matter amenable to measurement, and "values," conceived as wholly subjective desires. For Bayer, a proper understanding of language — particularly the relation between narration and explanation[8] — subverts this false polarization.

Bayer's work seeks to correct the existentialist matrix that has shaped contemporary views of the doctrine of justification, articulated particularly by Gerhard Ebeling.[9] Bayer draws on the conviction that for Luther, justification is not individualistic or egoistic, as criticism has long suggested. For example, Emanuel Swedenborg (1688-1772) sees the Lutheran as "locked up in a darkened room his entire life. Pacing back and forth in the room, unable to see anything, he searches for light by repeating only one sentence to himself: 'I am justified by faith alone; I am justified by

---

6. Bayer, "Justification as the Basis and Boundary of Theology," trans. Christine Helmer, *Lutheran Quarterly* 15 (2001): 273-92.

7. See J. L. Austin, *How to Do Things with Words,* ed. J. O. Urmson and Marina Sbisa (Cambridge: Harvard University Press, 1962), and especially "Performative-Constative," in *Philosophy and Ordinary Language,* ed. Charles E. Caton (Urbana: University of Illinois Press, 1970), pp. 22-54.

8. For Bayer, narration without explanation is empty, while explanation without narration is blind; see "Erzählung und Erklärung," in *Gott als Autor,* p. 254; see also "Wahrheit oder Methode?," in AK 89.

9. Ebeling, *Luther: An Introduction to His Thought,* trans. R. A. Wilson (Philadelphia: Fortress, 1983). It is Eberhard Jüngel's views that are most indebted to Ebeling.

faith alone; I am justified by faith alone!'"[10] In contrast, Bayer maintains that justification, when properly understood, offers social and cosmic breadth as much as existential depth.[11] According to Bayer, "Not only our relationship to God and ourselves is made new through justification by faith but at the same time our relationships with 'all creatures' are renewed."[12]

Indeed, justification has import for both the world and natural history. It offers a hermeneutics for interpreting God's action in nature and history as wrath or grace. The most decisive aspect of Bayer's thinking for Luther scholars, systematic theologians, and preachers is his unfolding of justification's significance as embracing external physical reality, history, and culture as mediums of God's hiddenness and self-disclosure. Justification then deals not primarily with a meta-experience but with language as "speech acts," illocutionary linguistic doings that alter not merely the "inner" life of the individual but also the "external" social world.[13] Bayer sees a point of contact between Luther's concept of *promissio*,[14] the gospel as a performative word, and J. L. Austin's view of language as illocutionary, as shaping life. Unlike Moltmann, who has a tendency to transform the gospel into a comprehensive *praxis* (a justifying behavior), Bayer believes the gospel is to be found as a "Categorical Gift" (not categorical imperative).[15] Unlike Pannenberg, who has a tendency to transform the gospel into a comprehensive *theoria* (a justifying thinking), Bayer sees the gospel as a word of promise, not a description of the totality of reality.

For Bayer, creation itself can convey this categorical gift, subverting all notions of merit that we might find either in a re-invigorated evangelical Catholicism, such as Jenson's, or in a Kantian "practical reason." Following the thinking of the Lutheran hymnist Paul Gerhard (1607-1676), Bayer notes that God does not "fairly" repay humans faithful to him. The "repayment" has *already been paid* and thus is a gift that is unearned

---

10. Bayer, "Justification as the Basis and Boundary of Theology," p. 273.

11. Bayer, "Justification as the Basis and Boundary of Theology," p. 274.

12. Bayer, "Justification as the Basis and Boundary of Theology," p. 274.

13. See Theologie, C, 3.2, pp. 440-42.

14. See Bayer, "Martin Luther," in *The Reformation Theologians: An Introduction to Theology in the Early Modern Period,* ed. Carter Lindberg (Oxford: Blackwell, 2002), pp. 54-55.

15. Bayer, "Justification as the Basis and Boundary of Theology," p. 276.

and solely granted: "As if your God had not already given to you!"[16] Drawing out the consequences of this line of reasoning, Bayer writes,

> Living in the poverty that accords with the gospel means allowing oneself to be determined by this kind of having. What do you have that you did not receive? Facing this question we are forced to change our outlook, we who are among the richest on this earth. Our hearts change when we acknowledge that we have received, and so do our being and having, and with them the distribution of the fruits of this earth.[17]

Bayer's work corrects the tendency to separate forensic and effective justification. Justification is not the allegedly fictive verdict of the divine judge upon the penitent, but is simultaneously effective in that it grants pardon, remission, and new life in its very institution, the words of absolution. As effective, it liberates the penitent's heart, which has been bound by incurvation. Bayer claims, "To be freed from judging or justifying oneself is the meaning of being justified by faith alone. And this means nothing less than being removed from the situation in which 'every "I" tries to be his own father and Creator,' in which one may — or even must — be also 'one's own killer.' The 'I' is freed, like Israel liberated out of Egyptian captivity."[18]

The doctrine of justification thwarts the systematician's tendency to seek an encyclopedic, "God's eye" view of all reality, from the most trivial puff of experience in far-flung space to God's very being itself, because when Luther's thinking is taken seriously, it subverts the tendency to unify all experience by means of making the finite infinite or the infinite finite, as structured by the Hegelian illusion that "the real is the rational and the rational is the real."[19] Configuring the thinking of Hegel, Kant, Schleiermacher, and their contemporary representatives is Aristotle's view of reason as "monarchic," that it independently rules as king over all other aspects of human experience.[20] In Hamannian fashion, Bayer contends that

---

16. Bayer, "Justification as the Basis and Boundary of Theology," p. 276.

17. Bayer, "Luther's Ethics as Pastoral Care," *Lutheran Quarterly* 4 (1990): 137.

18. Bayer, "Justification as the Basis and Boundary of Theology," p. 280.

19. "What is rational is actual and what is actual is rational." See Hegel, *Philosophy of Right*, trans. T. M. Knox (London: Oxford University Press, 1981), p. 10.

20. See Theologie, A, 1.1.2, p. 25.

there is no reason per se, only reasons.[21] Likewise, the quest for "system" is a hindrance to truth. Bayer lists four features from Luther's thinking that cannot be systematized by means of a unifying, overarching structure of practical or theoretical reason, but that likewise cannot be excluded from our understanding of faith. These four features are (1) the law as accusing, (2) the gospel as promising, (3) divine hiddenness as terrifying, and (4) divine providence as conserving the world.[22] Hence, with these four factors in play, one must walk by faith and not by sight in relation to God because they will never be harmonizable into a single, unified grand theory of the universe this side of the *eschaton*.

Hamann, Luther, and Hermeneutics

Bayer's thinking is significantly indebted to that of Johann Georg Hamann (1730-1788). Of course, this is true only with respect to the content, not the style, of their thinking, since Bayer submits his work to the highest standards of academic rigor as currently defined, whereas the rigor of Hamann's work is akin to that of the polyphony of a Baroque cantata, and whose pseudonymity conveys truth indirectly. Perhaps the most important aspect that Bayer learns from Hamann is that theology's task is largely discernment, not construction. Hamann yokes David Hume's (1711-1776) skepticism of metaphysics' ability to configure all reality, grounded in his empiricism, with Luther's theology of God, in which, if one attempts to decipher God (in a theology of glory), one will encounter the *deus absconditus*. For Bayer, theology is not done to integrate all knowledge, either theoretical or practical, into an abstract unity, but to limit reason to its proper fields. It is the art of discerning what God is saying to us, not peering into the divine. That said, Hamann, not as a counter-Enlightener or an irrationalist,[23] but as a "radical Enlightener"[24] (Enlightenment as configured in Christ, the "exegesis of God"[25]), is important for Bayer because

---

21. Bayer, "Bibliotherapie," in AK 39.

22. See Theologie, 2.1.

23. See Isaiah Berlin, *The Magnus of the North: J. G. Hamann and the Origins of Modern Irrationalism* (London: Fontana, 1994).

24. "Hamann ist kein Gegenaufklärer, sondern radikaler Aufklärer." See "Kreuzes-philologie," in LWRNK 112.

25. "In der von Jesus Christus, dem 'Exegeten' Gottes, hergestellten Vermittlung

Hamann's thinking offers a bridge whereby Luther can indirectly address concerns in the modern period that were only embryonic in Luther's own lifetime and about which we can only infer Luther's response. Bayer also brings Hamann into conversation with and critique of not only the Kantian tradition, which Hamann knew firsthand, but also with the theologies of Hegel and Schleiermacher, whose most fundamental assumptions about metaphysics and epistemology are situated by Kant. Through Hamann's work, Bayer is able to bring Luther's voice to bear upon the highly anthropocentric concerns of modern thinkers, ironically critiquing them as at heart spirit-infused *Schwärmer* who disdain the inability of sensuousness, physicality, and culture to be systematized.

Embedded in the Kantian framework (which also affected both Hegel and Schleiermacher) is a deeply Platonic dimension that vestigially remains in and contours all of modernity. This Platonism favors the supersensual over the sensual and can be found as the anamnesis (calling to memory) of the "pure categories,"[26] prior to language, by which the "transcendental ego"[27] shapes its experiences. Here, the mediation of experience by language is ignored. For Hamann, in contrast, without language there is no reason, no world.[28] Likewise the "substrate" of the "transcendental ego" — comparable to the Cartesian "ghost in the machine"[29] — is a pure spirit seeking explanations, impervious to physical enmeshment or narrative emplotment. Skeptical of the Aristotelian view of fourfold causality (material, formal, efficient, and final) assumed in the metaphysical undertaking, Hamann relocated God's agency outside the matrix of causality altogether (including the modern bias in favor of efficient causality), and in scriptural and creedal terms sees God as the "poet" who narrates life, our biography, and who through his word scripts our life history within that of the whole world, opening our lives as a "conversation" with God.[30] Given the

---

reden Natur und Geschichte als Schöpfung; Jesus Christus ist der Schöpfungsmittler." See "Schöpfung als 'Rede an die Kreatur durch die Kreatur': Die Frage nach dem Schlüssel zum Buch der Natur und Geschichte," in SA 25.

26. Kant, *Critique of Pure Reason,* trans. Norman Kemp Smith (New York: St. Martin's Press, 1929), pp. 111-19.

27. Kant, *Critique of Pure Reason,* pp. 157-61.

28. Hamann writes, in a letter to F. H. Jacobi (April 29, 1787), "Ohne Wort, keine Vernunft — keine Welt. Hier ist die Quelle der Schöpfung und Regierung." See LWRNK 113.

29. This is Gilbert Ryle's (1900-1976) phrase.

30. See "God as Author of My Life-History," *Lutheran Quarterly* 2 (1988): 437-56.

Lutheran supposition that it is Scripture that interprets us and not we who interpret Scripture *(sacra scriptura sui ipsius interpres)*, Hamann affirmed that it is God who gives human life meaning by interpreting it.[31] The self is no culture- and history-independent transcendental ego, but found only and thoroughly in narrative, particularly that of Scripture. Thus, Hamann sought to apply law and gospel as interpretive keys not only to preaching but also to all experience, even to theoretical science, and Bayer follows suit.[32] As such, neither Hamann nor Bayer abides the notion that nature and history are wholly opposite realities or that explanation and understanding are wholly opposite modes of knowledge. After all, in Bayer's interpretation, nature and history speak together as creation in Jesus Christ.

Hamann teaches metacritique as a response to Enlightenment critique. In its critique of authority, tradition, culture, otherness, and especially in its quest for a pure (non-contingent) knowing or doing, Enlightenment thinking represses sensuality, physicality, and tradition. Hamann brought these factors to the fore as inescapable features of experience that curtail the possibility of achieving an encyclopedic scope for the tasks of knowing or doing. It is a "rhetoric of assent,"[33] we might say, that allowed Hamann to interpret all of life and experience in light of Scripture, the key that unlocks the meaning of both nature and history.

Language is the connection that links Hamann to both Luther and J. L. Austin. For Hamann, language is the horizon of reality; we can seek nothing deeper than what language both discloses and conceals. Language is likewise creative of experience, since it shapes and orders it, opening horizons of possibility for human life. Language, in Hamann's terms, brings "nature" and "institution" together; thereby it shapes life.[34] Likewise, J. L. Austin helps us understand life as linguistically structured in his description of "how to do things with words." In his attempt to explain Luther's

---

31. AK 6.

32. "Hamann macht die Unterscheidung von Gesetz und Evangelium wissenschaftstheoretisch geltend, er macht sie geltend für die Methodenfragen — nicht nur für die Methodenfragen der Theologie, sondern der Philosophie, der Philologie, überhaupt jeder Wissenschaft, einschleißlich der naturwissenschaft. Dieses Verfahren ist überaus kühn." See "Text und Selbstbewusstsein," in AK 25.

33. See Wayne Booth, *Modern Dogma and the Rhetoric of Assent* (Chicago: University of Chicago Press, 1970).

34. See "Nature and Institution: Luther's Doctrine of the Three Orders," trans. Luis Dreher, *Lutheran Quarterly* 12 (1998): 125-59.

"Reformation discovery," Bayer sees that these two thinkers, in concert, offer an analysis of language as creative, unfolding life. That is, Luther's Reformation insight is profoundly hermeneutical. Bayer writes of Luther:

> His "Reformation discovery" happened in the wake of a deeply profound reflection on the sacrament of penance, which had been required of him by the monstrosity of indulgences. At first, Luther understood the priestly word of absolution: "I absolve you of your sins!" as an activity of declaration, which states something already present. The priest sees the remorse, takes it as a sign of the divine justification — the divine absolution occurring already in the one being absolved but unknown to him — and lets this appear as such. He states it for the assurance of the one being absolved. By this means the word of absolution is understood as a judgment in the sense of a statement.[35]

The result of Luther's Reformation discovery was that language is no longer to be viewed solely as a system of signs "that refer to objects or situations or of signs that express an emotion. In either case the sign is — as a statement or as an expression — not the reality itself. In other words, the linguistic sign is itself the reality; that it represents not an absent but a present reality was Luther's great hermeneutical discovery, his 'Reformation Discovery' in the strict sense."[36] It can be classified as a speech act that is an "effective, active word that establishes community and therein frees and makes certain. It does what it says. It says what it does."[37] For Luther, this effective word is also discovered in the sacraments of baptism and the Lord's Supper, the stories of Christmas ("Fear not!") and Easter ("Lo, I am with you always!") — "indeed in the whole Bible, including the story of creation, which Luther understood as a promise, as his translation of Psalm 33:4b indicates, 'what he promises, that he certainly does.'"[38]

Bayer's understanding of the meaning of the Reformation as inescapably hermeneutical is furthered by his work on Hamann. The Bible is (in Goethe's terms) a "mirror of the world."[39] But, for that matter, the

---

35. Bayer, "Martin Luther as an Interpreter of Holy Scripture," in *The Cambridge Companion to Luther,* trans. Mark Mattes (Cambridge: Cambridge University Press, 2003), pp. 75-76.

36. Bayer, "Martin Luther as an Interpreter of Holy Scripture," p. 76.

37. Bayer, "Martin Luther as an Interpreter of Holy Scripture," p. 76.

38. Bayer, "Martin Luther as an Interpreter of Holy Scripture," p. 76.

39. Bayer, "Martin Luther as an Interpreter of Holy Scripture," p. 73.

world is itself akin to a Bible in that God is constantly speaking to humans — through either judgment or grace — in all realities, however trivial or grand. This is Hamann's profoundly Christological conviction that "God speaks to the creature through the creature." It is Christological because in Jesus Christ, both the creator and the creature are one *(ibi creator et creaturum unus et idem est)*;[40] God addresses the rest of creation in Jesus. Focused through the lens of Jesus Christ, all things in creation are capable of mediating God's address. Properly understood, *creation is address.* "There are no creatures that God cannot use as his messengers: human beings and stars, animals and elements, a particular succession of notes in a fugue by Bach, Apollo's torso that says to you, 'You must change your life,' music, the beauty of art, and even the ugly. God can make everything that is created, the visible and the invisible, into his angels [interpreters]."[41]

This reading of creation as God's address to humans, an arena of God's justifying word and not a theater of *Heilsgeschichte,* has significant implications for both aesthetics and science. It subverts the fact-value split that has dogged the previous four thinkers. The believer is aesthetically permitted a "sense and taste for the finite," in contrast to Schleiermacher's quasi-Platonic "sense and taste for the infinite."[42] The new life in Christ is not reducible to ethics. Rather, the senses are opened; one can enjoy and experience the world as sheer gift. The world is not a carcass that is to be dissected. Nor is it an idol re-divinized by a romanticism of nature for the sake of providing meaning to a mechanical, impersonal world.[43] With respect to nature, moderns have taken the role of consumers and judges in their quest for control through measurement; the senses then remain closed to the immeasurable beauty of the world. Justification by faith alone opens the senses to the interconnectedness of oneself with all other creatures *(samt allen kreaturen),* as Luther put it in his explanation of the first article of the Creed in the *Small Catechism.* In hymns of praise and in lamentation, in all forms of worship (which is foremost and primarily God's service to us [*Gottesdienst*]) as centered in Scripture, particularly in praying and meditating on the Psalter, we find that our affections interpenetrate with the word, and vice versa, so that

---

40. Bayer, "Schöpfung als 'Rede an die Kreatur durch die Kreatur,'" in SA 18.

41. Bayer, "Angels Are Interpreters," *Lutheran Quarterly* 13 (1999): 271.

42. See *On Religion,* trans. John Oman (New York: Harper & Row, 1958), pp. 39, 36.

43. See "Schöpfung als 'Rede an die Kreatur durch die Kreatur,'" in SA 24. See also *Theologie,* C, 2.3.3.

they are remolded and reshaped in light of scriptural narratives and genres. With the senses opened to creation as God's address to us, the church itself, especially as praying and meditating on the Psalter, becomes a "universal community of communication,"[44] primarily with God, but also diachronically with all its past members, and synchronically with the entire cosmos. It is axiomatic for Bayer that all theology arises from the worship service and returns back to it.

Bayer believes that such communication can open a world in which we hear God's address in all created realities. We miss this communication when all that we seek in the creation is only to measure it for the sake of greater control. For Bayer, this approach to science ultimately is tantamount to a kind of theodicy in which we aim to protect ourselves from chaos by dissecting or "cutting up" nature in order to gain as much power as possible over nature's uncontrollable forces.[45] The sciences, like the Mosaic law, ought rather to be a "schoolmaster"[46] that leads us to Christ, who alone can set us free. In scientific method, we should acknowledge that all the sciences must assume a process of translation; there is no explanation apart from narration.[47] Otherwise, even mathematical concepts are arbitrarily defined, and their poetic character is forgotten.[48]

Metacritique and the Nature of Reason

One of Bayer's greatest contributions to theology is his intense engagement with the nature, limits, and focus of reason in light of Luther's view of justification. Reason is clearly affirmed in what it can offer. However, reason also has its limitations, given finite and incurvated human nature. The task of metacritique is to evaluate reason's powers and limitations, specifically within the Enlightenment project of critiquing tradition and authority. Too often justification's import is limited to an existential experience for the believer. We fail to recognize that taking justification seriously has bearing upon the nature of reason itself, especially since we are to love God with all our heart, soul, strength, and *reason*. In Bayer's perspective, we remain true

44. AK 7.
45. Bayer, "Schöpfung als 'Rede an die Kreatur durch die Kreatur,'" in SA 19.
46. Bayer, "Text und Selbstbewusstsein," in AK 23.
47. See "Wahrheit oder Methode?" in AK 89.
48. Bayer, "Wahrheit oder Methode?" in AK 92-94.

to a theology of the cross *(theologia crucis)* only in opposition to the Hegelian move to affirm a "natural theology of the cross" *(theologia crucis naturalis)*[49] with its implicit intellectualizing of experience and inherent theodicy, thus parting ways with Jüngel, Pannenberg, Moltmann, and Jenson. We offer our reason as service to the neighbor when it is unleashed as the capacity to understand nature and history for the sake of the flourishing of life, not as offering a flight into a pure, nonsensuous framework, independent of tradition, culture, or history. Thus, one must avoid all Platonically inspired notions of reason that situate it within an Augustinian and Anselmic "faith seeking understanding" *(fides quaerens intellectum)* approach. Understanding offers one no "higher" standing with respect to God than faith. It is faith that is pleasing to God. Faith liberates nature as love, and reason *coram mundo* is one form of love, pleasing to God. Thinking is to be seen as fundamentally *meditatio,* done in the context of *oratio* and within the experience of *tentatio.*[50] Faith liberates thinking for service. Bayer supports Protestant theology by challenging the critique of faith and understanding developed in the Enlightenment. He not only unmasks those aspects of human experience that Kant ignored, but also shows how Kantianism's weaknesses were absorbed into other antecedents of modern and contemporary theology.

Bayer's metacritique exposes what he names as the "Modern Narcissus."[51] Modernity has sought to see human agency as able to "ground" itself, independent of an external good, even the highest, which would by definition be heteronomous and thus threaten human liberty, now reconceived in terms of self-ownership and self-possession. Of course, this wholly anthropocentric view of life is at odds with Luther's view of life as a *vita passiva* and of human agency as free only when it is liberated from incurvation. Of the modern philosophers, Bayer notes,

> From Descartes to Kant the concepts of autonomy and freedom were based on self-ascertainment and do not claim to legitimize or ground the self. Since Fichte, Marx, and Sartre, however, what is human has been understood in a more radical light than what was thought to be human nature in the Middle Ages, with which Luther was concerned.

49. Theologie, C, 6.3, p. 514.
50. Theologie, A, 3.4.
51. Bayer, "The Modern Narcissus," trans. Christine Helmer, *Lutheran Quarterly* 9 (1995): 301-13.

The modern human being thinks of himself, from beginning to end, as a doer and maker. In the terms of Karl Marx, a human being produces him- or herself through work, "self-production" by "work."[52]

There is no Sabbath rest for this human. The onus of the entire world rests on his or her shoulders. One is thus doomed to be an Atlas.[53] Through "pure practical reason," moderns establish their own laws for themselves.[54] Nevertheless, they feel a burden or weight with respect to life and the world in that they, paradoxically, are not free in relation to their own expectation that they exercise their freedom. They are obliged to fulfill their potential, compelled to develop themselves, "condemned" to be free, as Jean-Paul Sartre (1905-1980) put it.[55] Moderns are no less "under law," to use Saint Paul's and Luther's term, than pre-moderns, although they have less recognition of their responsibility *coram deo*. Moderns are significantly more conflicted with respect to law and its final evaluation, since they find themselves with no *summum bonum* as an ultimate evaluator. They are thus positioned between an antinomianism which results from the belief that there is no objective final purpose to life, and a nomianism in which one is condemned to fulfill one's potential as the only way to extract meaning from life. This insight implies that the preaching of the gospel is no less "relevant" for moderns than pre-moderns. However, pre-moderns would far more easily be able to distinguish God as accusing from God as hidden, whereas for moderns, the two easily become conflated, since we are compelled to fulfill our potential on the horizon of an anonymous or even non-existent deity. With respect to the latter, the experience of God's wrath is captured, according to Bayer, in Friedrich Nietzsche's (1844-1900) phrase that a godless cosmos is composed of "a thousand wastes, silent, cold."[56]

Especially at stake for Bayer is the gospel as *promissio*, a speech act that delivers forgiveness of sins, life, and salvation, and that is not to be transformed into an ethical directive, a metaphysical description, or a meta-experience. It is a word of address that changes not only the reality of

---

52. Bayer, "Justification as the Basis and Boundary of Theology," p. 277.

53. Bayer, "Zukunft und Schöpfung," in SA 147.

54. See Kant, *Critique of Practical Reason*, trans. Lewis White Beck (Indianapolis: Bobbs-Merrill, 1956).

55. SA 147.

56. Bayer, "Martin Luther as an Interpreter of Holy Scripture," p. 82.

the addressee but also the entire web of interrelations which sustains that addressee and which is sustained by that addressee.

Dependent upon Hamann's evaluation of Kant's work, Bayer's metacritique extends to Kant, Hegel, and Schleiermacher. It also extends indirectly to the four other theologians with whom we have been dealing. Jüngel accepts the Kantian distinction between theoretical and practical reason, but opts to situate faith with respect to a meta-experience, an "experience with experience," similar to Schleiermacher's category of the "feeling of absolute dependence," all the while accepting the Hegelian "natural theology of the cross," in which God is wholly revealed through "identifying" with the human Jesus via a self-development which assumes a continuum between infinite divine reality and finite human reality. With respect to this divine identification, Pannenberg, like Jüngel, seeks to unmask the hidden God by adopting a Hegelian "natural theology of the cross," though he replaces Jüngel's incomparable meta-experience with a starting point in universal nature and history. Reason is embodied in history, and history is an expression of reason. Moltmann also accepts the Kantian dichotomization of pure and practical reason and, like Kant, favors the practical over the theoretical. Moltmann interprets the individual in highly experiential terms, like Schleiermacher does, all the while acknowledging that the individual is publicly subordinated to a "kingdom of ends" that will express the divine life in its fullness when it is finally materialized. Jenson aims to work outside of the Kantian framework altogether by appealing to a Catholic counterculture. But, for all that, his approach to God is still largely Hegelian, making the infinite finite and the finite infinite — to his mind, as we have seen, God is a "baptized God."

How can theology serve proclamation of the gospel, which finally alone legitimates theology? Seemingly, for these thinkers, theology's legitimation as a discipline in the university is determined by its ability to offer a way to cope with the world, or transform it on the basis of a set of ideals, or help it continue its cartography of all reality. What if none of these proposed salvations really saves? What if salvation is entirely in God's hands and not in ours at all? Is not the problem our ability to trust God's word to deliver the promise? In place of viewing theology as a task of integration that makes the Christian tradition conform to modernity, Bayer affirms that genuine theology is inherently conflictual, a continuous *disputatio* with those intellectual traditions that seek self-justification *coram deo*. One purpose of a theology faithful to the doctrine of justification is to challenge soteriological ramifications of the "secular" and allow the public square to be a forum for service.

Kant proposes an ethicization of life in which our being is to be found solely in doing, not in receiving, seeking to achieve a pure community, the "kingdom of ends." Schleiermacher proposes the task of the self as integrating itself via faith, having a *locus* primarily in the feeling of absolute dependence, not the word. Hegel proposes a *concupiscentia futurorum*[57] in which the finite and the infinite are reconciled through dialectics, the transparent rational monarchy in which the goal of *Geist's* history is mythically inscribed as the resurrection through the establishing of Christian community, beyond Jesus' crucifixion. In contrast, Bayer appeals to those four aspects of Luther's theology that simply refuse to be subordinated to monarchic reason's quest for unity. God's hiddenness itself especially thwarts our ability to map reality on the basis of theoretical or practical reason. Even Descartes's ploy of introducing an "evil genius" as the ultimate producer behind the theater of the cosmos is nowhere near as radically skeptical as the attitude resulting from affirming Luther's hidden God. Hence, Bayer writes,

> Yes, he [Luther] also encountered that God himself is at enmity with me and how God is my enemy: God becomes a demon to me if I do not look upon the crucified one. God is that omnipotence working life and death, love and hate. Both life-giving and life-denying, God works fortune and misfortune, good and evil. In short, God is all in all, entirely active in such a way that we cannot disentangle the opposite. "In short, God cannot be God unless he first becomes a devil."[58]

Even such standard divine attributes as *totum, unum, verum, bonum, perfectissimum,* and *necessarium*[59] are open to reason's challenge, and are acceptable to faith alone. The Incarnation should not be seen as the logical outworking of a prior predetermination of God to identify himself with humanity (Barth, Jüngel). Again, this is the attempt of reason to peer into the divine.

---

57. "tempus creatura verbi," in SA 132. The reference to Luther is WA 20: 59-60 (on Ecclesiastes 3:1).

58. Bayer, "The Rupture of Times: Luther's Relevance for Today," trans. Christine Helmer, *Lutheran Quarterly* 13 (1999): 37.

59. "Ich glaube, dass mich Gott geschaffen hat samt allen Kreaturen: Beispiel einer Katechismusszstematik," in SA 83.

For Bayer, theology stands between mythology — a comprehensive, though arbitrary, narrative framework which is unable to acknowledge conceptually that the biblical God discloses himself in the actual, concrete historical event of Jesus — and metaphysics: a scientific framework independent of all contingencies, which, ironically, is likewise threatened by specific, historical contingencies in which God is at work.[60] All encounters with God are mediated through the senses and language via a "physical word." What then becomes of Kant's quest for a priori "knowledge"? There is no pure a priori knowledge but rather a concrete "historical a priori." Scripture, nature, and history are all prior to the individual and provide the keys whereby individuals can interpret their experiences and life histories.[61]

This is of the utmost importance when comparing Bayer's views with those of the four previous theologians. All of the four prioritize the future tense as a way to specify truths about the divine being. For them, God's being is in coming; God will be fully himself only at the fulfillment of creation. Undoubtedly, Heidegger's prioritization of the category of possibility over that of actuality[62] and Hegel's notion of the *telos* of history as completing the divine life have contributed to this move in theology. As has been mentioned, this prioritizing of the future is pivotal for construing the doctrine of God as a field for theoretical and practical reason's quest to decipher the cosmos. However, it is a deadly move; it bypasses delivering God's good gifts that resurrect life in the present. God as the "world's fu-

60. Theologie, 1.2.

61. Christine Helmer explains this thus: "The a priori is joined to the 'historical' present tense. The present tense is privileged in order to make the claim that the divine word encounters its hearers in the concrete reality of the present. By combining the present perfect with the aorist present, Bayer can then move the 'historical a priori' into the space of God's continuous creative activity in creation. Bayer invents the term of an 'interweaving of times' in order to show that, from the divine perspective, all three modes of time are 'embraced' and 'permeated' by the present. The present tense continues to confront us as a perpetual present tense that cannot become 'past' in the theological concept, or anticipated in the 'future' as the logical extension of the present." See "The Subject of Theology in the Thought of Oswald Bayer," *Lutheran Quarterly* 14 (2000): 25-26.

62. "*Dasein* [human existence] is not something present-at-hand which possesses its competence for something by way of an extra; it is primarily Being-possible. Dasein is in every case what it can be, and in the way in which it is its possibility. The Being-possible which is essential for Dasein pertains to the ways of its solicitude for Others and of its concern with the 'world,' as we have characterized them; and in all these, and always, it pertains to Dasein's potentiality-for-Being towards itself, for the sake of itself." See *Being and Time,* trans. John Macquarrie and Edward Robinson (New York: Harper & Row, 1962), p. 183.

ture" stymies the preaching that delivers life, since only some of the goods are offered now. Instead, we must consider these words: "I came that they might have life and have it abundantly" (John 10:10) and "See, now is the acceptable time; see, now is the day of salvation!" (2 Cor. 6:2). Clearly a future is promised in the word delivered in the present. This future opens space and time for living securely today — God's giving of "daily bread" for those who ask, and even for those who do not. We hope for what we pray: "Thy kingdom come, thy will be done!" Nevertheless, the future is to be construed not as the fulfillment of deity or the realization of a pure human community, but as those events-to-come in which God will make good on the promise.

Creation Theology and Human Pathos

Few Lutheran thinkers have emphasized the doctrine of creation to the degree that Bayer does. In part, this is due to the fact that creation and justification, as well as ecclesiology and pneumatology, are so clearly yoked for Bayer. Bayer notes that in the explanation to the first article of the creed, Luther writes that God's activity in creating us is the giving of life, intertwined with the life of the world, as sheer gift. It is here, though, in this well-known explanation, that Luther points out that God's gift of creation is given apart from any worthiness or merit on our part. That is, the generosity of God's creative activity is akin to God's generosity in his saving activity. Insofar as both creation and salvation are gifts, they are similar with respect to God's agency in the world. In light of this "interweaving of times" *(Verschränkung der Zeiten),* which tells us that both past and future are also given in the present, it can be said that in justification the last judgment, the consummation of the world, and the creation of the world are perceived simultaneously.[63] The future of the world comes, then, from God's present and presence and not vice versa, in sharp contrast to the thinking of the previous four theologians.

From this same explanation, Bayer accentuates that God's creating, giving, and preserving are related. All three of these actions are one in God's relation to us. Hence, the divine creativity is continuous *(creatio continua),* the present act of sustaining us together with all creatures. Cre-

---

63. Bayer, "The Rupture of Times: Luther's Relevance for Today," p. 45.

ation loses its speculative connotation as a theory of origins. Instead, creation as gift is address. Sadly, incurvated humanity will not listen to creation as grace and thus experiences it as wrath. Bayer not only divests the doctrine of creation of a speculative, metaphysical aura; he also charges it with a deeply hermeneutical significance, as we noted earlier. This he takes from Hamann's reading of Luther and Scripture. For Hamann, God's address to us, on the basis of Psalm 19, is not only in Scripture but also in the "books" of nature and history. That is, God is speaking "to the creature through the creature." At its core, this way of interpreting creation raises an important metacritique of both ancient and modern ways of construing the God-human relation. Both ancient and modern ways of presenting this relationship have favored a "personalism" in which the God-human relation is, in Martin Buber's famous terminology, an "I-Thou" relationship. This "personalism"[64] can be found in the thinking of Augustine, Calvin, Descartes, Kant, and Kierkegaard. In contrast, Bayer points out that our identity is not to be found apart from the sheer sensuous physicality and diversity of experience. Following Hume's skepticism, the self is not to be construed as a supersensuous subjectivity, a Cartesian thinking thing, non-extended in space, since it is wholly composed as narrative, without any non-linguistic substratum. Bayer accepts the human as deeply mortal, not gnostically divine. Without a supersensuous spiritual bedrock for the self, the human's moment-by-moment personal identity is left in God's providential hands.

Bayer thinks that personal identity should be configured by means of an "I-Thou-it" relationship. God is only mediated in physicality — which, following Hamann, Bayer terms "nature" — by means of a word, which he terms "institution." With the categories "nature" and "institution," form and matter are indissolubly wedded together. Language imposes order on the world, but thereby grants possibilities of experience and intelligibility to creatures. This Hamannian approach rules out a Spinozistic cosmology that reduces all nature to one reality (God is the soul of the world, while the world is God's body), as well as a Manichean cosmology that posits a fundamental, dual opposition between a "good" spiritual reality and a "bad" physical reality. In opposition to every contemporary *Schwärmer* perspective, God comes to us only as mediated in a physical word or a linguistic body, thus sanctifying the world in all its

64. SA 1.

buzzing, blooming plurality. All too often, given modern views of scientific knowledge as "instrumental" and truth as "measurement," human ears are closed to God's address in creation. They must be "opened" by the gospel if creation is to be heard as address — as a visible sign of God's commitment in creation's rhythm. Contrary to what some Romantics think, the earth is not an object of worship but a sacramental vehicle of God's claim. The most important word that God would have humans hear in creation is that he will protect and provide for his children. In this regard, Bayer's constant retrieval of Luther's three estates of church, home, and government is offered as a corrective to contemporary appropriations of the "two kingdoms" doctrine. When the "two kingdoms" view is not corrected by the three estates, it easily permits the political to be abstracted from "private matters" such as sex, marriage, and family. It permits a separation between the personal and the political that Luther certainly never intended, the kind of separation we see in Moltmann. Bayer's focus on the three estates accentuates an unreserved theocentrism, in contrast to the implicit anthropocentrism of modern epistemologies. It is God at work in and through culture, language, and *cultus* to shape us as he, the author — the poet — of our lives wishes us to be.

Relation between the Locutionary and the Illocutionary

Reinhard Hütter has offered an important criticism of Bayer's theology that he believes indicates a significant weakness in Bayer's overall project and calls for theology to find a different basis than that of *promissio* as a speech act.[65] Hütter notes that for Bayer, theology is tied to a performative utterance and not a declarative statement. For Hütter, Bayer's work sets the gospel's locutionary, content-rich narrative in opposition to the gospel as a creative word within the logic of performative discourse. Yet, at this point, Hütter claims that Bayer is not being faithful to how truth is established in the Christian faith. The illocutionary form of the gospel presupposes a locutionary content. It is this locutionary content that plays an essential role for theology. The gospel is not only a promise but also a doctrine. It not only delivers Jesus Christ as a gift but also tells us who Jesus Christ is. In other words, the illocutionary must assume the locutionary for it to do

---

65. See Hütter, *Suffering Divine Things* (Grand Rapids: Eerdmans, 2000), p. 84.

its work. As Hütter sees it, Bayer does not give this aspect of doctrine its due. This is because Bayer lacks a supporting cultural-linguistic ecclesiology in which to situate theology. Hütter finds Bayer's work helpful in that he learns *pathos* from Bayer: theologians are created by the object of theology itself. In the *promissio,* the sign *(signum)* delivers what it signifies *(res).* Hence, for Bayer, salvation is *in* the linguistic form itself, while theology as "second order" discourse is a kind of morphology — a doctrine of forms that indicates the shape of worship, such as praise, lament, confession, and petition, all within the context of God working upon one's life.

Hütter compares Bayer's work to that of George Lindbeck. For him, doctrine is the "grammar" of Scripture, while theology results from the to-and-fro movement between interpreting Scripture and formulating doctrine.[66] For Bayer, by contrast, it is theology that is the grammar of Scripture, and there is no other independent *locus* of logic or value. In Hütter's judgment, Bayer fails to recognize that truth, for Christianity, is fundamentally descriptive, not performative. Truth is *outside* the promise in the narrative that permits the promise to be granted. This allows Hütter to reclaim theology as an integrative task, seeking a correspondence between narrative and reality, in that scriptural narrative corresponds to what is true about God and his dealings with humankind, as opposed to the *Konfliktswissenschaft* that Bayer proposes. Similar to Robert Jenson, whose thinking was explored in the last chapter, Hütter wants to link truth as the correspondence of the church's doctrine to the narrative truths of the triune life.

For Hütter, as for Jenson, the church is an extension of the Trinity, and the Trinity an abbreviation for the church. The story of God's ecclesial dealings with people provides a transparency by which to present doctrine. Culture and language are formative for Bayer's view of theology and truth, as they are for the views of both Lindbeck and Hütter. However, for Bayer they are not, as for Lindbeck, the matrix in which our theology is codified, as if they were pre-theological categories, but the theological frameworks through which God is creating. For Bayer, they are shapes of providential grace.

Hütter surely renders theology a service by raising the issue of the complexity of the relationship between locutionary and illocutionary types of discourse. But, for Luther, theologically speaking, must we not

---

66. See Lindbeck, *The Nature of Doctrine* (Philadelphia: Westminster, 1984).

assert that truth is never more evident than in the "solemn exchange" in which we, against our own reason, agree that God's judgment to embrace guilty sinners is just for Jesus' sake? Of course, the "solemn exchange," in *The Freedom of the Christian* (1520), is closely linked to the "happy exchange": God's exchanging Jesus' righteousness for our sinfulness, and vice versa. It is not fictive, but an actual transaction mediated linguistically in the promise. The promise, the illocutionary gift-word, is tied to the story, the locutionary narrative of God's redemption of sinners. Indeed, the illocutionary elements, such as the words of absolution, baptism, the Lord's Supper, and the promise in the sermon, depend on the locutionary. However, in response to Hütter, the locutionary is likewise inseparably tied to the illocutionary. Its whole point is *to make us people of faith.* The content of the faith, what faith is about, is for the sake of the reception of faith, the trust of the heart. The promise is tied to the story; however, the point of the story is to transmit the promise. Truth is not outside the promise because it is an abstraction to separate promise from narrative and vice versa. Proclamation and narration interpenetrate each other fully. It would not be an exaggeration to say that there is a *communicatio idiomatum* between proclamation and narration. That said, an exchange of attributes does not erase the real differences between narration, which describes reality, and proclamation, which delivers reality. The truth of justification is grounded in God's evaluation; this evaluation is mediated through an external word *(verbum externum),* an expression of God's fidelity to his love. Faith makes us true to God by allowing his righteousness to define our lives.

What then are we to make of truth? If we, like Hütter, should favor the locutionary over the illocutionary as the aegis for truth, and thus retrieve a notion of truth as a wholly descriptive enterprise either as correspondence or coherence, then we could not help but favor *logos* over *mythos.* That Hütter favors the locutionary over the illocutionary as the *locus* for truth raises the issue that *doctrina* could be developed in isolation from worship, the primary narratives of Scripture, and the various genres of Scripture. For Hütter, the locutionary is not only contrasted with the illocutionary, but is also to be preferred as the decoding of the inner logic of triune life as the source for doctrine, in opposition to telling the story as salvific. The conflation of the biblical story with God's being is permitted, finally by the "natural theology of the cross," with its deeply Hegelian suppositions. The consequence of this results in favoring *logos* over *mythos.*

But, again, favoring *logos* over *mythos* is exactly what we should not do, in either theology as a "science of conflict" or any other science, for that matter. Instead of favoring *logos* over *mythos*, we need to honor the differences between the two.

In any science, both *logos* and *mythos* inescapably interpenetrate each other, though this is often ignored. For example, contemporary theoretical physics is accomplished in tandem with a *mythos* about the "big bang," which as an (incomparable, unprecedented) "event" only has, at best, the status of an inference. Here, though, explanation and narration interpenetrate. Why a "big bang"? Narration must be included in explanation because physics presupposes a history to the cosmos. In matters of ultimacy, such as the very origin of the cosmos itself, our ability to test or control any answer is severely limited, and we are left to inference alone, accompanied with a plausible story. As Bayer has so helpfully said, explanation without narration is empty; narration without explanation is blind.[67]

Science indeed calls for a *logos*, and this is the quest of metaphysics.[68] However, scientific inference leaves much leeway. Again, why the "big bang"? Why not an appearance of age at the instant of creation? Informed by Leibniz (1646-1716) and Heidegger, we can ask, Why something rather than nothing? Only sheer prejudice would maintain that the question is meaningless simply because science is presently unable to answer such questions on the basis of empirical method. Surely we have moved a long way from the old verificationist ploy of dismissing metaphysical questions as meaningless. If we appeal to chance, the goddess *Fortuna*, as an answer to this question, then we must acknowledge that this answer is an Epicurean *credo*. In contrast, if we surmise that order, and not solely randomness, entails that there must be an Orderer as the efficient "cause" of this order, then we likewise enmesh ourselves in a theistic or deistic *credo*. Either way, we cannot avoid the fact that even our best "science" is packaged in inherently mythic forms of narration and description. We will not and cannot think apart from some version of faith. The question is always the content of faith: Should it be in an idol (of one's own power) or in the promising God? The secular assumption that there exists a religiously neutral dimension to

---

67. See "Erzählung und Erklärung," in *Gott als Autor*, p. 254.

68. See Roger Trigg, *Rationality and Science: Can Science Explain Everything?* (Oxford: Blackwell, 1993), pp. 219-34.

the human is to be disputed. Theology's dispute with metaphysics is not that it is a meaningless endeavor but that it neutralizes the promise by situating it within a comprehensive descriptive framework. Metaphysics quickly becomes the source of security, a theology of glory, for the old being. We should respond emphatically: Let the promise be free!

Again, Hütter is helpful in raising the issue of the complexity of the relation between the locutionary and the illocutionary, but he fails to make the case that the locutionary is properly the *locus* of truth in opposition to the illocutionary. Rather, we must affirm that the two are tied together like Siamese twins. Insofar as Bayer affirms that Christian theology is to be found between the two discourses of mythology and metaphysics, he may concur. Mythology is unable to see that theology is tied to the historical events of God's action, particularly in the historical life of Jesus Christ, rather than stories independent of such contingent specificity. Metaphysics likewise seeks a universality — albeit conceptually — that is independent of this finite, historical event. The story of Jesus Christ, to which both proclamation and theology refer, interweaves the finite and the historical along with the infinite and the eternal, not dialectically but wholly narratively, thus giving permission to the uniqueness of the contingent details to which it is committed and in which it is embraced. Hence, with Hütter, we must affirm that the locutionary as a *locus* of God's agency is not to be ignored in the affirmation that the word is performative. Yet, no non-mythic approach is available insofar as we seek a "correspondence" between narration and events (or shall we say between narration and other narrations?). Ultimately, however, truth in the Reformation perspective is an agreement with God against ourselves — to honor God's judgment, which must prevail, and to turn against our own set of standards by which to evaluate ourselves or others as sinners.[69]

---

69. With respect to the mythic nature of Christianity, we do well to listen to Gary Dorrien: "There is no compelling reason for Christian theologians to oversell the distinctiveness or antimythical character of Christianity, for the gospel uses and is an example of mythical speech. As Barth told Bultmann, 'there is no need for us to have a guilty conscience' about recognizing *and proclaiming* the gospel in all of its mythical character, for if all of the myth in the gospel were removed, it would be impossible to witness to Christ. Whether it is called myth or saga, mythical speech is intrinsic to Christianity. If Christianity is true, it is true as true myth." Dorrien explains that it was C. S. Lewis who particularly was able to understand and appropriate the mythic nature of Christianity. For Lewis, "if the Christ myth is true in the way that it claims to be true, it stands to other myths as the fulfillment of their

Bayer and Luther

More than any other scholar, Bayer has sought to establish Luther's voice outside the framework that separates theoretical from practical reason, nature and history, explanation and understanding, and other such Enlightenment polarizations that are particularly indebted to post-Kantian dichotomizations (especially as expressed in Max Weber's influential thinking). Existentialism, for instance, has been a major vehicle for presenting Luther's voice over the last several decades, as seen in Ebeling's interpretation, for example. In contrast, Bayer, not so different from Gustaf Wingren (1910-2000),[70] affirms the role of creation and law in its first use in Luther's thinking. He does so in a way which consistently subverts the latent Kantian favoritism of pure form over irrational sense that results in separating the inner and the outer, the private and the public, the phenomenal and the noumenal, and the spiritual and the secular. No dichotomies like these will do. Both elements must be held together in tension. The temporal is spiritual and vice versa, if we are to be faithful to Luther. Bayer offers a re-evaluation of Luther as a theocentric thinker: in all things God is at work, shaping life. This — rather than an analysis of spirituality, ethics, or metaphysics — ought to be at the forefront of our theology. In other words, Bayer actually bases his thinking about justification and theology on the notion of human life as fundamentally receptive, and then he develops everything else accordingly.

Bayer also accentuates the differences between Luther's age and our own. If we are to be rhetorically effective in delivering the gospel, we must reflect on the fact that there seem to be few anxious consciences today. As Bayer notes, our times differ from Luther's in that for many Europeans and North Americans, the law is no longer the law of God but at best the categorical imperative. Given current views of ethics as molded by subjectiv-

---

promise and truth. It is not an illustration of mythic truth, but the ground of its possibility and the realization of its fragmentary glimpse of the Real. The question is not whether Christianity is fundamentally mythical, but whether Christ became and fulfilled the great myth." Lewis went on to affirm that "the heart of Christianity is a myth which is also a fact." Hence, for Lewis, "the story of Christ is simply a true myth: a myth working on us in the same way as the others, but with this tremendous difference that *it really happened.*" See *The Word as True Myth: Interpreting Modern Theology* (Louisville: Westminster John/Knox, 1997), pp. 236-38.

70. See, for example, *Credo,* trans. Edgar Carlson (Minneapolis: Augsburg, 1981).

ism, personal choice, self-esteem, and other Epicurean modes of thinking, we must acknowledge that people indeed sense the hounding of the law to fulfill their potential. However, they see only themselves as the ultimate evaluators of their work. Christ as a coming judge seems terribly remote and unreal to many. Bayer notes,

> A gulf separates us from Luther's understanding of justification, a gulf greater than we can imagine. Our contemporaries do not experience
> v the law anymore as the law of God. Rather, the law is experienced as anonymous, or, in the best-case scenario, as the "categorical impera-tive." A sense of inescapable duty weighing heavily on every human heart is revealed to us by this anonymous law. Duty becomes deadly when the law coincides with the gospel, when they are not distin-guished from each other.[71]

To identify such subjective sentiment as the outworkings of God's objec-tive expectations of people is part of the Christian mission that would not need to have been articulated even a century ago. Where is God when the self seems to have taken center stage? However, anxiety resulting from the truth that the self can never be God, especially for itself, provides the social context for or rough equivalent to the medieval and Renaissance "anxious conscience." Admittedly, the thought that God will judge one for one's lack of merit, that in venial sin one faces significant "time" in purgatory, is quite different from the thought that one cannot fulfill the potential that one absolutely feels obliged to fulfill. However, this is the point of contact where we can challenge the self to center itself. God alone can center the self, and as we learn from Bayer, this will happen only in fellowship with all other creatures.

Like few others, Bayer raises the question of the hidden God, partic-ularly in a theological climate in which it is not popular to do so. Since the notion of the hidden God expresses an important reality with which peo-ple ultimately must wrestle — where is God in suffering? — Bayer has ren-dered contemporary theology an extremely important service. In Luther's thinking, however, we wrestle not only with a hidden God, who outside of Jesus Christ seems often to be indiscernible from the devil, but also with the devil. In other words, for Luther, the devil has agency that is to be dis-tinguished from that of the hidden God. Bayer, however, conflates the two:

71. Bayer, "Justification as the Basis and Boundary of Theology," p. 285.

"Luther's speech concerning the Devil may be understood in its radicality. The Devil, humankind's bitterest enemy, who constantly and everywhere assails and afflicts people, is nothing other than the mask of the Almighty God in his dreadful hiddenness."[72] Bayer is certainly right that God's hiddenness is manifest as the devil. However, the devil has agency over against the hidden God, at least at some level. For Luther, the devil is the "lord of this world," who, though subject to God's activity, wrestles against God's lordship. Admittedly, for Luther, in all things we ultimately deal with God. Whether evil is to be attributed to the devil or to the hidden God might, for Bayer, be a moot question. However, in the devil's quest to establish his own lordship in opposition to God's, he aims to have us serve him and not honor the First Commandment. The devil's attempt to establish his own deity is not an effect of the hidden God. To conflate the devil with the hidden God would too hastily toss out the exorcism rite, the renunciation of the devil, in the baptismal liturgy. This should not be done. Much ministry is exorcism, driving out devils for the sake of social health, especially in the modern world, with its unchallenged superstitions. It is a false lord with whom our Lord Jesus Christ battles, as we sing in all verses of *Ein feste Burg ist unser Gott.*

Why bother with talking about the devil? Is it not a concept too problematic — a license to demonize the other — or too mythological? The concept of the devil, who seeks to divide and conquer the church, helps us understand the origin of dissension within the church. Such discussion is not something for which talk of the hidden God is helpful. That we must contend for pure doctrine is a result of the devil's activity in the world. Talk of the devil, unlike the notion of the hidden God, plays little part in Bayer's thinking — but it would not be fair to suggest that the concept of the devil is an "outdated" doctrine, particularly because we must contend for truth in the church. The devil can never be an excuse to demonize one's opponents. Instead, the devil offers the recognition that our Lord contends with real, objective, evil forces in the church and in the cosmos.

The view of creation-as-gift is constantly upheld in Bayer's work. He too instinctually raises the "sense and taste" for finite beauty inspired in Reformation teaching. Bayer offers the affirmation of this life with all its ambiguities and challenges. Few thinkers can match Bayer's ability to im-

---

72. Bayer, "Martin Luther," p. 59.

part a benediction upon his readers. It is salutary that he accentuates an aspect of the Protestant tradition that is easily ignored. For all that, we dare not forget the penitential tradition of the church, not so that we can revel masochistically in our guilt, but so that we can simply be honest about our betrayal of creation and God's good gifts. Certainly Bayer does not deny this Lenten aspect of Christian life, and undoubtedly he corrects a feature that should never have been made secondary: the affirmation of creation. However, as solemn as it is, the acknowledgment that in life we are surrounded by death is simply a helpful reminder of a truth that people would, for their own perceived self-defense, suppress or ignore. The balance between the affirmation of created life and the mortality, finitude, and guilt of our experience would, ideally, be sought and found. Bayer helps us to realize that it is a false caricature of Lutherans to see them as "Unitarians of the second article [of the creed]." Implied in the doctrine of justification are also the first and the third articles, creation and ecclesiology. In contrast to Hütter, who sees Bayer as having a weak ecclesiology, we must affirm that ecclesiology — the church as an order of creation, though corrupted by sin and no longer church as such, as well as the church redeemed as a "community of communication" — is a remarkable strength of Bayer's thinking.

Bayer offers a theology of the cross, but often far more implicitly than explicitly. The theology of the cross looms in his writing as a critique of the theology of glory or a natural theology of the cross as moralism, intellectualism, or spirituality, as if we could approach the divine neutrally (and not as a struggle for recognition). However, the cross is the end of the theologian (and theology itself) too! While this is clearly affirmed by Bayer, it might not be central enough in his work. His emphasis on *promissio,* when not seen through the cross as our demise, can flatten out the discussion of the divine agency and create a neutrality with respect to God that he himself does not want to affirm.

There is always a danger in doing theology. It is the old being's favorite subject. We must be vigilant because if the cross alone is our theology, then the theologian too comes to an end. Faith alone saves. In Bayer there is always the systematic, constructive element of thinking at work, as is appropriate for a university theologian. Hamann knew the weakness of such construction; he sought for theology to be not primarily constructive but "therapeutic" — critiquing our theorizing not only with respect to content but also especially with respect to form. Hence, the unencyclopedic, proverbial Heraclitian style predominates in his thinking. Bayer's work helps us appreciate that with respect to the task of theological construction, the quest for systematization is unable to deliver a theology of the cross.

Finally, the introduction to the Ten Commandments is indeed gospel, as Bayer ever affirms, but it is also accusing law. If God is the Lord, then we are not the Lord. The voice of election is both law and gospel. While Bayer superbly critiques Barth's view of election (Jesus Christ as the electing lord and the elected human, the key that dialectically ties the infinite and the finite), Bayer seldom accentuates the doctrine of election as an important theme. He insightfully points out, on the basis of Genesis 2:17 ("you may freely eat"), that God promises freedom for the human, but he seldom emphasizes that the human as a captivated creature is threatened by and rejecting of Jesus Christ. Likewise, election is not an outdated doctrine; it is the flip side of our security in Christ: God holds our lives in his hands. The doctrine is a threat to the old being; creatures seeking ethical purity are bound to reject Jesus Christ. We will have nothing of Jesus' embrace of the outcast, the downtrodden, and the sinful. The doctrine of election as such is not to be preached, but we are to preach as though God is electing through our words.

Summary and Critical Assessment

Bayer's view of justification, compared to those of the previous thinkers, is markedly robust and thoroughly ready to assist the church in its mission. For Bayer, justification gives life and freedom to sinners through God's promise made physical in Jesus Christ, between whose manger and cross God is eternally for us.[73] God's promise in Jesus Christ establishes assurance for us with respect to God and opens us to harmony with nature and each other. It allows us to see that God is shaping us in various institutions, orders of creation, through which we are provided opportunities for service. Likewise, forensic justification and effective justification are not to be separated from each other, because God's word says what it does and does what it says. Justification discloses that human life is enveloped in *pathos;* God's word opens space and time for the human to enjoy life with all

---

73. "Tempus creatura verbi," in SA 132.

senses and aesthetically to walk in newness of life. Theology is not, then, grounded in human motives, ethical principles, or intellectual mappings of the cosmos. In Scripture, God interprets our lives, allows us to live freely. Justification helps us to disavow all quests for purity as seen in utopian communities, churches, and encyclopedic mappings of the self or the cosmos.

In contradistinction to each of the previous thinkers, Bayer teaches that conflict, not accommodation, is constitutive for theology. Bayer thus avoids "monarchic" reason, as he defines it, and gives us permission to embrace experience as highly pluralistic, transcending full comprehension. Surely we fail to understand the world if we suppress the sensuous aspect to experience that exceeds our ability to categorize. For Bayer, law and gospel cannot be harmonized into one schema. Properly understood, the being of the human then is in faith. The attempt to map God's being by appealing to the crucifixion as the union of the infinite and the finite in light of the *telos* manifest in the *eschaton* is soundly, and appropriately, rejected by Bayer. God's agency that orders memory and hope, past and future, is in the present. Overall, Bayer's is a holistic approach to life that disavows a separation between affect and intellect.

Bayer admirably takes on what arguably could be seen as the greatest weakness of Lutheran theology: If humanity as such is seen in terms of a fundamental passivity, a *vita passiva*, then how is agency to be construed? In sharp contrast to both reducing humanity to action and attempting to renew an ancient approach to agency as mimetic participation in greater patterns of the good, Bayer suggests that the promise permits redeemed humanity to hear creation as God's address, discerning it as wrath or promise, to enjoy life, and to offer its services spontaneously to others. Nor are we to affirm, as in Mannermaa, a "real-ontic" bond between the divine and the human, since Bayer points out that alien righteousness remains alien even for redeemed humanity.

Following Hamann, Bayer deftly takes on modernity, sharing in its assumptions, particularly the skepticism of George Berkeley (1685-1753) and David Hume, but also critical of the anthropocentric focus of modern epistemology and the purism of modern ethics. No one is more consistent than Bayer in disavowing Platonic forms as the essence of reality or Kant's re-envisioning of the forms as categories that shape human thinking. Language and culture mediate all experience.

Bayer's theological strategy, grounded on justification as its basis and boundary, avoids the accommodationist goal of mapping the cosmos, coping with the stresses of urban life, or creating a utopia on earth — all of which seek a purism within experience that is not granted to the human. If Bayer has a kind of "Lutheran sectarianism," it is one that orients the human to a universe that is truly catholic and theocentric, a cosmos on which God is continuously at work, shaping it to his glory and on the basis of his own goodwill.

CONCLUSION

Chapter Seven

Justification as the *Discrimen* of Theology

Many believe that the doctrine of justification ought to be limited to first-order discourse and preaching and should not structure doctrinal exposi-tions of faith. For these theologians, the doctrine of justification deals with how to represent the primary narratives of Scripture. It does not bear upon second-order discourse, which aims for coherence in theology's sub-ject matter. In this study, we can see why. Justification is corrosive to system-building, as either *theoria* or *praxis*. We have seen how the doctrine of justification unravels system in the theologies of Jüngel, Pannenberg, Moltmann, and Jenson. What this study indicates is that the attempt to po-sition justification within a comprehensive theory is not successful. Justifi-cation as *discrimen* undercuts these proposed methods of systematization by exposing their inability to deliver the promise with clarity. Thus theol-ogy is ever subject to pastoral discernment. Theory is subject to the proper distinction between law and gospel. Justification is a *discrimen* that cuts into the self-legitimating structures embedded in these modes of thinking; it does not limit itself to primary discourse.

Given that, we need to question the artificiality of the distinction be-tween first- and second-order discourse, even when it is made for the sake of establishing intellectual coherence for theology as a discipline given to criti-cal thinking. The quest of second-order discourse is to situate a place or role for theology in the academy. As such, theology is evaluated on the basis of its ability to achieve some good in the academy. If theology can deliver a unique meta-experience that helps us affirm the world in the establishing of its secularity (Jüngel), or if it is able to offer a sufficient reason for rationality on the basis of the ultimate union of all (Pannenberg), or if it is able to provide the pattern for an ideal moral community in which fairness prevails (Moltmann), or if it can provide the world with a meta-narrative on the basis of retrieving a Catholic perspective on God as the *summum bonum* (Jenson), then theology might be legitimated as a valid discipline in the university and be deemed socially relevant. It is these overarching theories that delineate the role of justification as helping us to cope, to think encyclopedically, to be moral, or to begin a journey in a countercultural Catholic identity. The role of justification in systematics as either a hub or one *locus* among many is tied to the question of theology's self-justification in the process of determining a worthy public investment of resources in the academy.

From all this, we can see that theology is a highly anxious discipline. Theology is a queen disowned in the modern quest for a secular space. She is potentially displaced altogether in the university. The onus is on her to prove her worth, and the only standards to which it seems that she can appeal are those of the academy itself. Undoubtedly, there are different degrees of accommodation in the typology outlined above. However, in light of the law-gospel distinction, should not the academy itself undergo critique? To what degree is it the epitome of human power — the attempt to master or control nature for the sake of human consumption or defense, particularly by means of measurement? At what cost has such progress or defense been borne? At what point is the academy complicit with and defined by the overall power struggles within society that unfairly favor some people over others? These questions make it clear that God's wrath operates not only outside but also inside the university system.

However, must not the ambiguity in our experience of creation as a *locus* of *both* wrath and grace be acknowledged? To what extent does the academy offer possibilities of God's generosity to people — a providential grace helping them to cooperate with God's creativity? To what extent does the conquest of chaos by means of developing new medications, tools, technologies, and models of reality concomitantly offer God's hand of consolation and support? Providential grace is operative, though not often acknowledged, in the university.

The current academy is an expression of modern European and American culture and as such shares in the ambiguities of that culture. As we have seen, it fails to secure the secular space it seeks. Accordingly, culture should not be seen as a pre-theological category that can frame the agendas of theology. It is not a concept independent of an appeal to religious legitimation but is itself the locus of that legitimation. However, culture is far more than something that is human-generated. It is primarily a vehicle whereby God is shaping the world, even if this is not universally acknowledged. Culture should be seen as a theological category. It is tied to creation. It is not only a medium of human creativity and self-legitimation but also a means whereby God invests in people-making and world-making, an agency through which God speaks either wrath or grace.

All too often, the sciences become reductionistic in their attempts to chart reality. Must not our quest for scientific understanding be tempered by humbly acknowledging that the buzzing, blooming manifold of experience, and the criteria of thinking itself, transcend a total conceptualization, either through *contemplatio* or *actio?* Theologically speaking, the greatest peril of the university, with all its various disciplines, is the attempt to establish — by whatever means — an encyclopedic "God's eye" view of reality, walking by sight, not by faith. It is this temptation, whether mediated existentially, ethically, theoretically, or via a Catholic *ethos,* that besets four of the thinkers investigated in this study. As we have seen, the various guilds that determine the way knowledge is generated each have their own alternative faith systems, even their own soteriologies.

Relativizing the Relationship between First- and Second-Order Discourses

When one asserts that the doctrine of justification must be limited to first-order discourse, one is saying that the gospel, while certainly necessary, is not sufficient for life. Instead, faith must be supplemented by understanding, as defined by the academy, if it is finally to offer value. Here, the gospel is necessary as a foundation for the edifice of theology; the entire edifice is planned on the basis of situating theology in relation to knowing, doing, or feeling. It is accountability to one or more of these three that would give the doctrine of justification its passport to relevance. However, our study indicates that justification is necessary *and sufficient,* not only as the basis of but also as the hub for theology, since faith constitutes human nature at its core.[1] Receptiv-

1. See Bayer, "Justification as the Basis and Boundary of Theology," *Lutheran Quarterly* 15 (2001): 275.

ity, the passive life *(vita passiva)*, is the most primordial stance of the human. All knowing, doing, and feeling come from this. Thus, justification is the lens through which all Christian truth must be presented.

The line of thinking challenged here over-accentuates the differences between primary and secondary discourses. As stated in Chapter Six, *mythos* and *logos*, as well as locutionary and illocutionary discourses, interpenetrate and imply each other. *Logos* is not done apart from *mythos* and vice versa, and the illocutionary is not spoken apart from the locutionary and vice versa. The one always accompanies the other, even if the other is sometimes more hidden, withdrawn, or not in focus. They can be discerned as extremes along a continuum, and we cannot get around this. For this reason, the risen Lord's mandate to preach the gospel, which entails that we distinguish words that convey gospel from those that do not, is to be applied not only to first-order discourse but also to second-order discourse. *Logos* is to operate a test to distinguish false *mythoi* as self-justifying, in distinction to true *mythoi* that adequately convey or are compatible with God's word, both law and gospel. Scripture is our compass in this regard. Scientific disciplines, which the university seeks to establish, can be seen as forms of wisdom — albeit as law, not gospel — in both worldly and political uses.[2] Their power is capable of being channeled and harnessed for overall good. And in them God can offer providential grace. However, the university establishes no pure realms of theory or ethics abstracted from history and experience. Thinking and willing are not foundations for knowledge but responses to God's creativity. Knowledge in any given discipline results from this response. The goal of theology, as a theoretical, reflective discipline, is to support proclamation. While not to be divorced from the academy, the proper cultural focus for the distinction between proclamation and reflection about proclamation arises in the church.

Theology's Eschatological Limit

Having allowed Luther to speak to us as a contemporary, we have heard his concern that outside faith, God may appear as a devil. Doing theology outside faith imperils us. That way of doing theology inanely thinks that the-

2. See Theologie, C, 2.3.4.

ology can be done neutrally. It cannot. The supposition that it can invites demonic *Anfechtungen* to govern both life and thought. More than that, delivering the word of the cross effectuates the end of the old being. The old being suffers its power to be squeezed away in both the accusation of and the affirmation from the cross. In either case, law or gospel, the ego directed by *ambitio divinitatis* is negated. For the new being called forth by the gospel, the world is opened as creation, as address. The self is opened to this address and as such is opened to others. The last judgment ("Come you blessed of my Father . . ."), similar to the word that primordially creates ("Let there be light . . .") and that heals ("Ephatha, be opened . . ."), is spoken, delivered, and granted now. The last judgment, creation, and forgiveness are all one and the same in God's action. The limit to our thinking is not the inestimable distance between the finite and infinite, being and becoming, and eternity and time, which four of our theologians presume can be bridged by a "natural theology of the cross"; rather, the cross itself suspends the attempt to unmask the hidden God through *contemplatio* or *actio. Coram deo*, faith alone in the promise suffices for our relation with God. Metaphysics offers no neutral turf on which to do theology. Theologians (as all people are) practice either as old beings who do not fear, love, and trust in God above all things, or as new beings who do. The neutrality assumed in most constructive theological work is wrongheaded. In this regard, the quest for a system hinders truth. It is tantamount to the attempt to unmask the hidden God or to transform the cross into a symbol of human power. It is inevitably self-defeating.

The Positive Role of Theology

Theology should not be about providing an overall system, but instead should deconstruct systems. Undoubtedly, it is desirable for the church's catechesis to seek rhetorically a structured presentation of the faith. Excellent examples of this are found in Luther's *Large Catechism* and *Small Catechism*. The Catechisms explicate the faith in terms of God's requirements, Jesus Christ as good news, our expression of faith as prayer, and the sacraments of baptism and the Lord's Supper. They do not offer a "God's eye view" of all reality as based on God's or our future experiences. Theology should deconstruct such overly ambitious systematizing for the sake of preserving the doctrine of justification's role as *discrimen*. We should forego encyclopedic systematizing not because it is inherently irrational, as is often maintained by proponents of the old fact-value split (like Bertrand Russell), but rather because both systematizers and their opponents claim a "God's eye" perspective. The task of professional theologians is on a continuum with that of all the faithful. It is to offer that "discretion of spirits" (*discretio spirituum* [1 John 4:1]) that archaeologically and methodically examines the sources of the church's teaching and proclamation in order to discern how law or gospel is to be proclaimed wisely and pastorally. The most important task in theology is not construction but discernment. All construction needs to subordinate itself to this discernment, and not vice versa.

The Relevance of Justification
and the Irrelevance of Relevance

If our being itself is in faith, then the question of what our faith rests on is always relevant. Insofar as one's humanity consists in seeking legitimation for behaviors in the social context of responsibility, accountability, and the competitive struggle for social recognition, then the question of one's ultimate justification is always relevant. In this regard, the problem is not an absence of anxious consciences such that the doctrine of justification is irrelevant, but rather that people fail to discern and critique the idols by which they justify themselves. The doctrine of justification ever looks to the First Commandment, with both its promise — "I am the Lord your God" (I will provide for you) — and its threat: "Since I am the Lord your God, you are not your own god or goddess for yourself — nor can anything else serve as god for you!" Sadly, in today's highly humanistic context (like many ancient philosophers: the human is the measure for all things), it is this commandment that has been ignored. The First Commandment is really the summation of all the commandments, and its fulfillment in faith would entail their observance.

That people are unaware that they are under God's wrath does not mean that they are unaffected by it. That people substitute creatures as their "higher power" in place of the creator implies by definition that they subordinate themselves to an idol and suffer the consequences of separation from their true source of life. They thus experience God's wrath, which hands them over to their sin. This wrath, for Europeans and North

Americans, is finally nothing other than the apparent meaninglessness of it all — an "eternal recurrence of the same" (Nietzsche) outside of Christ. However, with the promise, with Christ unbound from the chains of death, raised by the Spirit, liberating us from incurvation, we can, like him, call God "Father." In this, all things are new (2 Cor. 5:17). We are free from the drudgery of the (eternal recurrence of the) same. Adventure is permitted and unfolded by the giftedness of life, the new horizon of an identity shaped and interpreted by God, who as the ever-imaginative, caring artist restores us to harmony with creation and allows creation to be restored to harmony with itself. We are delivered from the need continuously to re-establish our merit, worth, and value, which cannot be established on the basis of our own self-evaluation, since no ultimate standard is available other than God's as the measure of a worthwhile life.

Articulating the gospel can never be anything other than "catholic," since to be "catholic" is found only in the quest for fidelity to the gospel. The Catholic tradition has always been a debate about gospel fidelity. Luther is a chief participant in this debate. So is Saint Paul. If we perceive that churchly identity is becoming postdenominational, it is not the preservation of denominational identity that is at stake for the confessionally minded, but the preservation of the promise. To seek to honor this distinction is to seek to honor the God who restores us to creation.

In the theologians examined, we have found much that is good. With Jüngel, we can affirm several things as helpful theologically: (1) the critique of modernity as the compulsion (not freedom) to establish an identity, (2) the affirmation of a fundamental passivity *coram deo*, (3) the distinction between person and works, and (4) the word as effectual. Pannenberg offers insights for theological anthropology with his view of the human as exocentric, and the recovery of genuine humanity in the acceptance of finitude. Moltmann affirms that good fruit can be expected from a good tree; faith gives birth to and embraces an active life on behalf of the neighbor and the cosmos. With Jenson, we need not be naïve about the modern promotion of individualism and the attendant loss of an overarching "story" for human meaning. The church, if it is true to the gospel, can offer an alternative to the nihilism that enmeshes the world. That said, the critique of these thinkers is that they, unlike Bayer, fail to see that the church's distinctive task, role, and mission, more than anything else, is to deliver the promise, Jesus Christ as *sacramentum* for the world, and that in the face of the hidden God, our faith never becomes sight, but instead the gospel alone gives us the assurance that God is for us. What we must eschew in the above system-builders is the attempt to develop a totalizing system, whether through theorizing, existentializing, ethicizing, or various combinations thereof. Such attempts transgress the boundary set by the doctrine of justification and therefore are untrue to its basis.

The Task of the Church

The church today is trying to do so many tasks because it has forgotten the task for which it exists: delivering the good news. The gospel is a word that frees. In this regard, the gospel is not "whatever" frees but is tied to a specific liberator, Jesus Christ, and offers a specific liberation — from sin, death, wrath, and the devil. It allows us to be restored to creation, to be the caretakers of God's beautiful garden, and to treasure and savor the delights of this garden as well.

What then is freedom? In the gospel, we are free *from* the wrath of God as it is exhibited in its various manifestations, including our indifference to holy things, our seeking to control our destinies, and the pervasive meaninglessness that has been widespread for the last hundred years and more, to which God has given us up. We are free *for* sheer enjoyment of God, the world, and our very lives, which, as created, are intertwined with others. Acknowledging God to be God allows us to be free from *ambitio divinitatis,* allows us to accept our humanity, including those aspects of ourselves that apart from God's affirmation of us in our entirety we would find unacceptable. In such trust that God is for us, and from the assurance of God's present commitment to us, the future is promised as a space for the flourishing of life, not only personally but also socially and cosmically. In God's provision, there will be enough for us. We need not be driven by the anxiety that results in greed. Furthermore, the past is not something from which we must flee in shame or guilt, but instead can become an integral part of our histories and identities. We are free from the compulsion of establishing our own worth and security, because these are in the hands of a trustworthy God. As free, we can be free for others — genuinely open to their needs and concerns as well as the needs of the earth. Independent of secular mythologies that legitimate human autonomy, we can see that the freedom of the gospel permits a new outlook on the social realm as an arena for securing human dignity, freedom of conscience, and the right to education,[3] important democratic ideals, expressions of God's providential grace in history. Luther's rediscovery of the gospel helped permit an acknowledgment of these ideals.

Other than Bayer, the theologians examined tend to ask the church to adopt agendas that confuse the church's mission. Thereby the church becomes a confessional church of many different, even conflictive confessions. Such fundamental theological pluralism within the church subverts the confessional loyalty that can foster the collegiality that could uphold a vibrant ministry in the midst of today's increasing individualism and secularism. The church's leadership tends to manage this theological diversity, mimicking the diversity within the American Academy of Religion. But such management can be only so successful. Various agendas compete with each other within the church, undermining the one distinctive agenda, delivering the promise, which would allow the church to actually make a difference in the world. Under these circumstances of bureaucratically managed confessional pluralism, it becomes difficult to discern the shape of faithfulness, in opposition to faithlessness, with respect to Scripture and the church's confessions. The question of heresy has been overridden by the goal of novelty. What should we make of Luther's concern for pure doctrine which he expressed so emphatically?

> Doctrine and life are to be distinguished. Life is as bad among us as among papists. Hence we do not fight and damn them because of their bad lives. Wycliffe and Hus, who fought over the moral quality of life, failed to understand this. I do not consider myself to be pious. But when it comes to whether one teaches correctly about the Word of God, here I take my stand and fight. That is my calling. To contest doctrine has never happened until now. Others have fought over life; but to take on doctrine — that is to grab the goose by the neck! . . . When the Word of God remains pure, even if the quality of life fails us, life is placed in a position to become what it ought to be. That is why everything hinges on the purity of the Word. I have succeeded only if I have taught correctly.[4]

North Americans are apt to find talk about doctrine cold and impersonal. Thereby they keep themselves ignorant of the very Romantic doctrines

---

3. See Wilfried Härle, "Zur Gegenwartsbedeutung der 'Rechtfertigungs'-Lehre," *Zeitschrift für Theologie und Kirche,* Beiheft 10 (1998): 135-37.

4. LW 54:110 (WA TR 1:294-95).

that favor the personal over the impersonal (a distinction which is often artificial) that so define their lives. A service crucial for the church's mission is to make the world aware of the various *mythoi,* with their concomitant doctrines, by which the world legitimates its power and interprets its behavior. Analyzing doctrine is always at the forefront of the church's mission.

The task of the church is not, paternalistically and patronizingly, to do the world's work for the world, as if the world were incompetent to do it, or as if God has abandoned the world. While it is difficult for many to trust that God is working in the world for good, since we are confronted with so much violence and pain in the world, the church can undertake no more important task than challenging the world with the claim of the First Commandment — a claim of both law and gospel, threat and promise — and in this way allow God's claim to have its effect, trusting that a new heaven and earth will be fulfilled.

Restoring Creation

What concrete difference does the gospel make in the world? Reflection about this question is important because many church leaders simply are unable to specify why the church should be in mission. Undoubtedly, in Luther's time, the gospel answered the problem of the anxious conscience. For us, that anxious conscience is less public though no less real. People are far less apt to perceive that God is the final judge of their deeds or that they could spend an eternity in hell. Few are endeavoring to gain sufficient merit in exchange for less punishment in purgatory. However, is the gospel only time-conditioned to the penitential piety of the late medieval era? Does it address only men and women who were obsessed with their fate in the afterlife? While belief in the afterlife is widespread throughout the world and in North America, it would seem that it is hardly the focal point of life today as it was for many medieval folk.

Must we not say that fidelity to the gospel entails that it has never solely dealt with saving people from a future hell, as important as that is, but also, and significantly, from present hells? What are such present hells? They are expressions of the wrath of God as actually experienced in daily life, such as the cycle of violence and exploitation of others and the earth that invariably comes back to haunt us. They are the "death God finds,"[5] which robs us of the very joy and vitality with which nature as such pulses. Is not this violence, so enmeshed with our present economy with its exploitation of workers and the earth, legitimated by those very symbols of freedom to which we so tenaciously cling? Contemporary men and women are every bit as much "works driven" as their ancestors were, even if they fail to have the proper fear of God as judge. Indeed, they are even more burdened than people in the past for the very reason that they see themselves as their own judges. They carry the weight of establishing worth within themselves.

To live by faith is to live as a creature. It is to accept that only God can be God for oneself and the world. To pretend to have a say in ultimate matters — to take a finite thing and to give it an ultimate symbolic worth in order to justify our very being — is to deny our dependence on God, who is the source of life. Thereby all of life becomes crushed in moralism. All transactions become translatable into legal ones. However, none are righteous before the Creator. The cross must so be preached that our rejection of God's generous offer of forgiveness implicates us in the murder of Jesus.[6] This accusation deflates the false power of the old being. Yet, the message of forgiveness, life, and salvation is to be spoken to the sinners that God is making us to be. "You belong to me" is the claim of the Resurrected to the penitent. The crucified Jesus Christ alone is our righteousness before God.

Thus nature does not need perfecting by grace such that we could climb to a higher level on the heavenly ladder. Rather, nature needs liberation from human incurvation. Thereby it is freed so that it can work in harmony with God's moment-by-moment creativity. It is the message of the cross that liberates nature and allows creation to be restored. Restoring creation through the message of the cross is God's activity. Receiving this restoration liberates us so that we can listen to God in nature as guided by Scripture. Liberated from incurvation, our senses are opened to nature in all its dimensions as sheer gift, a promise of God's faithfulness to us.

Perhaps for many this sounds far too optimistic. The gospel always appears as a problem to the old being. It is too pessimistic about human

5. Martin Luther, *The Bondage of the Will*, trans. J. I. Packer and O. R. Johnston (New York: Fleming H. Revell, 1957), p. 170 (WA 18:685).

6. See Gerhard Forde, "Caught in the Act: Reflections on the Work of Christ," in *A More Radical Gospel*, ed. Mark C. Mattes and Steven D. Paulson (Grand Rapids: Eerdmans, 2004), pp. 85-97.

potential and too optimistic about God's activity. Is not nature a vicious circle of big fish eating little fish *ad infinitum?* And if it is not the strongest who survive, then it is the cleverest. Is not nature a never-ending cycle of violence in which those most adapted survive and pass on their genes? How can we so rosily picture nature as the vehicle of God's promise to which the person of faith is restored, since it is "groaning in travail" (Rom. 8:22), feeling the consequences of human sin?

We need not deny violence within nature for the sake of affirming the gospel. The gospel offers no theodicy. The hidden God is never deciphered. Only faith secures the anxious conscience in dealing with the masks of God's hiddenness. However, we must ask, What does one make of such violence in nature? Does it allow us to condone personal violence: I'm only hurting you because I'm doing what comes naturally? To see such violence in nature — a truth that should not be denied — is to experience God in hiddenness. Indeed, we should expect that most people, most of the time, in fact deal with God in such hiddenness. We too eat and live at others' expense. The good news is that God wants us to eat, and even enjoy our daily bread, because thereby God is providing for us. There is enough sustenance for all. The problem is that in our incurvation we lack the faith that God will provide for us. We are never secure enough; we greedily hoard so-called limited resources. In this violence, the accusing law defends our neighbor: Thou shalt not steal. It also is spoken, along with the cross, to end our incurvation and invite us to Christ so that a new life is created.

Is this a life freed from law? Would such lawlessness restore us to creation? *Coram deo,* we need no law. Christ replaces law as the mediator between God and people. However, *coram mundo,* it is appropriate that we seek civil righteousness for family, community, nation, and world. It is appropriate that we attend to the garden over which we supervise as caretakers. It is appropriate that we seek, in our vocations, an economy that globally serves people and not one that solely prioritizes our own "self-interest," which is so very often self-defeating (tantamount to God's wrath in action). The gospel that awakens faith liberates us from incurvation and allows us to become more human — indeed, ever more human. It invites us to treasure this world as gift and opens the possibilities of rendering love as justice to the neighbor. Free of establishing virtue *coram deo,* we can live our lives heedless of securing the identity of the self and the community in the face of death and meaninglessness.

Who does not hope for a better world, given the ignorance and violence that surrounds us? With respect to the church's mission, the answer for a better world is not social engineering for a millennial kingdom dreamed of by either the political right or the political left. Rather, it is delivering the word that liberates from incurvation and restores creation. Who would not want to be clued into the grand unified theory of everything? Who would not want to know the mind of God? Such secrets might unlock unlimited human potential. However, it is not human potential that is problematic, but the direction that such potential takes. We ever seek a security before the ultimate that we cannot have. Life is only in faith because faith restores our sanity and our realization that we can never be our own gods for ourselves. Faith renders God his due and unleashes the genuine creatureliness that embraces creation as address, promise, and gift. The cosmic dimension of justification is opened when creation is heard as promise. The social dimension is opened when the gospel is received as communication renewing that community, the church that meditates on God's address in creation and primarily in Scripture.

We should not seek to return to the pre-modern world. That would not be possible in any case. However, we need to decipher the codes of modern superstitions as legitimating a control in the world that is not ours to have. Rather than accommodating to these codes, in which theology is so tempted to secure its place, we need to discern spirits, so that we might hear God's voice as distinct from those of false idols and false prophets. The distinction between law and gospel is pivotal for discerning God's restoration of creation. It is an art that needs to be both treasured and nurtured.

Index of Names

Index of Names

Hume, David, 149, 161, 172
Hütter, Reinhard, 118n.9, 162-66, 170

Iwand, Hans Joachim, 69, 71

Jenson, Robert, 8-9, 18-19, 117-44, 163, 177, 178, 183; Bayer and, 146, 155, 157; Moltmann and, 101
Jüngel, Eberhard, 8-9, 17-18, 23-55, 177-78, 183; Bayer and, 146, 155, 157-58; Jenson and, 119-20, 134, 143-44; Moltmann and, 86, 91, 98, 100, 102; Pannenberg and, 62, 73

Kant, Immanuel, 18; Bayer and, 147-48, 150, 155, 157-59, 161, 167, 172; Jenson and, 120, 127, 131; Jüngel and, 33, 100, 157; Moltmann and, 89, 94, 100, 108, 119; Pannenberg and, 72, 100
Kierkegaard, Søren, 18, 34, 161

Leibniz, Gottfried Wilhelm von, 165
Lewis, C. S., 166
Locke, John, 132, 108
Löhe, J. K. Wilhelm, 138
Luther, Martin, 10, 11n.21, 15-17, 183, 185; Bayer and, 10, 145-46, 148, 154-55, 158, 160, 162-63, 167-71, 185; Finnish School and, 127-30; Hamann and, 149-54, 161; Jenson and, 120, 127-28, 131, 137-42; Jüngel and, 25-27, 34-35, 38, 40, 42, 47, 50-53; Moltmann and, 87, 89, 91, 94-96, 105, 108, 109-13; Pannenberg and, 57-58, 60-64, 67-71, 74, 77-79, 80-83

Mannermaa, Tuomo, 47n.95, 66, 78, 127-31, 172
Marx, Karl, 36, 90, 119; Moltmann and, 86-87, 93, 104, 108, 111
Moltmann, Jürgen, 8-9, 17-18, 85-113, 177-78, 183; Bayer and, 146-47, 155, 157, 162; Jenson and, 119-20, 134, 143-44

Müntzer, Thomas, 50, 91, 94-95, 109, 112

Nietzsche, Friedrich, 41, 140, 156, 183

Osiander, Andreas, 67

Pannenberg, Wolfhart, 8-9, 17-18, 56-84, 137, 177-78, 183; Bayer and, 146-47, 155, 157; Jenson and, 119-21, 123, 127, 134, 143-44; Moltmann and, 86-87, 91, 98, 100, 102
Paul, Saint, 183; Bayer and, 156; Jenson and, 121n.15, 127, 140, 142; Jüngel and, 45; Moltmann and, 93, 111; Pannenberg and, 57-58, 61-63, 67, 79
Plato: Bayer and, 150, 153, 155, 172; Jenson and, 119-20, 121n.15, 134, 139, 144; Jüngel and, 27, 39, 41-42; Moltmann and, 96, 112; Pannenberg and, 73, 79

Rahner, Karl, 32, 118
Ratzinger, Joseph Cardinal, 118n.7, 126n.38
Ritschl, Albrecht, 33, 71-72, 99, 106-7
Russell, Bertrand, 182

Sartre, Jean-Paul, 8, 155-56
Schleiermacher, Friedrich, 18; Bayer and, 148, 150, 153, 157-58; Jenson and, 120; Jüngel and, 29, 33, 52; Pannenberg and, 72
Spinoza, Baruch (Benedict), 27, 39, 138, 161
Swedenborg, Emanuel, 146

Troeltsch, Ernst, 90

Walther, C. F. W., 4n.5
Weber, Max, 17, 19, 38, 120, 146, 167
Wingren, Gustav, 167

Yeago, David, 110n.67, 118n.9

192

Index of Subjects

absolution, 8, 164

ambitio divinitatis, 13, 14, 29, 33, 55, 63, 81, 113, 181, 184

analogy, 35, 38, 49, 50

anthropology, theological, 64, 108, 183

antinomianism, 62, 130, 156

apostolicity, 79, 122

atheism, 28, 30, 40-41, 44, 54, 102, 129, 137

Augsburg Confession. *See* Lutheran Confessions

baptism, 62-63, 71, 79, 152, 164, 169, 181

Catholicism, 11, 119; evangelical, 82, 147; Jenson and, 126, 128-29, 130-33, 135-36, 157, 178; Jüngel and, 24, 27; Moltmann and, 109; Pannenberg and, 57, 78-79

catholicity, 79, 143, 183

Christian life, 61, 68, 70

christology, 51, 88, 153

church: Bayer on, 154, 162; Catholicism and, 132; countercultural community, 95-96, 119, 126, 135, 137, 140; creature of the gospel, 3, 9, 36, 80, 82, 87, 122, 133, 140; hell against, 82, 169; Jenson

on, 118n.6, 121-26, 130, 136; Luther on, 105; Moltmann and, 85, 111, 113; order of creation, 74, 99, 135, 140, 170; Pannenberg and, 78; Protestantism and, 132; purpose of, 33, 86-87, 89n.16, 107, 124-25, 143, 171, 183, 184-86, 189; relationship to world, 103, 136, 141, 143; theology as servant of, 55, 60, 72, 180; visible unity in, 80, 119, 137

communicatio idiomatum, 73, 164

cooperatio, 14, 68, 75

coram deo, 9, 11, 14, 24, 29, 45, 51, 54, 60, 65, 66, 67, 74, 81, 83, 94, 95, 100, 102, 109, 113, 125, 139, 144, 156, 157, 181, 183, 188

cosmos: explanation of, 7, 120, 159, 172; transformation of, 62, 77, 140, 160, 173

counterculture (Moltmann and), 89-90, 103, 106, 111

creation: as address, 153-54, 162, 181, 189; Bayer on, 15; doctrine of, 88, 161; fulfillment of, 58, 68, 92, 159, 186-89; gift of, 19, 50, 55, 81, 169-70, 183, 189; God's action in, 8, 43, 74, 135; Jenson on, 125; law as belonging to, 10, 106,

Index of Scripture References